The Collected Works of
William Howard Taft

The Collected Works of
William Howard Taft

David H. Burton, General Editor

VOLUME V

POPULAR GOVERNMENT

AND

THE ANTI-TRUST ACT AND THE

SUPREME COURT

Edited with Commentary by

David Potash and Donald F. Anderson

OHIO UNIVERSITY PRESS

ATHENS

Ohio University Press, Athens, Ohio 45701
© 2003 by Ohio University Press
Printed in the United States of America
All rights reserved

Ohio University Press books are printed on acid-free paper ⊗ ™

09 08 07 06 05 04 03   5 4 3 2 1

Popular Government copyright 1913 by Yale University Press; first printed November 1913 Kraus Reprint Co.
The Anti-trust Act and the Supreme Court copyright 1914 by Harper & Brothers; published October 1914.

Publication of *The Collected Works of William Howard Taft* has been made possible in part through the generous support of the Earhart Foundation of Ann Arbor, Michigan, and the Louisa Taft Semple Foundation of Cincinnati, Ohio.

Photograph of William Howard Taft courtesy of William Howard Taft National Historic Site.

Library of Congress Cataloging-in-Publication Data

Taft, William H. (William Howard), 1857–1930.
  Popular government and the Anti-Trust Act and the Supreme Court /
edited with commentary by David Potash and Donald F. Anderson.
      p.   cm.— (Collected works of William Howard Taft ; v. 5)
  ISBN 0-8214-1457-7
  1. Constitutional law—United States. 2. Constitutional law—United
States—Interpretation and construction. 3. Antitrust law—United
States. 4. Competition—Government policy—United States. I. Potash,
David. II. Anderson, Donald F. III. Title.
  E660 .T11 2001 vol. 5
  [KF4550]
  352.23′8′097309041 s—dc21
  [343.73/07   2003040571

Dedicated to
the Taft family,
for five generations serving
Ohio and the nation

The Collected Works of William Howard Taft

David H. Burton, General Editor

VOLUME ONE
Four Aspects of Civic Duty and *Present Day Problems*
Edited with commentary by David H. Burton and A. E. Campbell

VOLUME TWO
Political Issues and Outlooks
Edited with commentary by David H. Burton

VOLUME THREE
Presidential Addresses and State Papers
Edited with commentary by David H. Burton

VOLUME FOUR
Presidential Messages to Congress
Edited with commentary by David H. Burton

VOLUME FIVE
Popular Government and *The Anti-trust Act and the Supreme Court*
Edited with commentary by David Potash and Donald F. Anderson

VOLUME SIX
The President and His Powers and *The United States and Peace*
Edited with commentary by W. Carey McWilliams and Frank X. Gerrity

VOLUME SEVEN
Taft Papers on League of Nations
Edited with commentary by Frank X. Gerrity

VOLUME EIGHT
"Liberty under Law" and Selected Supreme Court Opinions
Edited with commentary by Francis Graham Lee
Cumulative Index

Contents

POPULAR GOVERNMENT

Its Essence, Its Permanence, and Its Perils

Popular Government

Commentary

———

David Potash

For those interested in William Howard Taft's political philosophy and, on a larger scale, in exploring the tensions inherent in progressivism and direct democracy, *Popular Government* is an invaluable source. The book offers critical insight into Taft's conceptions of democracy, republicanism, and the federal Constitution, as well as an introduction to his political beliefs, values, and habits of mind. Written at a critical juncture in American political history, the work encapsulates Taft's relationship with the progressive movement. Above all, *Popular Government* allows for a clear understanding of Taft's political philosophy.

Context is of critical importance to understanding *Popular Government*. The book consists of eight lectures Taft gave at Yale University Law School during the spring of 1913 and two speeches he delivered before the American Bar Association the prior autumn. Following his failed presidential bid in 1912, Taft joined the faculty at Yale as the Kent Professor of Constitutional Law. However, the former president did not take up residence in New Haven until well after the start of the 1913 spring academic semester. The dean of the law school and Taft decided that a series of lectures over a four-week span in May would serve both as a replacement course and as a means of heightening his presence on campus. In 1914 Yale University Press published the lectures in book form as *Popular Government.*

Taft organized his addresses around a common theme, the preamble to the Constitution:

> We the People of the United States, in Order to form a more perfect Union, establish Justice, insure domestic Tranquility, provide for the common defence, promote the general Welfare, and secure the Blessings of Liberty to ourselves and our Posterity, do ordain and establish this Constitution for the United States of America.

Analysis of the Constitution, while an appropriate activity for a law school, was not an academic exercise alone. The role of the Constitution, its proper interpretation, and even its status as a fundamental or national document were highly contested in the progressive era. Taft's intent was not pedagogy or scholarship, but persuasion.

Enthusiasm for progressive reform was perhaps at its zenith during the spring of 1913. Democratic president Woodrow Wilson had just embarked upon a path of domestic reform, and Theodore Roosevelt's Progressive Party was a significant presence on the political landscape. In contrast, under the leadership of Taft and the Old Guard, the Republicans in 1912 had staked their party's precepts to the Constitution, the sanctity of the judiciary, and opposition to Roosevelt. The battle for the heart of the Republican Party was, for many, the central story of progressivism at the national level. Six months after the election, though, the struggle was not yet over. *Popular Government* was Taft's first post-election effort at articulating conservative republicanism and justifying traditional Republican values.

The emergence of a conservative Republican Party in the progressive era was not ordained. In fact, many Republicans supported most of the hallmarks of progressivism—reform, good government, control of special interests, efficiency, conservation, the social gospel, and so forth. Theodore Roosevelt effectively balanced the desire for reform and the need for stability during his tenure in the White House. In 1908, Taft was elected president as Roosevelt's hand-picked heir. Committed to continuing Roosevelt's policies, President Taft reinforced and expanded his predecessor's agenda. The political terrain was changing, however, and Taft's brand of reform proved to be markedly different from Roosevelt's. Within a short period of time, reform-minded and insurgent Republicans were in open conflict with conservative Old Guard Republicans. Roosevelt and Taft's friendship disintegrated, as did many alliances among party leaders. Taft's presidency was a political, professional, and personal trial for the chief executive and much of the Republican leadership.

The most conspicuous source of disagreement within the Republican Party in 1909 was the tariff. Insurgents sought lower rates, and the Old Guard wanted protectionism. Establishing a pattern he would repeat on several occasions during his presidency, Taft mediated unsuccessfully between these two wings of the party. The resulting tariff legislation, the Payne-Aldrich Act, did not cause interparty conflict; instead, it served as an excuse for it. Various insurgent and progressive groups wanted the pace of change to quicken and the scope of reform to widen. In addition to the tariff, numerous proposals were advanced to increase government's police power in the workplace and economy. Many suggested ways of restructuring government itself. Insurgent Republicans openly challenged established party leaders in Congress. The Old Guard, free of Roosevelt, became increasingly antiprogressive or antireform. President Taft attempted to chart his own course, which pleased neither brand of Republican. The party was trounced in the 1910 elections, and Roosevelt's return to the political arena further complicated matters. At debate was the meaning of republicanism. What were the party's basic tenets?

As the progressive wing of the party fell under the leadership of Roosevelt, the conservative wing of the party united in opposition. Importantly, though, conservatives learned that antipathy toward Colonel Roosevelt was not their only basis of accord. Old Guard and moderate Republicans discovered a surprising intensity of agreement on fundamental principles: the Constitution, the status and prerogatives of the judiciary, liberty, order, and the preservation of the rights of private property. Speeches and articles by men such as Nicholas Murray Butler, president of Columbia University, Henry Cabot Lodge, historian and longtime senator from Massachusetts, and Elihu Root, senator from New York and former secretary of state under Roosevelt, provided the intellectual groundwork for conservative republicanism. The movement toward direct democracy and constitutional reform quickly became the focus of conservative Republican attacks. Initiative, referendum, and recall undermined the American way of life, conservatives warned, and, if not checked, could lead to revolution and anarchy.

In the summer of 1911, Taft charted much of the conservative Republicans' program in a lengthy veto of Arizona's statehood. Arizona, reflecting strong labor and Democratic elements, submitted a constitution containing provisions for the initiative, referendum and recall of elected officials, including judges. Taft believed that he had a constitutional duty to reject Arizona's application to the Union. In a lengthy message accompanying his veto, he argued that the recall of judges was "so pernicious in its effect, so destructive of independence in the judiciary, so likely to subject the rights of the individual to the possible tyranny of a popular majority, and, therefore, to be so injurious to the cause of free government." Taft's stand was a clarion call to moderate and conservative Republicans. A carefully drafted document, the special message was reprinted as a campaign document and quoted in *Popular Government*.

Notwithstanding Taft's determination, the desire for direct democracy did not abate. Initiative, referendum, and recall were adopted in several states and municipalities. The results were mixed: anarchy did not result, but neither did honest and responsive government. Were it not for Theodore Roosevelt, it is possible that the issue might have faded away. In a speech before the Ohio Constitutional Convention in February, 1912, Roosevelt introduced a plan for the recall of judicial decisions, revived interest in direct democracy, and linked progressive reform to his candidacy for the Republican presidential nomination.

Moderates criticized Roosevelt's proposal; conservatives reacted with horror. Though Roosevelt would soften his plan, the very notion of a recall of judicial decisions galvanized conservative Republicans. Speeches and editorials lambasted Roosevelt as an enemy of American values. Taft told an audience in Toledo that the recall "lays the ax at the foot of the tree of well-ordered freedom and subjects the guaranties of life, liberty, and property without remedy to the fitful impulse of a temporary majority of an electorate." Roosevelt's popularity exacerbated conservative Republican anxiety. It is difficult to overstate the concern with which conservatives viewed another Roosevelt presidency. Not only did they fear the end of the Republican Party, they also feared for the rule of law under the federal Constitution and an American way of life.

Conservatives' immediate goal was to find a way to stop Roosevelt and the recall of judicial decisions. Their longer-term objective was to educate the public, or rather to inoculate it from anticonstitutional measures. The emerging Republican plan was not orchestrated by one man, but rather emerged on several fronts through the spring and summer of 1912. Taft subscribed to the strategy, writing a friend: "If I were nominated, even though I were to go down to defeat, I should be on a conservative platform and rally the conservative forces in this country and keep them in a nucleus of party strength, so that after four years the party could gather itself together and probably reestablish itself in control." In other words, Republicans viewed the possibility of defeat in 1912 as little more than a setback, provided Roosevelt was thwarted. Without Roosevelt, the party could be reconstituted around basic conservative principles, such as constitutionalism, rule by law, and republican mechanisms of government. The tactic was successful. Taft's control of party machinery insured his renomination. Roosevelt, frozen out of the party, ran for president on his own ticket as a Progressive. And finally the Republicans moved to the right and defined themselves as conservative.

William Howard Taft's presidency was rife with ironies. Even as he led the conservative charge for fundamental principles, his administration pursued a host of reforms in other arenas. Furthermore, while Taft's efforts to prevent Roosevelt's nomination garnered the backing of many conservative

Republicans, Taft's own candidacy and initiatives received lukewarm support. His fall campaign was carried on primarily in the press. By default, Republican efforts in 1912 centered on two issues, stopping Theodore Roosevelt and promoting fundamental principles.

Running third behind Wilson and Roosevelt, William Howard Taft left the White House a soundly defeated politician. Not since Grover Cleveland in 1888 had a president failed to be reelected. Taft's unpopularity and his ineffectiveness as a campaigner were evident to himself and the public at large. Nonetheless, he viewed his course as both just and right, as he explained in *Popular Government*. Taft genuinely believed that Roosevelt posed a great danger and that his success at the polls was of secondary importance to the preservation of a Republican Party championing republican ideals. These values, as exemplified in the Constitution, were the backbone of American culture and progress.

Following his defeat, Taft, only fifty-five years old, wanted to work but was sensitive to propriety. America had never really known what to do with its ex-presidents. By definition cast in the role of elder statesman, they usually flitted on the edges of the spotlight, aware of their diminished authority but eager to retain whatever influence they might possess. Many wrote memoirs, including Theodore Roosevelt, who had more difficulty than most in deciding what to do with himself after the White House. A member of the Yale Corporation and an active alum, Taft was approached about a faculty position a few weeks after the election. He agreed, finding the prospect of a professorship a "dignified retirement."

Taft was genuinely enthusiastic to return to Yale. He counted his undergraduate years at New Haven among the happiest of his life. Furthermore, he envisioned a mission as an academic. In February of 1913 he wrote the student newspaper, the *Yale Daily News,* saying that "there is a need that our young men should appreciate the Constitution of the United States, under which we have enjoyed so many blessings." Despite his strong predisposition toward his new professional home, Taft had grave doubts about his effectiveness in the classroom. He confessed to his brother that he was "looking forward with considerable trepidation to beginning the business of instructing." The transition from executive to scholar was not easy. Taft did not start working on the lectures, his only academic assignment at Yale for the spring term, until a few weeks before they were due. Complicating matters, Taft's library was unavailable and somewhat out of date. Complaining to a friend about the assignment, he admitted, "I don't feel competent to instruct anybody on anything."

Taft approached the lectures in the same manner as he would a draft of a judicial decision—by marshaling evidence in support of an opinion. He purchased books, asked Yale librarians for help with research, and drew upon the expertise of colleagues both in and out of academia. Nicholas Murray Butler responded to Taft's call for assistance by referring him to his book, *Why Should We Change Our Form of Government?* Republican attorney Harry M. Daugherty, who would later guide Warren Harding into the White House, provided Taft with information and published lectures on Ohio's Constitutional Convention. Senator Root steered Taft to a series of lectures he had given at Princeton University. Perhaps most important was the advice of Professor Max Farrand, a constitutional historian and colleague at Yale. Farrand helped Taft with historical development, sociological jurisprudence, and provocative new scholarship, such as Beard's *Economic Interpretation of the Constitution.*

Taft's lectures, published in *Popular Government,* were a critique of direct democracy initiatives and other progressive trends, as well as a spirited defense of traditional conceptions of constitutionalism and republican government. Without the time or inclination to prepare a profound work of scholarship, Taft instead argued and persuaded. The arguments in *Popular Government* were so deeply influenced by the election of 1912 that they can be read as highbrow or "educational" campaign literature. In fact, Taft borrowed liberally from his own and other Republicans' campaign speeches.

Taft's *Popular Government,* however, was not a simple paean to the Republican Party. In his discussions of the Constitution, private property, and the judiciary, Taft drew upon a well-respected line of Anglo-American scholarship. The key inspiration and model was Sir Henry Sumner Maine. A book of essays, also entitled *Popular Government,* was published in 1885, at the end of a prominent academic career and a few years before his death. Maine's *Popular Government* was the Oxbridge scholar's most widely read effort. Maine was a legal scholar whose expertise was in the development of classical law. However, in *Popular Government* he cast a critical eye on the development of modern democracies. The work anticipated many of the arguments made by scholars on both sides of the Atlantic Ocean.

Democracies often impeded progress, placed liberty and equality into irresolvable conflict, and endangered justice, Maine argued. He claimed that human nature was democracy's most fundamental obstacle, even though many believed that democracy had "an inherent superiority over every other form of government." Furthermore, the historical record demonstrated that "popular government, since its reintroduction into the world, has proved itself to be extremely fragile." In addition, democracy's successes "have arisen rather from skillfully applying the curb to popular impulses than from giving them the rein." Maine's intent was not the advocacy of a different form of government, but a serious appraisal of democracy's strengths and weaknesses. The clarity of Maine's thought, the force of his exposition, and the elegance of his prose inspired Taft.

The first lecture, which examines the phrase "We the people of the United States," emphasizes the difference between all Americans and the electorate. Taft was at pains to distinguish between a democracy, in which all citizens participate in government, and a republic such as the United States, in which a relatively small percentage participates. He made this argument several times in his campaign for the Republican nomination in the spring of 1912, despite criticism from Progressives and Democrats, who castigated him as elitist. He never understood the charge. In chapter 1 Taft stresses that American progress and development had stemmed not from direct democracy, but form a hierarchical society in which a small group promoted justice and the rights of all. Building on a line of thought advanced by Maine, Taft argues that democracy is not an end but a means.

Chapter 2, "The Representative System," continues the assault on direct democracy. Proper representative government allows for popular government and efficiency, Taft claims, invoking Edmund Burke for evidence and support. Moreover, modern government demands expertise and specialization; parties are necessary to bridge general sentiments and specific needs. America's growth and prosperity are clear evidence of the superiority of representative government. However, progressives, direct-democracy advocates, and socialists all pose a threat to the system. Their weapons are the referendum, initiative, and recall. Taft takes up the first two of these measures in chapter 3. Acknowledging the lengthy history of the referendum, he cautions not to make it compulsory. Borrowing here from Henry Cabot Lodge and some of his own speeches, Taft argues that reliance on the referendum takes power out of the hands of elected officials and representative government. Furthermore, he cites poor electoral participation as further proof that the people "are far better able to select candidates than they are to pass upon complicated questions of legislation."

In chapter 4 Taft critiques the recall of judges, which he believes would undermine government by law and place power directly in the hands of the people. "Unrestrained tyranny of the majority will lead to anarchy, and anarchy will lead the people to embrace and support the rule of one." Taft theorizes that the recall, in conjunction with the initiative and referendum, would greatly weaken the rights of private property.

The issue of the direct primary is the focus of Taft's next lecture. The potential for abuse and corruption in the nominating process was common knowledge, and the popular solution was to replace closed conventions with open elections. However, Taft was concerned that changes would weaken the party system and hence representative government. In the fight for the Republican presidential nomination in 1912, Taft benefited greatly from state conventions, especially in the South. Roosevelt, in contrast, drew support from primaries. While admitting to the value of primaries at the local level, Taft makes three complaints: direct primaries may be adversely affected by the participation of those who do not subscribe to a party's tenets; conventions often select more moderate leaders; and lastly, direct primaries give an inappropriate advantage to ambitious men of wealth.

Taft examines the phrase "in Order to form a more perfect Union" in chapter 6, looking at the relationship between state and federal governments. The theme, however, serves as little more than a pretext for Taft to comment on contemporary political issues. He follows a similar path in chapter 7, "To Establish Justice." Moving quickly through a variety of historical and constitutional issues, Taft focuses upon the recall of judges and the recall of judicial decisions. While both are soundly criticized, Taft reserves especial scorn for the latter, Roosevelt's plan.

Taft was passionately interested in ways of strengthening bench and bar. Chapters 8 and 9 consist of two addresses on judicial reform Taft delivered in the autumn of 1912. The first speech looks for ways to improve the process by which judges are selected and tenured; the second speech calls for increased legal standards. The final chapter, "To Insure Domestic Tranquility, Provide for the Common Defence," examines the role of the president as commander-in-chief of the armed forces.

The ten chapters constituting *Popular Government* share an anti–direct democracy message and reveal the workings of a mind conservative in both principles and practice. In terms of content, Taft makes his attachment to traditional values extremely clear. The work, though, is also illustrative for what it does not contain: penetrating questions or surprises. Taft was not interested in challenging established customs; nor did his thinking run to historical or political analysis. Instead, he sought elucidation and development through incremental change. Reform, in other words, was sound conservative practice. Taft's message as president, judge, and professor was remarkably consistent. He sought the continuance of constitutionalism, liberty under law, and representative government.

Introduction

I came to Yale to assume my duties as Kent Professor of Law near the end
of the school year, when it was not practical to add my courses of constitutional law to the then curriculum. It was suggested, therefore, that during the spring term, I prepare and deliver a course of lectures on some
questions of modern government. This I did, making my text the preamble
of the Constitution of the United States. In explaining the meaning of
"We the people," used to describe the source of political power, I thought
it relevant and important to discuss the proposed changes from our republican form of government to a more direct, democratic government, and
this led me to consider the initiative, the referendum and the recall, and
also the direct primary, which, while not necessarily involved with the
other issues, properly suggested itself for consideration with them.

Under the clause of the preamble "to form a more perfect union," I
considered very briefly the historical issue between those who favored the
broad construction of the Federal powers under the Constitution, and
those who took the States' rights view.

Under the clause "to establish justice," I discussed the subject of recall
of judges and the recall of judicial decisions.

Under the phrase "to provide for the common defense," I considered
the question of war and peace, under the Constitution, the army and the
navy and their present needs, and the question of settlement of international controversies through diplomatic negotiation and by arbitration.

At the meeting of the American Bar Association, at Montreal, in September last, I read two addresses, one on "The Selection and Tenure of
Judges," and the other on "The Social Importance of Proper Standards for
Admission to the Bar." In the latter, I dealt with "judge-made" law. These
addresses were closely related to the subjects treated of in my lecture on
the establishment of justice under the Federal Constitution, and seemed
an appropriate supplement. The Yale University lectures were eight in

number, and, with the addresses at the American Bar Association, make the ten chapters which follow.

Since I have prepared this book for the press, the valuable and interesting volume of President Lowell of Harvard, on "Public Opinion and Popular Government" in the American Citizen Series, has been issued, in which he discusses in a most satisfactory way the actual operation of the initiative, the referendum and the recall, and gives a valuable résumé of the result of the use of these processes of direct government in Switzerland and in the states where they have been adopted.

I have not had the time to support the views that I have stated by such citations from official sources, but I am glad to be advised that the specific instances of record he gives are in general accord with my conclusions.

I am very hopeful that while this movement for more direct government now seems to be spreading, actual experience under it in the states that have tried it longest is convincing the members of the various electorates who have seen it work that it is not a panacea, and that it is developing evils of its own that will require at least a partial retracing of their steps.

1

The Meaning of "We the People of the United States," in the Preamble of the Constitution

It is my aim to discuss the subject of popular government under the Federal Constitution, and certain current issues as to the wisdom and soundness of the principles upon which its provisions are based.

If I had attempted the treatment of this subject ten years ago, my task would have been easier than it is today, for in the last decade a school of political thinkers has arisen by whom the wisdom and equity of our fundamental law have been seriously questioned and the justice of the common law, inherited from England and modified by judicial decision and statute, is attacked as not squaring with the proper civic and social and economic ideals of today.

It is difficult, therefore, to enter upon this discussion without taking up political, sociological and economic questions. As one reads the slashing criticism of everything which he accepted without argument when a student of constitutional history and governmental law twenty years ago, he finds himself suffering dizzy sensations for want of stable ground upon which to stand. Not only are the views of those who made the Constitution said to be unsound and outworn, but these Fathers of the Republic are themselves severely arraigned because of their alleged class feeling as land owners and creditors. We have been accustomed to muckraking in the case of living public men, but it is novel to impeach our institutions which have stood the test of more than a century by similar methods with reference to their founders, now long dead.

I cannot think that this school of political philosophy will ultimately triumph. That some of its views may contain elements of truth and useful principle, requiring some changes and amendments in our fundamental law, may well be; but that it can justify and secure a radical change in the structure of our Government, and do away with its character as a Republic, based on the principles of popular representation, I cannot believe.

The doctrines of the new school have been put into practice in a number of the States, and have acquired a vogue that is likely to extend their application. But one of the saving qualities of the American people is their ability to make mistakes, to take a wrong course, and then to retrace it when the results and facts show them the truth. They frequently have to incur a very considerable cost in learning these lessons, but, as a people, they are quick to appreciate them, and do not seem to have pride of opinion that will keep them from a change, even in the short period of a presidential term. Therefore, while we may expect this "remedy of infusing more democracy in our existing democracy" to continue for a time, we have reason to hope that its obvious inconveniences, the appearance of new evils in its use and the probable return in possibly different forms of the old grievances for which these changes are now regarded as a sovereign cure, will ultimately convince the people that the difficulty in the operation of our present machinery has not been in its lack of adaptability to our needs, but it has been due to the failure of a majority of the people to discharge their duty as responsible members of a political community. Upon those of us, therefore, who appear to be in the minority in opposing these new governmental devices, the duty is plain of pointing out their defects and awaiting the event to demonstrate the truth of what we say. I would not say that one kind of political machinery is not better than another for securing good government and the expression of sober popular will, but I would say that, generally speaking, between the two systems, if the real reason why one does not work is the failure of the people to discharge their duty thereunder, a new system is not likely to work any better, when if properly discharged, the duty of the people is more onerous than before.

In examining the Constitution, the first clause that one reads is the preamble. The preamble is a general declaration of the Convention as to the purposes of the Constitution. The preamble has been much used in argument in the Supreme Court to aid the construction of the Constitution. The title of an act—and I presume the preamble of the Constitution comes within such a description—can hardly be used to change the actual language used in the body of the instrument which is to control. Still it throws light upon the document. It will be useful to follow its phrases as a general plan for my discussion of popular government in the United States, its advantages, its purpose, its essence, its safeguards and its perils.

The preamble is as follows:

> We the people of the United States, in order to form a more perfect union, establish justice, insure domestic tranquility, provide for the common defence, promote the general welfare, and secure the blessings of liberty to ourselves and our posterity, do ordain and establish this Constitution for the United States of America.

I ask your consideration, therefore, of the first phrase, "We the people of the United States."

These words became very important in the controversy that arose as to the construction of the Constitution soon after its adoption, and which continued until the end of the Civil War. The theory of those who construed the Constitution so as to restrict and minimize, as far as possible, the powers conferred upon the National Government, contended that the Constitution was in effect not much more than a mere compact between the several sovereign States, who retained their independence and sovereignty as to everything except that which was expressly or by inevitable implication conferred upon the central government.

The other view was that taken by those who wished to enlarge the national power by every reasonable and useful implication from the powers expressly conferred in the Constitution. The strict constructionists, like Mr. Jefferson and Mr. Calhoun, contended that the use of the words, "We the people of the United States," meant that the peoples of the several States, as different state units, were entering into a compact with each other to part with some of their faculties to form a central government in order to accomplish the purposes stated in the preamble. On the other hand, Chief Justice Marshall and the Supreme Court of the United States, in many decided cases, held that the words indicated that the body of the whole people of the United States, assembled, it is true, in the different States, because they could not assemble together, but acting as a whole people, were forming a new government of their own by ordaining and establishing the Constitution, and were to be recognized in the adoption of this fundamental instrument as the original source of the newly created Federal powers. This view made the whole people a possible depositary of some of the powers not granted to the National Government, and prevented the inference that the States were necessarily the depositary of all such reserved powers.

It is noteworthy, as a matter of history, that when President Jefferson was in the Presidency, and felt called upon to fill a vacancy in the Supreme Court, he appointed Mr. Joseph Story, of Massachusetts, a member of the then Republican party, evidently with the expectation that his view of the Constitution would be opposed to that of Chief Justice Marshall. The personality and the great ability of the illustrious Chief Justice, however, exercised great influence over the brilliant young Justice, appointed at thirty-two, and when he came to pronounce his first great constitutional judgment as the organ of the Supreme Court, in the case of *Martin vs. Hunter's Lessee,* in 1816, 1st Wheaton 324, he announced the view of the Court that the Constitution of the United States was ordained and established, not by the States in their sovereign capacities, respectively represented by the different peoples thereof, but by the people as a body of the United States as a whole, and that this was the meaning of the preamble. This was confirmed by other judgments of that Court, notably by Chief Justice Marshall in the great cases of *McCulloch vs. Maryland,* 4th Wheaton 316, and *Osborn vs. the Bank,* 9th Wheaton 738. All these cases gave the Constitution liberal construction in favor of the powers of the National Government, and as the views expressed were opposed to those of Mr. Jefferson and the then Republicans, Mr. Justice Story was attacked as a renegade of the party. His views and those of his colleagues were regarded as most heretical by Mr. Calhoun and by his disciples. It is not very important now, except from an historical standpoint, to review the distinctions that were made before the Civil War in this all-absorbing issue, because the view taken by the broad constructionists was vindicated and made permanently to prevail by the arbitrament of the sword, and the theory of the Federal Constitution as a compact between sovereign States has as fully disappeared as the constitution of the Southern Confederacy itself.

The use of the words, "We the people," was an indication on the part of the makers of the Constitution that they thought they were establishing a popular government, because a popular government may properly be defined to be a government established and maintained by the authority of the people. We are in favor of popular government because we believe that the fact that the people govern themselves will make them constant in its support and will secure obedience to the laws their representatives make and the executive they elect. This is likely to make the government strong and its protection of its individual citizens effective.

Moreover, experience sustains the view that every class of citizens in a community—and by a class I mean those who are similarly situated and conditioned—is more certain to look well after its own real interests than any other class, however altruistic. Hence a government in which every class has a voice, that is, a popular government, is more certain to do justice to each class and make proper provision for its welfare. This has only one exception, and that is, where a class has not intelligence enough to understand its own interest or rights.

Now popular government is not an end. It is a means of enabling people to live together in communities, municipal, state and national, and under these conditions to secure to each individual and each class of individuals the greatest measure of happiness. It was to aid this ultimate purpose that our Constitution was adopted. It was not thought by the people who made and ratified it that the majority could always be trusted certainly to accord to the individual just and equitable treatment in his pursuit of happiness. The people, themselves, imposed the restraints upon their own political action contained in the Constitution, the chief of which were the guaranties of individual rights. The security of these rights and all our civil institutions are nothing but means for the promotion of the happiness of the individual and his progress and are to be so regarded.

I know that the so-called individualistic theory of rights and duties has been attacked as not broad enough and that pressure is now being exerted to introduce into practical jurisprudence the view that class or collectivist rights and obligations should be more clearly recognized and enforced at the expense of the present so-called rights of the individual. I am not now considering this issue and am not intimating any opinion on it. Whatever the proper view, whether we should continue to preserve individualism intact, or qualify it by collectivist amendment, the ultimate purpose of government and its limitations must be conceded to be the same, the promotion of the happiness of the average individual and his progress, whether this be effected by exalting individual independence, or by giving more power to society to secure greater happiness to a greater number of individuals.

The effect of these restraints to secure justice and right for the individual reacts in favor of the strength and permanence of the government of the people. The tyranny and injustice of a majority would be certain in the end to stir those individuals suffering it to revolt, and would lead to a change in the form of government, perhaps to a one-man control. Such was the fate of Greece, of Rome, and of France. The rule of the people which is just and equal to all should endure forever. Of course this permanence reciprocally promotes individual happiness.

If, then, the distinction between what is the end of government and what are the means by which that government is to be bettered and may more nearly reach its end, is kept clearly in mind, we shall eliminate from the difficulties of political discussion a good many fetishes that now lie in wait for the unsophisticated reformer.

The preamble of the Constitution uses the phrase "We the people of the United States," and I have been attempting to state the advantages of a popular government and its purpose. What is its essence? What is meant by "We the people"? What is meant by "popular government"? If these terms are to be construed as referring to a government by all the people, then there never has been, and there never will be, and there never can be, a truly popular government, because it is impossible that all the people, i.e., all the individuals in the community, municipal, state or national, should have either the capacity or the opportunity to take actual part in its government. This is a fact the importance of which has not always been fully recognized.

Who were "the people" in the days when this Constitution was adopted? They were not the whole 4,000,000 of those who lived in the thirteen colonies. At least that four million did not select the members of the Constitutional Convention. The members of that Convention were selected in popular colonial conventions in some colonies and by the legislatures of other colonies, and in the latter some of the delegates were confirmed by popular conventions. Now who voted to select the delegates for those conventions or legislatures? They were the qualified electorate of each colony, or at least a majority of the members of the electorate who took the trouble to vote. We know from the colonial laws who were qualified to vote, and we have an estimate made by those who have investigated it as to the ratio of that part to the total population.

Generally in the thirteen colonies, those who could vote were limited to men who owned a certain amount of property or paid a certain amount of taxes, and in some of the States they were required to be believers in the Protestant Christian religion.

In New Hampshire the voter had to be a Protestant and a tax-payer. In Massachusetts he had to be possessed of an income from a freehold estate of £3 a year, or to own a personal estate worth £60. In Connecticut he was obliged to have an annual income of $7 from a freehold estate, or real estate rated on the tax list as worth $134. In New York he was required to have a freehold estate of £30, or a house rent of 40s. In New Jersey any person, male or female, black or white, native or alien, was permitted to vote, if only he or she owned real estate worth £50. In Maryland the voter had to have in the county in which he wished to vote a freehold of £50, or personal property of £30. In Virginia the voter had to own twenty-five acres of land of cultivated property, and a house at least twelve feet square on the foundation, or he had to have fifty acres of wild land, or a freehold or estate interest in a lot in some of the towns established by law. In North Carolina the voter had to be a tax-payer. In South Carolina the voter had to be a free white man, acknowledging belief in God and in a future state of reward and punishment, and had to live one year in the state, have a freehold of fifty acres, or own a town lot, or have paid a tax equal to the tax on fifty acres of land. In Georgia any mechanic, any male white inhabitant owning £10 of property and paying a tax not only might vote but had to vote, under penalty of £5.

The estimate of historians is that out of the four million of people in the thirteen colonies, including slaves, women and children and other citizens who were non-voters, there were only one hundred fifty thousand qualified to vote, and therefore we may properly say, that in one sense the people whose delegates and representatives framed the Constitution of the United States were not one twenty-fifth part of all the people of the United States at that time. Judge Sharswood, a great jurist of Pennsylvania, said: "It is to be remarked that in the various nations, even in the representative government of the United States, the consent of the entire body of the people has never been expressed, as 'the people' comprise all of the women and children of every age and class. But they were not 'the people' in the same sense, until the Constitution was adopted. A certain number of men have assumed to act in the name of all the community." (1 Sharswood Blackstone, 147 N. 11; 2 Wilson's Works, 566 Andrew's American Law, Sec. 122.) Yet the Government of the United States became the typical popular government of the world and has been made the chief model of many popular governments since established.

The political history of each State since the Constitution was adopted shows a gradual enlarging of the electorate so as to eliminate religious and property qualifications, and to reach manhood suffrage. Until recently the electorate in each State was limited to males over twenty-one years and the result has been, as seen in the presidential elections when the vote was the highest, that the qualified electorate in the United States has not amounted to more than 20 percent of the total population. If this number is to be increased by allowing women to vote, it would probably increase the percentage of the electorate to 35 or 40 percent of the total number of the people resident in the United States. As we must govern by a majority or a plurality of those who have the right to vote, we may properly say that this must always be a government by a minority of all the people of the country.

These are mathematical facts that no one can escape, and it thus appears that there is a large part of the people who are governed and in whose interest government is maintained, to whom it is impossible safely to extend the electoral franchise. No one proposes to do so. No one proposes, for instance, to extend the electoral franchise to children or minors, to aliens who live here and do not wish to be naturalized, to aliens who live here and who cannot by law be naturalized, to the insane, or to those who have shown themselves by crime to be unfitted to vote.

These facts do not make against government by the people as we understand it. It only shows that approval of so-called popular government is not worship of a fetish. We are not in favor of the rule of all the people as an end desirable in itself. We love what is called democracy not because of the name but because of what it accomplishes. We are in favor of a rule by as many of the people in a democracy as will secure a good government and no more. The result will be good because it secures the happiness of the individual. Government is a means to an end, and the means are to be selected on account of their adaptability to the end.

I will illustrate the point I am making if I say that women should be accorded the privilege, and given the duty, of voting, not because they have an inherent and inalienable right to vote, but because, by giving them the franchise, their own welfare or that of the whole body of the people will be thereby promoted. If the advocates of female suffrage can show that they, as a class, have been unjustly prejudiced by governmental measures or by lack of them, and that they could remedy this by their vote, or if they can show that, by the extension of the franchise to women, either the general Government would be better or stronger, or the existing electorate would be improved in its average moral tone, its intelligence, its political discrimination, its patriotism and attention to political duties, they make their case; and they do so because they thus establish that the addition of them to the electorate is a useful means to secure the happiness of the individuals.

While it is impossible to escape the proposition then that we have not a Government by all the people, in the sense that we do not include in those who exercise the power of control all the people, or a majority of them; nevertheless, in fixing our federal franchise we do seek to make our voters in a true sense representative of all the people. The theory of manhood suffrage is that after a man becomes twenty-one he represents in a true sense some of the same class as himself—that is, of those similarly situated—who are related to him. The husband represents his wife; the father the children; the brother the sister, and even though we make our electorate as wide as possible by giving all women of adult age the franchise, we must still have the principle of representative authority in the practical carrying out of popular government. Jameson Constitutional Conventions, Sect. 335, 336, 337; Andrews' American Law, Sect. 122.

The theory of an original contract between those who made the Government and those who were to live under it, in which each member gave up some so-called natural rights and consented to the exercise of governmental authority, on condition that he enjoyed certain other rights under the protection of the Government, is of course not a true statement of what has happened in history. It was advanced by Rousseau for the basis of a rightful government. As a working formula the theory is sometimes useful to test the correctness and justice of institutions which are made part of governmental machinery. When we all theoretically consent to, and actually acquiesce in, a popular government, we say to ourselves, "This is a good government, and we can count on its efficacy, its honesty and its high ideal, and on its practical protection of our rights because the governing body, to wit, the electorate, is composed of citizens of varying intelligence, self-restraint and patriotism, the average of whose political capacity is sufficiently high to justify the belief that the majority will in its political control be fairly wise, prudent and patriotic." Now if we find that the burden involved in the political activity legally required of the average citizen, leads a large number of the electorate and those the more intelligent utterly to neglect their political duty and not to vote, because there are too many elections, or because they feel unfitted to vote on the subjects submitted, with the result that a minority of the electorate of less average intelligence and capacity than the whole is in control, it seems to be clear that the man who is held to consent to this form of government is not receiving the benefit of the government which he had a right to expect.

What is the remedy for this? The Government should either adopt measures which will compel the delinquents to vote, or we must change the law by calling on the electorate for political action less frequently, so that with a lighter burden they may be induced to carry it and give the attention that the interest of the State requires from them in the matter of elections.

Can we meet this difficulty by requiring all the citizens who can cast a vote, to vote, under penalty? This has been attempted in Switzerland and

Belgium. I am not fully advised as to the operation of such a law in Belgium, but in Switzerland its result has not been satisfactory. One man can take a horse to water, but fifteen cannot make him drink. The men who were compelled to vote in Switzerland on issues referred to them under their referendum law, voted blanks in large percentage, because either they were not interested, or did not feel that they had knowledge enough to express an opinion, or for some other reason. The difficulties as to enforcing such a remedy, therefore, would seem to remit us to the only other one that I know of, which is that we should limit the political duties of the average elector to those which experience shows he is likely to perform. This will prevent too numerous elections. It will lead to a government more representative and less direct, and it will make possible the short ballot, because it will limit the elective offices to a small number and will impose the responsibility of appointment of all other officers upon the few who are elected.

A system which leads to a continuous neglect by a majority of the electorate of their political duties, conclusively shows its unfitness. It is condemned—negatively, it is true, but none the less emphatically—by the very electorate upon whom the safety of the Government depends. The Government becomes one of an active minority. Experience does not show that such a minority is the wisest part of the electorate or the part best adapted to secure good government.

Of course the argument advanced at once is that men who do not care to take part in the government and do not care to discharge their political duties must be regarded as forfeiting their right to do so and must be held responsible for all the ills that come. But the difficulty of this argument is that it ignores altogether the rights of others who do perform their political duties and who vote on every occasion required, and also that large part of the people who are not entitled to vote at all. Both classes have a vital interest in the character of the Government which is imposed on them, and may justly insist that in such a Government it is the general character of the whole electorate that they have a right to rely upon, to secure to them proper and efficient administration and the maintenance of right and justice.

It is altogether an error to assume that a man who neglects his own political duties is only injuring himself. He is injuring everybody who has a right to the exercise by him of his intelligence and experience in the decision of the questions presented to an electorate. It is a just cause of complaint against the laws if they provide electoral duties so heavy that they necessarily discourage his political activity.

Of course the effort should be to strike a mean. It may be necessary, where his duty is light and his neglect of his duty is unreasonable, to institute personal penalties against an elector. But where the practical working of the law is to keep away from the polls a majority of the electors, such penalties would be impracticable, and it is only fair to assume in such a case that the duties imposed are unreasonable and should be entrusted to representatives. When we find, as we often do, in the same election a large vote for candidates and a small vote on legislative issues, it is the best evidence that a majority of the electorate have neither interest nor information enough to lead them to vote on such issues, but do feel themselves competent to select representatives for the purpose.

2

The Representative System

In my last lecture, I sought to show that we should not worship democracy or the rule of the people as a fetish, that government of any kind is only a means to an end, that the end is the happiness of each individual, and that the reason why we favor popular government is because we believe that it is more effective in securing the happiness of each individual and each class of individuals than any other. I invited your attention to the fact that there is, and can be, no truly popular government, in the sense that all the people have a voice in the government as part of the electorate; that a great many more than a mere majority must always be excluded from the electorate, and this, for the purpose of adapting the government better to the end in view; that on the same ground the political duties of each elector ought to be made light enough to secure the attention and activity of the majority, so that the average intelligence of the electorate may exert its proper influence at the polls, and that a system which wearies the mass of voters and keeps them from the polls is condemned by that fact.

These premises were necessary in my judgment to a proper consideration of the question of the wisdom of the changes in our present government, involved in the adoption of the devices known as "the initiative, the referendum and the recall." These are proposed either as a substitute for, or by way of improving the representative system of, popular government. Before coming to a detailed description and discussion of the new devices, I believe it to be germane and relevant to describe the representative system and to point out why it was adopted and what purpose it served.

Mr. Root, in one of his lectures at Princeton, says of the system:

"The expedient of the representation first found its beginning in the Saxon Witenagemot. It was lost in the Norman conquest. It was restored step by step, through the centuries in which Parliament established its power as an institution through the granting or withholding of aids and taxes for the king's use. It was brought to America by the English colonists. It was the practice of the colonies which formed the Federal Union. It entered into the Constitution as a matter of course, because it was the method by which modern liberty had been steadily growing stronger and broader for six centuries as opposed to the direct, unrepresentative method of government in which the Greek and Roman and Italian republics had failed. This representative system has in its turn impressed itself upon the nations which derived their political ideas from Rome and has afforded the method through which popular liberty has been winning forward in its struggle against royal and aristocratic power and privilege the world over. Bluntschli, the great Heidelberg publicist of the last century, says:

"Representative government and self-government are the great works of the English and American peoples. The English have produced representative monarchy with parliamentary legislation and parliamentary government. The Americans have produced the representative republic. We Europeans upon the Continent recognize in our turn that in representative government alone lies the hoped-for union between civil order and popular liberty."

The problem of popular government is difficult. In a pure one-man despotism, the machinery is simple. It needs only to express the will of one individual. In a limited monarchy in which the power of government is divided between the King, at the head of the state, and representatives of different classes in the community, it is less easy to frame a satisfactory plan. Finally, when the King and privileged classes are dispensed with, the complications of government are increased. The problem in a popular government is so to arrange its organization that, with due protection to individual and minority rights, which experience has shown to be useful to society and its progress, the expressed will of a majority of an electorate may be truly interpreted and executed in effective action by the government. The business of administering and legislating for a government is not an easy task. Men of experience in governmental affairs and special knowledge are certainly better able to carry it on than those who have neither. In ordinary life, when we wish a man to draft a will, or a contract, or a deed, or some legal document that is to meet legal requirements, we employ a lawyer. When we would have a member of our family who is ill attended by anyone, we employ a physician. When we would have our children educated, we employ professional teachers. When we wish to build a bridge or a road, we employ professional engineers. When we would build a house, we employ an architect and a competent contractor and carpenter. When "We the people," have an object in view, we are generally lacking in the knowledge and practical experience to devise a practical measure to secure it. It would seem wise on our part to employ in such matters men who have the special knowledge and experience enabling them by amendment and discussion to shape measures that will receive the judicial interpretation that we wish to have them bear, and to employ others who know how to enforce them.

Take the question of currency and banking. We know generally that we would like to have a currency issued under a plan automatic in operation, by which the volume shall increase to meet the wants of trade in times of prosperity and expansion, and shall be reduced when the conditions of business require less. If there is too little currency in circulation at times when the timidity of people lead them to hoard it, we are likely to have a money panic that causes a disastrous halt in business, and if, at other times, we have too much idle currency, its unnecessary volume may lead to unhealthy speculation and unwise investments. In drafting such a law and its enactment, we should have men representing us in Congress who by reason of their experience and their studies and their discussions and their knowledge of government finance and banking can properly prepare, discuss and enact the law. It is obviously impossible for the electorate of fifteen millions to meet together and to deliberate with any hope of reaching a satisfactory conclusion as to such legislation.

As government increases in its functions—and the tendency of modern times is to increase the variety of the functions of government—the necessity for the employment of agents who have a specialized knowledge in carrying out such new governmental functions is much greater than where the office of government was limited, as Jefferson would have limited it, largely to the preservation of order and the administration of justice—that is, to a simple police system. What is true in respect to legislation is equally true as to the selection of governmental administrators to execute the laws. In the maintenance of a modern government, it is necessary to employ a vast number of public agents. In the Federal Government, the number runs up into the hundreds of thousands. Now it is obviously impossible for the 15,000,000 of voters, or a majority of that body, carefully and intelligently to select the hundreds of thousands of those who are to execute the laws and the general policy determined by an election. Therefore, our Constitution provides for the appointment of all of these officers, and that chiefly by the President, who, representing all the people, does the best he can to secure good appointees.

This is a representative democracy, in the sense that the people ultimately govern, but they make their government effective by the use of competent agents whom they elect as their representatives.

What the duty of the representative is, of course, has always been a subject of discussion. Undoubtedly when a man permits his name to be submitted to the people as a candidate for their suffrages, with the announcement, either by himself or through a party, that he is in favor of certain governmental policies to be embodied in executive or legislative action, he is bound to conform to those policies or is guilty of deceit. But in the discharge of the functions of a representative, it often occurs that issues arise which were not the subject of discussion at the time of the election, and it often occurs also that even though the general object was the subject of discussion, the particular means to be selected furnished so complicated a question that it played no part in the election. Under such circumstances, I conceive that the representative is to act on his own best judgment, even though it may differ from that of many of his constituents.

This was the view that Edmund Burke took, as shown in his letter to his Bristol constituents. Indeed, Burke went further and insisted that a member of Parliament elected by a district, when elected, ceased to be the representative of the people of that district only and became a representative of the whole Kingdom. I fully concur in that view. Members of Congress owe their allegiance first to the people of the whole community whenever there is a difference between the interest of the country and that of the district. The representative ought not to be the mere mouthpiece of his constituents. He is elected because presumably he is well fitted to discharge the particular duties in respect to which he is to occupy a representative capacity, and he knows more about them than his constituents. In carrying out their general purpose, in accord with his promise, he is still within his authority if he selects his own means of executing that promise according to his conscience.

Again, popular government is impossible without parties. If you have 15,000,000 voters, and every voter is going to have a different view, or every voter differs from every other voter on something, and so they do not agree politically on anything, you will have a chaos that will result in simple negation. In a proper system of party government, the members of each party must agree on certain main doctrines in respect to governmental policy and yield their views on the less important ones, in order that they may have united action, and in order that these main and controlling doctrines, when the party is successful at the election and controls the Government, may furnish the guide for governmental action. But parties cannot be organized and cannot give expression to their views without having leaders, captains, lieutenants and file leaders, without taking the advice of those leaders, and without being influenced by their leadership.

Parties thus in turn adopt the representative system, and the people of the parties appoint delegates to conventions that are supposed to express the party will in the selection of candidates and the declaration of principles. The leaders of the party, the delegates who represent the people of the party, meeting in convention, are charged with the responsibility of nominating fit men for office and of adopting principles that will unify the party and will properly appeal for the support of the entire people.

This is the way in which our representative government down to within a few years has been carried on, not only in the general Government, in the State governments, but also in the organization and maintenance of parties; and there are but few who will not admit that theoretically it is a plan admirably adapted to the creation of efficient government by competent representatives, carrying out in good faith the general purposes of the party which has received the mandate of government from the majority of the electorate.

We have had 125 years of this system, but now we are told that it has failed, and that either it must be changed in a radical way and abolished, or else it must have a supplement which shall correct its evils and give to the people and all the people a more direct control of the laws passed, and of the executive action taken. What is the reason and what the necessity for this change? I wish to be as fair as I can in the statement of the arguments in its behalf. Many books have been written to show the growth of capitalistic control, by corrupt means, of State legislatures and other local tribunals in which and through which charters and special privileges have been voted. They set out in detail the political influences which railroad and other great public utility companies have been able to exercise in politics. From 1865, immediately after the war, until 1900, there was a remarkable expansion of population and commerce. The movement did not take place in the South until the eighties, or later, but certain it is that from 1880 to 1900, in the prosperity and expansion that manifested itself on every hand, the whole attention of nearly all the people was devoted to commercialism. I remember in 1878 when I was graduated from Yale College, the Class of 1853 had its twenty-fifth anniversary, and President Andrew D. White, of Cornell, a member of the class, delivered an address. He took for his subject "The Commercial Spirit," and he prophesied, if it were to continue unabated, the evils which have come. By seizing the opportunities which the corporation laws in various States offered, combinations were increased and added to, and became, in the flush times of the McKinley Administration, after the hard times of the Cleveland Administration, all commanding in business, in politics, and, it would seem, in society. I am the last one to minimize the critical nature of the conditions which prevailed in politics and business and society after the Spanish War, and which seemed to have crystallized into a rigid control of all by great business combinations which could not be shaken. Then there arose a protest, or rather a chorus of protests, which called public attention to the danger that was confronting the people and their government in the control of those artificial creations of the law which circumstances had fostered and permitted to grow into Frankensteins as they were. Leaders arose and led a popular crusade to destroy the undue power of wealth in politics, and to bring these great quasi-public corporations within the regulative influence of legislative and executive action.

The indignant spirit of the people thus aroused is what has prompted the demand for a change from a representative government to one in which the people are to act directly and immediately in legislative and executive matters. That the occasion for the general alarm was justified, no one who has studied the situation can deny. That we were thus saved from the continued corrupt and subterranean control of legislatures and other depositaries of the privilege-granting power, every careful observer must admit. We should rejoice as patriots from the bottom of our hearts for this popular rising, even though it has projected these new questions into politics and has for the time being raised queries as to the wisdom of our present form of government. The inconveniences and the possible excesses which may come from the rousing to action of a leviathan like the people are inevitable. The advantage derived from their quickened conscience, however, is worth all the incidental mistakes or injustice that may be done, before the sobering effect of experience produces a reaction carrying conditions back, not to the abuses of old, but to that point where the original movement might wisely have ended.

The initiative, referendum and recall were proposed in order to clinch the reform I have been describing. It was thought that they were instrumentalities which would prevent forever a recurrence of the abuses. This result, if it could be attained, would certainly be real progress. The advocates of these new institutions, confident of their efficacy, therefore denominated them as progressive measures, and themselves as Progressives.

There is another form of progressivism which calls for notice here. It has grown out of the conditions I have referred to, and operates not only upon the collective conscience of the public but also upon that of individuals who have come to see clearly the folly of devoting themselves exclusively to the mad chase for money and to realize the greater happiness they can attain in making themselves useful to their less fortunate brethren. The accumulated wealth has created a leisure class that recognizes, in the opportunity that their circumstances afford, a responsibility to society to lessen the burden and suffering of the poor and the oppressed under our present economic and social system, and render opportunities for self-betterment in society more nearly equal. There has arisen, as a reaction from the commercial spirit, a greater social consciousness. The organization of social settlements, the expansion and increased effectiveness of charitable organizations and the greater social responsibility of men of wealth—already alluded to—manifest a stimulated fraternity of feeling among members of society toward each other.

This has led to a demand for increasing the functions of Government to relieve the oppressed and the less fortunate in society. The *laissez faire* school would have opposed such functions as paternalistic. Undoubtedly, the Government can wisely do much more than that school would have favored to relieve the oppressed, to create greater equality of opportunity, to make reasonable terms for labor in employment, and to furnish vocational education of the children of the poor. But on the other hand, there is a line beyond which Government cannot go with any good practical results in seeking to make men and society better. Efforts to do so will only result in failure and a waste of public effort and funds. But many enthusiasts, whose whole attention has been so centered on the poverty and suffering in cities or elsewhere as to lead them to disregard the general average improvement of the individual in the community in comfort of life and happiness, have lost their sense of due proportion and spend their energies in pressing forward legislative plans for the uplift of the suffering and the poor and for the mulcting of the fortunate, the thrifty and the well-to-do that are impracticable and will only result in defeat, and increased burden of taxation. This attitude in favor of such measures among the well-to-do, and the propaganda they have made in unjust denunciation of general social and economic conditions, have found ready response in the classes among whom penury, want and misfortune exist.

The elements I have been describing have worked together to produce a school of political philosophers and a large group of followers who call for a change in the fundamental structure of our Government which shall give to the majority of those voting immediate and direct control of new legislation and immediate and direct power to remove all limitations which the fundamental law may present, with a view to the adoption of legislation supposed to be needed to carry out the three purposes: first, to prevent the corruption of politics by corporate wealth; second, to further equality of opportunity, to alleviate penury, want and social and economic inequalities and injustices, and third, to change or qualify the right of property so as more nearly to equalize property conditions.

The plans of this new school of progressives involve much in their general purposes that all good men sympathize with; but the methods they propose and the bitter class spirit they encourage are dangerous in the extreme, and if carried to their logical result will undermine just and enduring popular government. We all sympathize deeply with a purpose to destroy the possibility of plutocracy and we welcome the quickened social consciousness, but because we object to the proposed remedies, and insist that they are sure to fail and will lose for all the people the solid foundation for safe progress in our present form of government, we are relegated to the position of reactionaries, and of men who do not sympathize with progress. Those of us who are thus unjustly classed must be content to be so until vindicated by the event. But we must fight for our principles and maintain them without fear, because unless we do, as I verily believe, our form of representative democracy will be destroyed and its power to aid and maintain the happiness of the individual will cease.

There is nothing to show that all legitimate governmental purposes sought by the so-called Progressives may not be promoted and brought about under the representative system. Admitting that it may be somewhat more slow in its results, it will insure wiser action in detail because of greater deliberation. Great reforms should not be brought about overnight. They need time. They should be marked by careful consideration.

It is said that the representative system is a failure because it gave rise to these evils. Of course the evils did come and they came under the representative system, and it is true that, in the working out of the political evils, politicians adopted means which were fitted to succeed under the representative system. But it does not follow that politicians might not, if we had the other system, address themselves to its weaknesses and bring about a result quite as disheartening. The truth is that what we all utterly ignore in the growth of the abuses which have given rise to this demand for a change in the structure of the government is that the real defect, deeper down than mere machinery, was the sluggishness of the people and a sort of tacit sympathy of the people with those who were promoting the expansion and the material progress of the country in which the people expected to share. People voted without hesitation bonds for the construction of a railroad equal to many thousand dollars a mile, to be paid for by the county or some other local subdivision, in order to secure better transportation in that vicinity. Then when the railroad was built, and the people had to pay the bonds, the whole public attitude was changed and the bitterest antagonism to the railroad company was shown. This is human nature. First, in order to resist injustice, then to acquire unjust advantage, the railroads and other franchise holders used corrupt means. The continued success of such methods with state legislatures and municipal councils was possible only because of the original sympathy of the people with those building up the country by their investments and enterprises, and of their unwillingness at that time to devote proper care to their political duties in selecting and watching legislators and councilmen. In other words, instead of blaming the character of the representative system for recent conditions, we must put the blame where it belongs and not upon a system of government that has stood the test of experience for centuries as the best and wisest means for giving effect to the popular will. Of course, the means used to make corruption successful for a time were cunningly adapted to take advantage of the prominent features of the representative system. The promoters of corruption used the party convention and the party caucus to further their purpose, and they deceived the people as to the character of their candidates. They might have to change their methods under the proposed changes to a more direct democracy, but if the people neglect their duties in politics the same manipulators could learn to turn the new system to their use quite as successfully as the old.

There is no warrant for the assertion that the representative system cannot be made to serve the purposes of honest government and of legislative and executive reforms just as well as the new devices proposed.

One of the strongest reasons for saying so is what has happened. With the heart of our people sound and honest, the dishonesty of their agents has awakened them. Under the influence of their awakening a wonderful change has taken place in every legislative body in the country, and reform laws, many of them meritorious and useful, have been promptly enacted. Indeed, even where the initiative, referendum and recall have been adopted under this impulse, it had to be done through purely representative government machinery.

If this was the case then, why condemn the representative system as not sufficiently responsive to the will of the people when aroused to action?

But it is said that the people will be lulled to inertia again, and then the corruptionists and the politicians will again be working their evil schemes and binding the people as the Lilliputians bound Gulliver. This is certainly inconsistent with the widespread announcement that there is a permanently aroused public and an awakened social conscience. I am glad to believe that the people have learned a permanent lesson from bitter experience in the necessity for holding their representatives strictly responsible for protecting the public in all forms of public grants, whether of money, property, franchises or privileges. I hope to be able to show that the new devices are more likely to produce neglect of the voting part of the people to attend to their duties than this representative system under which, by the method of what is known as a short ballot, we can lessen the electoral duties of the people and secure their general attention at moderate intervals for concentrated and effective action.

3

The Initiative and the Referendum

I now come to the consideration of the system which it is proposed to substitute for the representative system. The new system embraces three parts: the referendum, the initiative and the recall. Let us take them in their order. The referendum, speaking generally, is nothing but a reference of an issue to a decision by a popular election. It has long been known in the political machinery of this Government, and has long been used for certain purposes; and while its operation has not been entirely satisfactory, it seems the only feasible plan to accomplish that for which it is used.

In the first place, after a proposed constitutional amendment has been formulated, discussed, amended and modified in some deliberative assembly, like a constitutional convention or legislature, and has been recommended for adoption by the convention or legislature, or, as some constitutions provide, after it has twice received such examination and favorable vote at successive legislative sessions, it is then submitted to the people for them to determine, by a majority vote, whether it is to be finally adopted. Under some systems a constitutional amendment is not adopted unless a majority of all those voting at the election shall vote for it. Under other systems, it is enough if a majority of those voting on the issue shall be in its favor. Of course, if there is no other issue pending at the election, and there are no candidates running for office, then a majority of those voting at the election and a majority of those voting on an issue are the same, but often at such elections candidates for office are voted for, and it has usually resulted that the votes for candidates are largely in excess of those cast on a constitutional issue. The difference, therefore, between a majority of those voting at the election and those voting on the issue is generally a very material one. I have no hesitancy in saying that I think the requirement that the vote should be a majority of those voting at the election is the safer and better one. In Minnesota the former rule prevails and some four or five amendments proposed have failed, though more voted for them than against them, because the favorable vote was not a majority of the total vote cast for candidates for office at the same election. It too often happens, as we shall see, that the vote on constitutional issues thus taken awakens so little interest that the total vote on the issue is hardly more than half the usual vote cast for candidates for office. The total vote *pro* and *con* on the issue is hardly a majority of the electorate, and a majority of those voting is thus a comparatively small minority of the whole electorate. The constitution is the fundamental law adopted after deliberation, discussion and final vote of the people. It embodies the self-imposed restraint by the people upon those who act for them in passing laws or executing laws or policies. Those solemnly enacted restraints that have been tried for years, and upon the faith of which so much of business and individual action has been based, should not be lightly changed, certainly not by less than a majority of the electorate. The small vote by which in some States the most marked changes are brought about in their constitutions, does not show the stability in our Government which we were wont to think we had, and which gave us such pride in the proven efficacy and permanence of popular rule. Thus in California the vote which carried most radical amendments to the constitution, with changes of immense importance in the structural framework of the State government, was considerably less than that of the vote a year before cast for the minority candidate for the Presidency, who lost the State by sixty thousand (60,000) and it was less than one-third of the total vote for the Presidency. In Ohio there were forty-one different constitutional changes voted on at a special election in September, 1912. The total vote was very little more than 500,000, and the prevailing vote was generally less than 300,000. In the November following the total vote was over 1,100,000, showing that these radical constitutional changes were effected by less than 30 percent of those electors who turned out at a presidential election and considerably less than 25 percent of the total electorate. I have already pointed out how important it is that a large part of the electorate shall discharge their duties, and how unfair it is that so large a proportion of the electors avoid elections when they concern the adoption of legislative or constitutional changes. Still, under the systems that have prevailed, preliminaries are required of a character to advise the whole people of the issue, and delays are enforced to secure deliberation. Thus in the process of adopting such constitutional amendments, the final action of the people has usually been preceded by the detailed discussion, in a deliberative assembly like a legislature or a convention, of every clause and by the proposal of amendments of every clause for the purpose of betterment. The public are advised of the character of the amendments by the discussion in the assembly or convention, and substantial time elapses in which to enable the public to acquire knowledge of what is proposed in the change of fundamental law. Sometimes, indeed, two years are consumed in the necessary preliminaries for a constitutional amendment. Where, however, the referendum is associated with the initiative, we shall see that no such safeguards are provided to give the public the benefit of amendment by persons of experience or of time for information and deliberation.

Second, the referendum has been used for years as a condition upon which local legislation enacted by a state legislature shall go into effect. For instance, when the question is whether a prohibition law ought to be put into operation in a municipality, district or county, it has become frequently the custom on the part of the legislatures to provide that the law shall go into operation in such municipality, district or county, if, in a local election, a majority of the voters lawfully residing therein shall vote in favor of its operation—otherwise not. This is what is called the local option arrangement, and has the advantage of making the going into effect of the law depend upon the question whether it can be really enforced. Experience has shown that a law of this kind, sumptuary in its character, can only be properly enforced in districts in which a majority of the people favor the law, and, therefore, favor its enforcement; but in a district where the majority of the people are opposed to the law, and do not sympathize with its provisions, a sumptuary law is almost certain to become a dead letter. Now everyone must recognize the demoralizing effect of the enactment of laws and their attempted enforcement and their failure because of the lack of public opinion to support the officers of the law in attempting such enforcement. It ought to be said that localities have interest enough in such a local question as liquor selling to make the vote much nearer that on candidates in a general election. The issue is simple and thoroughly understood, it is sharp, and the people know their minds.

Attempts have been made in courts to impeach the constitutionality of a referendum law like this, on the theory that the legislature cannot delegate its legislative power to the people without special constitutional authority. Courts have sustained the law, however, on the theory that the legislation was the act of the legislature, and that the legislature had the authority to impose such conditions as to its going into effect as the legislature might choose, and that the question of the referendum and the issue in the referendum were nothing but the conditions upon which the law was to go into effect.

The referendum has been used in other cases. Wherever the local legislative body has the power to act in such a conclusive way that the people are unable by electing a successor to reverse the action, it is a security against precipitate or corrupt action to require that there shall be a referendum before the action of the local body becomes effective. Thus where the legislature authorizes a city council to issue bonds, binding the municipality to pay a large debt twenty or thirty years hence, in such an important matter as this, the approval of the people may well be had. And so in the issuing of franchises to corporations that may not be amended or revoked, for the same reason the opinion of the people may usefully be invited on the question of the grant before it becomes binding. I may add that in such cases also, the questions thus referred are simple and easily understood and the people can vote with a clear idea of what the election means.

The new school of political philosophers proposes the referendum for far wider uses than I have described. It will be observed, in the instances I have mentioned, that the use of the referendum was voluntary, that is, the legislature could invoke its use but they were not compelled to do so. The new theory, however, is that we are to have a compulsory referendum, that the legislature shall be compelled to refer all laws of importance to the people, and that this referendum may be effected, without the intervention of the legislature at all, but through another instrumentality which I have mentioned, to wit, the initiative. By the initiative is meant an institution under which a certain percentage of the voters signing and filing a petition in some named state office, are enabled to require the state authorities to submit for adoption, by referendum to the lawful voters of the State, any bill for enactment into law of which the petitioners set forth a copy in their petition. The percentage of the registered voters required to make such a petition effective in many of the States is 5 percent; in others 8 percent, and in some others is higher, but 8 percent is usually the requirement. Under this system, as it is actually employed in a great many States, legislation of the most complicated character, embodied in bills, numbering as high as thirty-five or forty, has been submitted at one regular election to the people for their consideration and adoption. In such cases, if the people by a vote of a majority of those voting on each issue shall favor the proposed legislation, it becomes law, and this without being subject to a veto by the Governor or to any interference or change by the legislature.

The question is whether this system is one that ought to approve itself to the public for general adoption. It is argued that, in this way, subterranean influences of corrupt character can be avoided because the whole electorate cannot be corrupted. It is argued that in this way prompt action is secured in deference to popular will, and that legislation, beneficial to the public and avoiding or abolishing special privilege, cannot be obstructed or prevented by the hugger-muggering of political bosses acting under the inspiration of corrupt corporate managers.

I do not mean to say that in the early use of such a device as this upon legislation, the results may not seem to be more directly under the control of the people than under the representative system when it was being used and abused by corrupt methods. However, the ease with which the so-called pure democracy can be turned to the advantage of the corruptionist has yet to be shown. His opportunity will be in the failure of the majority of the people to perform their heavier political duty under the new system, and human nature has greatly changed if such opportunity will not be improved. With the legislatures now in the chastened condition to which the

indignation of the people has brought them, they are not any less responsive in respect of legislation which the people desire than the people themselves. More than this, the great advantage under the representative system
is that it gives room for intelligent discussion and amendment, whereas
under the initiative and referendum such opportunity for bettering the
proposal and making it practical and useful is wholly wanting. Under the
initiative, those who sign a petition frame the bill just as they wish to have
it, and then the public must accept or reject it. To such an audience as this,
it is hardly necessary to point out the fact that, in the history of legislative
measures, the original bill is often so changed and perfected for the good
of the public, and to promote the real and beneficial object, that the bill as
introduced can hardly be recognized in the bill as passed. The bill as passed
accomplishes its purpose, because it has been made over by men whose
knowledge fits them to frame legislation to accomplish a particular purpose, while the original bill is quite likely to have been impracticable and
a failure. The opportunity for amendment is one of the most important
steps in securing proper laws.

Again: Representative government is said to be a failure because the
people are not capable of selecting proper representatives, and yet the
whole system of referendum and initiative rests upon the assumed intelligence and discretion of the people, sufficient to pass upon the wisdom of
the details of thirty complicated bills at one election. The official explanation of these bills in fine print filled a pamphlet of 300 pages. Now I submit
whether the people as a whole may not more certainly select honest and
intelligent agents to act for them in considering and adopting such difficult
legislative measures than they can exercise a discriminating and intelligent
choice in respect to the approval or disapproval of such measures. I commend a perusal of the laws submitted to the electors of Oregon at the last
general election, and if the reader does not lay down the book containing
them with fatigue, confused mind, tired eyes and a disgusted feeling, I am
mistaken. If it has that effect on the reader, consider how much more tired
and confused the perceptions of the voter of average intelligence must be.
It is not too much to say that only a small percentage have the patience to
read through the proposed bills, much less the knowledge and persistence
to learn what they mean and decide upon their effect and value.

We have had societies organized by conscientious reformers for the

purpose of simplifying issues at an election. The platforms of various organizations have approved what is called the short ballot. Now, what is the
principle of the short ballot? What does it mean? It means that the number
of electoral offices to be voted on by the people shall be reduced to as few
as possible, and that all other offices shall be filled by appointment by the
few to be elected, so that the persons elected may be held responsible by
the people, and the people may, by selecting a few honest and intelligent
agents, be sure that all the other officers to be appointed will be selected
with a care, knowledge and discrimination that the people have not the
means of exercising. Now if that is a reform that ought to be adopted, does
it not necessarily follow that the submission to the people of such matters
of complicated legislation as have been offered to the voters of Oregon and
the other States where the voters at a general election are invited to pass
upon a very volume of proposed laws, is directly in the teeth of the principle upon which the short ballot is founded? Is not the advocacy of the short
ballot a conclusive admission that a system by which a small percentage
can foist upon an unoffending electorate the burden of passing on complicated and voluminous legislation is to be avoided? An examination of a
ballot in Oregon, or in South Dakota, or in Colorado, yards long and feet
wide, will at once convince any reasonable man that the system which
makes such a ballot possible is a travesty upon practical methods of ascer-
taining the deliberate will of the people either in legislation or in the selection of candidates.

Again, the people themselves have indicated that they are far better
able to select candidates than they are to pass upon complicated questions
of legislation, and they have done so by the withholding of expression of
any opinion at all upon these many legislative issues that have been submitted to them in the same elections where they have in full numbers expressed their opinion on the selection of candidates for office. This very
act of the people themselves shows that they think that the intricate legislative issues submitted are not proper questions to be submitted to a popular
election. Could any system be devised better adapted to the exaltation of
cranks and the wearying of the electorate of their political duties than the
giving of power to 5 percent or even 8 percent of the voters to submit all
the fads and nostrums that their active but impractical minds can devise,
to be voted on in frequent elections? They invented this initiative in Switzerland and when a considerable percentage of voters refused to vote on

the issues presented, they imposed a fine for failure to vote, with the result that the voters, to avoid the fine, cast their ballots, but they were blank. Examine the record in referendum states and you will find that the total vote on legislative referendums varies from 75 percent to 25 percent of the votes cast for candidates at the same election.

I have a letter from Governor Buchtel of Colorado, chancellor of the University of Denver, in respect to the initiative and referendum in Colorado and Denver, which was written in response to my inquiry as to how the system was working there. It is as follows:

> University of Denver,
> Denver, Colo., April 25, 1913.
> My dear Friend:
>
> I send you herewith report on two state elections and two city elections, held recently, in which the actual vote for initiated measures is shown in connection with the available vote. It is all very depressing. We changed our form of government here in the city of Denver with a total vote of 26,842, when the available vote was somewhere between 65,000 and 70,000. The fact is that our people are disgusted with these programs and so they do not vote at all. We had a day for registration yesterday.
>
> Most faithfully in high regard,
> Henry A. Buchtel.

General Election, November 5, 1912

The vote for Presidential Electors was	265,991
Average for other officers about	260,000

The votes on Initiated Measures at this same election were as follows:

Initiated Constitutional Amendment for State-wide Prohibition:

For	*75,877*
Against	*116,774*
Total	*192,651*

Initiated Constitutional Amendment.

Recall from Office:

For	*53,620*
Against	*39,564*
Total	*93,184*

Initiated Constitutional Amendment.

Recall of Judicial Decisions:

For.. 55,416

Against *40,891*

Total 96,307

Referred State Law.

Building Moffat Tunnel:

For.. 45,800

Against *93,183*

Total 138,983

City of Denver Election, May 21, 1912

The vote for Mayor was.. 71,922

Charter Amendment:

Playground Commission, total 34,403

Charter Amendment:

Mountain Parks, total.. 37,119

Charter Amendment:

Liquor Question, total... 34,096

City Election, February 14, 1913

The actual vote over most serious matters was:

Telephone Ordinance:

For.. 25,784

Against *3,315*

Total 29,099

Holding Charter Convention to Adopt Non-Partisan Commission Form of Government:

For.. 7,632

Against *15,647*

Total 23,279

Initiated Measure to Give Immediate Non-Partisan Commission Form of Government:

For.. 15,841

Against *11,001*

Total 26,842

Non-Partisan System of Election:

For... 15,601

Against *11,012*

Total 26,613

Again, in the city of Cleveland, Ohio, the immensely important question whether they should approve a new charter was submitted and resulted as follows:

Registered electors... 97,000

For charter 24,037

Against charter... 12,077

Not voting 60,886

The charter was thus approved by less than one fourth of electors. It was the result of four months' work of fifteen commissioners.

Such instances might be cited in great number. But it is said by the proposers of this new system, "we propose to teach the people the problems of government and to interest them in matters that they ought to understand. We believe that by continuing we shall ultimately succeed in securing the action of a large majority of the electorate." It is enough to say this has not been the result whenever the attempt to have people vote on complicated legislative measures has been tried. Their interest has decreased. They have been tired and have avoided voting. Is it not much easier to rouse them to their duty to vote only between long intervals and then for a few competent representatives? If education of the people is necessary to make the new system work, does it not seem the course of common sense to retain the old system in which the lesson to be learned is so much simpler and so much more easily taught?

We live in an age of reform—I hope of real reform, but the sham reformers and the crank reformers, the men who have no practical sense with reference to what reform is, will seize upon an opportunity like this initiative to bring the people to the polls so often, and to increase the questions to be submitted at the polls to such number as utterly to disgust the voting public, and ultimately to reduce the numbers of those who do vote on such issues to a point where a very small minority can carry them. Now is this wise? Is it not turning over our Government to the cranks? Is it not giving the decision whether nostrums shall go into operation to the very inventors of those nostrums? When the careful student of history shall read over the legislative measures proposed by the initiative for referendum in the various States and the steps taken under them, his amazed interest, on one hand, and his humor, on the other, will all be roused, as ours now is, by considering the wild propositions that were made and seriously entertained and for a time put into operation during the French Revolution.

One of the features of present-day politics is the lively fear that those engaged in executing the laws and enacting them entertain of temporary popular condemnation and criticism. The man from whom the people really secure the best service is the man who acts on his own judgment as to what is best for his country and for the people, even though this be contrary to the temporary popular notion or passion. The men who are really the great men of any legislative body are those who, having views of their own, defend them and support them, even at the risk of rousing a popular clamor against themselves.

Take an instance recently noted in the dispatches from Washington. A member of the House has justified making incomes of $4,000 a year exempt from the proposed national income tax on the ground that, if the line of immunity were reduced to incomes of $1,000 and less, it would create such an opposition to the tax that it would defeat the party responsible for passing it. If an income tax is a good thing, and ought to be imposed, then the line of immunity ought not to be determined by the question how many votes it would drive away from the controlling party, or by the justice and economic wisdom of the limitation. Personally, it seems to me that the lower the line of immunity the better, from the standpoint of public policy. In all the nations of Europe the immunity is below the line of $1,000 incomes, and the advantage of this is that it makes as many as possible contribute something directly to the Government, and such a contribution rouses an interest on the part of the tax-payer in the expenditures of Government, and gives him a motive for being economical and for wishing to reduce governmental expenditures as much as possible. But if the great majority of the voting population pay no taxes at all, and the taxes are paid by the comparatively few, then the great majority in supporting or voting appropriations of the Government are unaffected by the expenditures and have no sense of responsibility as to their amount.

The reason given by the member of Congress, whom I have quoted, sufficiently illustrates my point that Congressmen do not permit themselves to think independently on subjects entrusted to their judgment and action, but they keep their eyes constantly on the question of how the votes of the people may be affected by such legislation toward the authors of it.

No one ought to minimize the danger there is of corrupt corporate control of legislatures and obstruction to popular will. These are serious evils to be provided against, I fully admit, but, on the other hand, I think that the slavish subordination of the representative, against his better judgment, to temporary, popular passion is also a serious evil. The disposition of politicians to coddle the people, to flatter them into thinking that they cannot make a mistake, and to fail to tell them the truth as to their own errors and tendencies to error, is a growing difficulty in the matter of successful popular government. The assumption that all the defects in our body politic and social which have manifested themselves are due to the machinations of wicked men, and are not due in any degree to the fault of the people in discharging their political obligations, is a misrepresentation of the truth, but flattering to the people. Ultimately the people learn the truth; ultimately they see through the hypocrisies of those who flatter them, and without hesitation they reverse their action, although it seems as if the entire population had been irrevocably committed to its wisdom. If some of our politicians pursued the course of telling the truth at all hazards to the people about themselves, and about those who wish to mislead them, they might not lose as many votes as they fear.

To all these objections, which seem to me to constitute conclusive reasons against this proposed return to direct government, the answer is: "We do not intend to destroy representative government. We value it highly. We wish merely to better it and make it more responsive to the people's will." The effect of the initiative and referendum upon the legislative branch of the Government, even if it be retained, is necessarily to minimize its power, to take away its courage and independence of action, to destroy its sense of responsibility and to hold it up as unworthy of confidence. Nothing would more certainly destroy the character of a law-making body. No one with just pride and proper self-respect would aspire to a position in which the sole standard of action must be the question what the majority of the electorate, or rather a minority likely to vote, will do with measures the details of which there is neither time nor proper means to make the public understand. The necessary result of the compulsory referendum following the initiative is to nullify and defeat the very advantages of the representative system which made it an improvement upon direct government.

The strongest objection to these instruments of direct government, however, is the effect of their constant use in eliminating all distinction between a constitution as fundamental law, and statutes enacted for the disposition of current matters. When exactly the same sanction, without any greater formalities or deliberation, is given to a statute as to a constitution, to an appropriation bill as to a bill of rights, so that the one may be repealed as easily as the other, the peculiar office of a constitution ceases to be. It minimizes the sacredness of those fundamental provisions securing the personal rights of the individual against the unjust aggression of the majority of the electorate.

We are told by this new school of political thinkers that there are no inalienable rights of an individual which the people may not, in the interest of the people and the government at large modify, impair or abolish. The contention is that a man has no rights, independent of the will of the people with whom he lives, that he does not inherently possess personal liberty, the right to property, the right to freedom of religion, the right to free speech or that protection secured to him under the title of "due process of law," and that these can be taken from him by legislative or executive action, if sanctioned by a popular vote, with the same ease and dispatch that the repeal of any ordinary law could be effected. Now this is a very different doctrine from that which our forefathers laid down in the Declaration of Independence and exemplified in the provisions of our Constitution and the amendments called "the Bill of Rights" which immediately followed its adoption.

I don't know that a discussion would be productive of much good as to whether such rights are in the moral sense inalienable. I don't care whether they are called inherent rights, or whether it is conceded, as it must be conceded, that experience has shown that in the use of popular government for the promotion of the happiness of the individual and of society, these things which are called rights must be accorded to the individual, if government is to attain the great end of government. In *Loan*

Association vs. Topeka, 1874, 20 Wall 655, Mr. Justice Miller, speaking for the Supreme Court, used this language:

> A government which recognizes no such rights, which held the lives, the liberty and the property of its citizens subject at all times to the absolute disposition and unlimited control of even the most democratic depository of power, is after all, but a despotism. It is true it is a despotism of the many, of the majority, if you choose to call it so, but it is none the less a despotism. It may well be doubted if a man is to hold all that he is accustomed to call his own, all in which he has placed his happiness, and the security of which is essential to that happiness, under the unlimited dominion of others, whether it is not wiser that this power should be exercised by one man than by many.

The great heritage and glory of the American people has been that their English ancestors first invented representative government and first established these individual rights as against their kings. When, as Americans, they came to establish a government of their own in this country, they developed even more perfectly the representative system and recognized the possibility and probability of error and mistake on the part of themselves in their temporary action, and they therefore imposed upon themselves, and upon their agencies represented in their government, certain limitations in protection of the individual and of the minority. They saw a possible tyranny in a majority in popular government quite as dangerous as the despotism of kings and they prepared a written constitution intended to preserve individual rights against its exercise. It is this fundamental law of popular self-restraint that has aroused the admiration of the world, has commanded the praise of those historians who have studied governments and has led them to the conclusion that it was this that has given such stability and success to the American nation. Lord Acton, one of the greatest historical authorities of any age, in speaking of the Constitution of the United States, said:

> It established a pure democracy, but it was democracy in its highest perfection, armed and vigilant, less against aristocracy and monarchy than against its own weakness and excess. Whilst England was admired for the safeguards with which, in the course of many centuries, it had fortified liberty against the power of the crown, America appeared still

more worthy of admiration for the safeguards which, in the delibera-
tions of a single memorable year, it had set up against the power of its
own sovereign people. It resembled no other known democracy for it
respected freedom, authority and law. It resembled no other constitution, for it was contained in half a dozen intelligible articles. Ancient
Europe opened its mind to two new ideas—that revolution with very
little provocation may be just and that democracy in very large dimen-
sions may be safe.

Now it is proposed to dispense with all the limitations upon legislation
contained in the Constitution, and it is proposed to leave to the initiative
and the referendum, without regard to the character of the law, or what it
affects, and without limitation as to individual rights, the absolute power
to legislate according to the will of the people. This was the principle that
prevailed in the pure democracies of ancient times, and we know with what
disastrous results.

The same great historical authority, Lord Acton, describes it as follows:

The philosophy that was then in the ascendant taught them that there
is no law superior to that of the State—the lawgiver is above the law.

It followed that the sovereign people had a right to do whatever was
within its power, and was bound by no rule of right or wrong but its
own judgment of expediency. On a memorable occasion the assembled
Athenians declared it monstrous that they should be prevented from
doing whatever they chose. No force that existed could restrain them;
and they resolved that no duty should restrain them, and that they
would be bound by no laws that were not of their own making. In this
way the emancipated people of Athens became a tyrant; and their Government, the pioneer of European freedom, stands condemned with a
terrible unanimity by all the wisest of the ancients. They ruined their
city by attempting to conduct war by debate in the market place. Like
the French Republic, they put their unsuccessful commanders to death.
They treated their dependencies with such injustice that they lost their
maritime empire. They plundered the rich until the rich conspired with
the public enemy and they crowned their guilt by the martyrdom of
Socrates.

When the absolute sway of numbers had endured for near a quarter
of a century, nothing but bare existence was left for the State to lose;
and the Athenians, wearied and despondent, confessed the true cause of

their ruin. . . . The repentance of the Athenians came too late to save the Republic. But the lesson of their experience endures for all times, for it teaches that government by the whole people, being the government of the most numerous and most powerful class, is an evil of the same nature as unmixed monarchy, and requires, for nearly the same reasons, institutions that shall protect it against itself, and shall uphold the permanent reign of law against arbitrary revolutions of opinion.

The result in the Roman Republic for similar reasons was the same.

The question which is really at issue in the adoption of the initiative and the referendum is whether we shall abolish constitutions, shall abolish the standard of individual rights and shall justify the action of the majority of an electorate which is a minority of all the people as necessarily the only guide to right and justice. When it becomes apparent, as it undoubtedly will later, what the real meaning of this issue is, as I have stated it, I doubt not that the American people will end this movement, formidable and popular as it now seems, and reverse their present tendency. It is said that this cannot be; that the people have felt the pleasure of the exercise of the power which they have under the system and that they never will willingly give it up again, lest they may be obstructed and hampered by the intrigues and corruptions of politicians. It is possible that the people may never formally repeal provisions for referendum, but my judgment is that the movement will come to an end by the non-use of the referendum, as the people shall see the absurdities into which it is likely to lead them. That the initiative as an instrumentality in the hands of cranks to impose unnecessary political duties upon the whole body of the electorate will become unpopular, it is easy to foretell. When the initiative is abolished as an institution, and the referendum left to the option of the legislature, with the experience that the people are likely to go through with before this result is reached, we can be confident that the use of the referendum will be so infrequent as not to endanger the representative system, or to change materially its useful character.

4

The Initiative, the Referendum, the Recall

I have pointed out in the last chapter a number of objections to the new system of direct government by a majority of those voting, who are usually a minority of the electorate, but I did not exhaust the arguments which can be urged against the proposed radical change in our form of government.

I must not fail to notice an argument against the introduction of the system into the state governments, which has been made by some very able opponents of this so-called reform, in which, however, I cannot concur. Senator Bailey, on the floor of the Senate, contended that the proposed change would be a violation of the guaranty contained in Article 4, Section 4, of the Constitution, the language of which is:

> The United States shall guarantee to every state in this Union a republican form of government and shall protect each of them against invasion, and on application of the legislature, or of the executive when the legislature can not be convened, against domestic violence.

The insistence of Senator Bailey was, and of others who have supported him in that view, that the use of the expression "republican" form of government indicated the intention upon the part of the framers of the Constitution to secure in the States, by guaranty of the general Government, a representative form of popular government. He pointed out that the debates of the Constitutional Convention, so far as we can get at them, and the language of *The Federalist,* a contemporaneous comment on the Constitution before it was adopted by the people, showed conclusively that all the framers of the Constitution understood clearly the difference between a representative government and one in which the people exercised the power of government directly; that they had constantly in mind the difference between a republic under a system of representative government and a pure democracy, and that they were anxious to avoid the dangers which in their judgment would flow from a pure democracy.

A number of times Madison gave his definition of republicanism, and he described it as a popular representative government. In Chapter 10 of *The Federalist,* which Madison wrote, he pointed out the dangers of faction in a popular government, and then he said:

> If a faction consists of less than a majority, relief is supplied by the republican principle, which enables the majority to defeat its sinister views, by regular vote. It may clog the administration, it may convulse society; but it will be unable to execute and mask its violence under the forms of the constitution. When a majority is included in a faction, the form of popular government, on the other hand, enables it to sacrifice to its ruling passion or interest, both the public good and the rights of other citizens. To secure the public good, and private rights, against the danger of such a faction, and at the same time to preserve the spirit and the form of popular government, is then the great object to which our inquiries are directed. Let me add, that it is the great desideratum, by which alone this form of government can be rescued from the opprobrium under which it has so long laboured, and be recommended to the esteem and adoption of mankind.
>
> By what means is this object attainable? Evidently by one of two only. Either the existence of the same passion or interest in a majority at the same time must be prevented; or the majority having such co-existent passion or interest, must be rendered, by their number and local situation, unable to concert and carry into effect schemes of oppression. If the impulse and the opportunity be suffered to coincide, we well know, that neither moral nor religious motives can be relied on as an adequate

control. They are not found to be such on the injustice and violence of individuals, and lose their efficacy in proportion to the number combined together; that is, in proportion as their efficacy becomes needful.

What does Madison mean by faction here? It is clear that he means that spirit either of a majority or minority of the electorate when it allows its action to be controlled by passion, selfish desire for its own benefit even through unjust treatment of others, and by absence of responsibility in the use of political power.

With this suggestion, let us follow Mr. Madison further in his discussion. He continues:

> From this view of the subject, it may be concluded, that a pure democracy, by which I mean a society consisting of a small number of citizens, who assemble and administer the government in person, can admit of no cure from the mischiefs of faction. A common passion or interest will, in almost every case, be felt by a majority of the whole; a communication and concert results from the form of government itself; and there is nothing to check the inducements to sacrifice the weaker party, or an obnoxious individual. Hence it is, that such democracies have ever been spectacles of turbulence and contention; have ever been found incompatible with personal security, or the rights of property; and have, in general, been as short in their lives, as they have been violent in their deaths. Theoretic politicians, who have patronized this species of government, have erroneously supposed, that by reducing mankind to a perfect equality in their political rights, they would, at the same time, be perfectly equalized and assimilated in their possessions, their opinions and their passions.
>
> A republic, by which I mean a government in which the scheme of representation takes place, opens a different prospect, and promises the cure for which we are seeking. Let us examine the points in which it varies from pure democracy, and we shall comprehend both the nature of the cure and the efficacy which it must derive from the union.
>
> The two great points of difference between a democracy and a republic, are, first, the delegation of the government, in the latter, to a small number of citizens elected by the rest; secondly, the greater number of citizens, and greater sphere of country, over which the latter may be extended.

I have read this passage from Madison not only to show that he, as one of the leading spirits of the Constitutional Convention, and, therefore, probably all the others, were advised of the distinction between a republic and a pure democracy, but also to enforce the arguments of my last lecture as to the danger of direct government of a majority or a minority of the electorate, without any restraint as to the rights of the rest of the people and of individuals. But its real relevancy at this point is with reference to its bearing upon the meaning of the word "republican" used in the Constitution to support the argument of Senator Bailey and others, to which I have already referred. To Senator Bailey's argument that provision for legislation by referendum in a State government destroys its republican form, there are, it seems to me, two conclusive answers. One is that the use of the word "republican" at this point in the Constitution was not by way of contrast to a pure democracy as Madison used it in the passage quoted, or by way of emphasis upon the distinction between the two, but that it was used to describe generally the character of the governments which the embryo States had, at the time the Constitution was being formed, and that the contrast intended to be emphasized by this language was the contrast between a republican form of government and a monarchical form of government, a government in which the people had control, and in which they did not have control; and this clause was a guaranty by the National Government that every State should have a form of government which rested upon the will of the people. The second answer to the argument is that the question of what is a republican form of government in this clause is a question which was evidently committed to the discretion of Congress ultimately to decide, because under the form of the article the guaranty is by the general Government, and that guaranty the general Government must necessarily enforce, if it is to be enforced. The method to be pursued by the general Government in the enforcement of such a guaranty is by legislative and executive action, and this necessarily relegates to Congress and the Executive the power, political in its nature, to determine when a State government is republican within the meaning of this article. To such a decision the judicial branch of the Government must necessarily bow and can exercise no jurisdiction in enforcement of the guaranty. One of the most frequent questions which Congress has been called upon to decide is whether the constitution of an embryo state (that is a territory asking Congress for admission into the Union and tendering a constitution) secures to the State a republican form of government. Congress has acted a number of times in respect to this matter so as to leave no doubt as to the decision by this competent authority that a republican form of government guaranteed to each State by the Constitution is not limited to one which is strictly representative and may extend to one in which, by provisions for the initiative and referendum, there is an assimilation to the pure democracy and direct government.

In the case of *Pacific States . . . Co. vs. the State of Oregon,* 223 U.S. 118, the Supreme Court was called upon to consider the defense made by a defendant telephone company against the collection of a tax, that the tax was invalid because authority was found for it in a statute enacted into law directly by the people under the procedure by initiative and referendum, and that the statute by virtue of Section 4, Article 4, was the act of a State not having a republican form of government and was void. The Court, speaking by Chief Justice White, held that the question whether Oregon had a republican form of government was political, and was for the judgment of Congress, and that until Congress acted upon any change in the government of Oregon, and declared it to be a violation of the Constitution, the Court would accept its status as determined by Congress when it admitted Oregon into the Union.

In passing, it may be useful to call particular attention to the action of the Supreme Court in declining to decide this purely political question and in remitting it to the political branch of Government as represented by the legislature. The Supreme Court has been attacked vigorously in this recent and current agitation as an arbitrary repository of political power, legislative in its character and prejudiced in its exercise, this for the purpose of laying the foundation for the abolition of the constitutional restraints and the remission to the result of a popular referendum the question of the validity of a legislative act rather than to the decision of a court. Not only in this case but in a great many other cases arising under the Constitution, the Supreme Court has refused to assume power to differ with the political branches of the government in the decision of political questions.

Recall

In coming to the question of recall, we are brought to the consideration of something said to be new in the instrumentalities of government, although the Athenians certainly exercised it in effect. The initiative and the referendum were inventions of the Swiss, and had been put into operation for a number of years before their adoption here, but the Swiss never had the recall. The recall is part and parcel of the plan of direct government by the people acting at once, and, as the Latin phrase has it, *dum fervet opus,* i.e., "while the issue is raging" (to give it a free translation). It is a part of what has not infrequently been called the "hair trigger" form of government, by which, immediately upon the presentation of an issue, it shall be passed upon by the electorate. The recall is an institution under which, by the petition of a certain percentage of registered voters, the question whether any elected officer shall continue in office during the term for which he was elected shall be submitted to the electors, with the feature added that any other aspirant to the office, having complied with certain formal preliminaries, may become a candidate against him in the same election in which his qualifications for office are to be reconsidered by the people. The opportunity is given in the petition for a statement of the reasons why the officer against whom the petition is filed ought to be recalled, and generally in some form or other an opportunity is given to the incumbent to state a short answer to the charges made.

It seems to me that the arguments against this method of changing the popular agents are as strong as those against the initiative and the referendum. The useful part of the plan can all be accomplished by a provision that if the officer has neglected his duty, or is guilty of malfeasance, he may be removed after a hearing by a court or by the Chief Executive. This could be made as expeditious as a fair hearing would permit and need not drag through all the courts with the officer still holding his office, but the action of the first tribunal, whether judicial or executive, could oust him, and an appeal, if taken, need not suspend the effect of the ouster until a final reversal of the first decision.

The objection to the recall is not at all the injustice to the officer in taking away from him that which the people had given him. We have lost the idea in this country that an office is the property of the officer, and such a provision as recall does not, therefore, in any way interfere with a vested right. His comfort or enjoyment does not figure in the matter at all. The objection to the recall is its injury to efficient government and the possibility that an honest and effective official may be prevented from doing his duty by the use of such an instrument in the hands of malignant enemies, or aspiring rivals who seize the opportunity of a momentary un-popularity to deprive the public of a useful public servant. It takes away the probability of independence and courage of official action in the servants of the people. It tends to produce in every public official a nervous condition of irresolution as to whether he should do what he thinks he ought to do in the interest of the public, or should withhold from doing anything, or should do as little as possible, in order to avoid any discussion at all.

What do we have government for? It is not merely for the purpose of elections. It is not merely for the purpose of inviting the people constantly to express their opinion on issues just as an amusement. We have govern-ment for the purpose of accomplishing something, of doing something for the benefit of the people, of achieving the greatest good to the greatest number, and preserving to the individual his happiness and progress. Now I submit it is not to contribute to that end to have mere puppets in office who cannot enter upon proper public policies and carry them out, because they fear that their purpose will be misunderstood before their patriotic and public objects are accomplished.

If we have the recall in the case of local officers, there is not any logical reason why we should not have the recall in the case of all officers, and therefore that whenever proper preliminaries are established, we should have the recall of Presidents. Look back, my friends, through the history of the United States and recount the number of instances of men who filled important offices and whose greatness is conceded today, and tell me one who was not subject of the severest censure for what he had done, whose motives were not questioned, whose character was not attacked, and who, if subjected to a recall at certain times in his official career when criticism had impaired his popularity, would not have been sent into private life with only a part of his term completed. Washington is one who would have been recalled, Madison another, Lincoln another and Cleveland another. These were the highest types of patriots and statesmen, who adhered to a conscientious sense of duty to the public. They are men for whom today the verdict of history is, "Well done, thou good and faithful servant" and this, too, in respect of the very matters that at the time had subjected them to the doubt and suspicion and antagonism of a temporary majority of the people. Indeed the recall is nothing but the logical outcome of the proposition embodied in the referendum and the initiative, to wit, that government must follow the course of popular passion and momentary expression of the people without deliberation and without opportunity for full information. I am now referring to the recall of executive officers and legislative representatives, and what I have said is applicable to them. I am not now dealing with the judicial officer and the recall of the judge. That is associated with another proposition known as the recall of judicial decisions, and I shall later consider those two propositions together under another clause of the preamble.

The adoption of the initiative, referendum and recall, and the change of the character of our Government which they will involve, is but flying in the face of the indisputable verdict of history, and the plainest inference that the logic of circumstances can enforce. These "hair trigger" popular verdicts are said to be progressive, and to be the means of a growth toward better things. They are advocated as necessary steps in advancing civilization. The facts contradict altogether such a view. It is a case of atavism. It is adopting a theory of government that was rejected thousands of years ago because of its utter failure to survive the inherent difficulties presented in its practical operation.

I would not minimize in the slightest degree the advantage that will doubtless arise in our Government from the stimulated interest of the people in stamping out certain evils of our political system to which I have referred. Those evils were largely possible because of the lack of that popular attention which is now being more or less roused to the consideration of our Government, our social condition and those inequalities of opportunity and condition which it is wise for our Government to attempt to modify and remedy. But the warning in which all practical and patriotic men must join is that these so-called novel methods, approval of which is now made a test of the real progressive spirit, mean only a reversion to a type that has been proven to be a failure and will necessarily lead to a defeat of all the good purposes and real benefits of popular government. Unrestrained tyranny of the majority will lead to anarchy, and anarchy will lead the people to embrace and support the absolute rule of one rather than the turbulent and unreasonable whim of a factional majority.

Of course, I understand the penalty that one has to undergo in taking this position, of being charged with prejudice in favor of special interests, and against popular government, and with failing to recognize the great change which has come over the people. The leaders of the movement dwell upon the regeneration of the political character of the people, and their really religious enthusiasm and the growth of self-abnegation among them. Therefore, it is said that we must not look to the past as an evidence or a proof of what will happen by the introduction of these old methods.

I had the pleasure of listening to a sermon in New York preceding the last election, in which it was pointed out that, except in respect of the slavery issue, politics in America had since the foundation of the Government been commercial, sordid and concerned with the material side of life, but that from this time on the issues were not to be merely commercial and economical, but were to present the higher aspirations on the one side, and a retrogression on the other, and that all that was necessary was for the people to choose; that we had escaped from the dominion of the slavish accumulators of wealth, and that we were now moving on to a higher level and to the cultivation of the pure brotherhood of man. This view was not very complimentary to the great men that established this government, or the patriots and statesmen who have figured since in American history, and it struck me as unduly optimistic. No one should hold in contempt the aspiration for better things nor employ ridicule to confute argument based upon it, but the plain facts cannot be destroyed by mere eloquence.

The character of the people is made up by the character of the individuals that compose it. The truth is that the conscience of the crowd is never as sensitive, and never represents as high ideals, as the conscience of the individual, and the soundness of the view that the people are now ready for a form of government which, in the past, they have not been able to exercise with any utility to themselves, must rest upon our knowledge of the individual. I would not deny at all that there are enthusiasts who conscientiously feel the spur of brotherly love and of anxiety to bring about a condition in which that sentiment shall be embodied in our statutes and in our governmental policies, and in all relations in life between individuals, and that there are those who are willing to make real sacrifices to bring about such a state, even to the giving up of the advantages of comfort and wealth and position that they now enjoy in society. But has sin left us? Has the principle of enlightened or other kind of selfishness ceased to operate on the individual? Are we not all subject to the weaknesses of human nature that we have known for six thousand years? And do those weaknesses not manifest themselves in elections as well as in other phases of individual duty? Is it the wise part of statesmanship to ignore these truths and the character of the individual and of the people as we know them today, and proceed to adopt a form of government on the theory that they have entirely changed, and that each man bears to the other a feeling of altruism and of brotherly love that will make him ignore his own condition and look after his brother's only? We know this is not so. Though we accept the proposition that the people have grown more sensitive than they were when they permitted corruption and corrupt control of state legislatures and other instrumentalities of government by their inertia and their failure to act, must we not admit that in the States where the new direct system has been introduced, we find a majority of the voters neglecting their public duties so that measures are being adopted by a comparatively small minority, and not by the majority?

This movement back of the referendum, initiative and recall does not find its only promptings in a desire to stamp out corruption. There is another basis for the movement today which gives strength to the proposal to put unrestrained and immediate control in the hands of a majority or minority of the electorate. It is in the idea that the unrestrained rule of the majority of the electors voting will prevent the right of property from proving an obstacle to achieving equality in condition so that the rich may be made poorer and the poor richer. In other words, a spur, conscious or unconscious, to this movement is socialistic. It may not be recognized, even by those who are acting under its influence, but it is there, and ultimately it will manifest itself so plainly that no one can be blinded as to its real meaning and purpose.

I cannot at this time consider properly the wisdom and soundness of the doctrine that lies at the basis of socialism, or put a true and full estimate upon the value of the preservation of the right of property in our political, governmental and economic systems. Nor do I impeach the good faith or intentions of socialists. It is sufficient for me now to say that next to the right of liberty, the right of property is the most important individual right guaranteed by the Constitution and the one which, united with that of personal liberty, has contributed more to the growth of civilization than any other institution established by the human race. If it is to be eliminated from the rights secured to the individual, then we shall see disappear from our community the mainspring of action that has led men to labor, to save, to invent, to devise plans for making two blades of grass grow where one grew before, to increase the production of all human comforts and to reduce their cost; we shall see a halt in thrift, providence, industry, mental and physical activity and energy because they will no longer command the rewards that have heretofore stimulated them, and society will sink to a dead level of those who will seek to get along with the least labor, least effort and least self-sacrifice. Socialism proposes no adequate substitute for the motive of enlightened selfishness that today is at the basis of all human labor and effort, enterprise and new activity.

There is reason to believe that the tendency of much of what has been termed "unrest" in society has been fed and stimulated by the jealousy of those who with envious eye are now looking upon the rewards of thrift and saving and enterprise enjoyed by others. Then, too, these proposed radical changes in our political and social structure have found ready support from those sincere lovers of their kind whose judgment has been led astray by a constant contemplation of the suffering and misfortune in the world, and whose sense of the due proportion of things has thus been affected so that they cannot see the real progress that has been made in the comfort and enjoyment and opportunity of the average individual today over that which the average individual enjoyed fifty, one hundred or two hundred years ago.

Do we find in the propaganda of this modern school of thinkers who are engaged in organizing the new millennium, any appeal for industry, thrift and the discharge of duty by all the people? Is not the picture constantly held out to the people that they are the victims of a conspiracy against them by those who appear to be the more fortunate? Is there not in every line of the addresses and the speeches and the platforms that are issued to arouse the people, the assumption that they have discharged their duty in every regard? Are not those who achieve under modern conditions the greater comfort by hard work and prudential virtues held up as in some way to blame for the fact that those who are not so thrifty, and who have not labored with the same assiduity and with the same self-sacrifice do not have the same comforts?

I would not minimize the number of the unfortunate who in the struggle for existence have fallen behind through the hardness of conditions rather than through their lack of industry and thrift. Wherever the present law by reason of its ancient derivation fails to square with the just requirements of modern conditions, I would amend it, and one good thing that this present movement is accomplishing is the modification of the harder and narrower provisions of the common law so as to put the employees of little power and means on a level with their employers in adjusting and agreeing upon their mutual obligations. Indeed, no objection exists to the proposal to introduce what is called "collectivist" legislation, if sensibly and practically conceived, in which the rights of classes against each other may be recognized, and the classes placed on such an equality as to opportunity as the law can properly effect. But it is a real injury to society to emphasize constantly the necessity for ameliorating the conditions of the less fortunate and the people of little means, without at the same time dwelling upon their duties as citizens, their obligation to render a full day's work for a full day's wages, their duty to sympathize with the enforcement of law and to render justice even to the more fortunate members of the community. Instead of this, appeals are really being made to the majority to use the power that their being a majority gives them to compel equality, not only of opportunity but of condition and of property, and, by silence on the subject, to ignore all difference in point of merit between thrift and industry on the one hand, and shiftlessness and laziness on the other.

Let the movement in favor of purer and better government go on. Let it disclose itself in the effective attention to the election of our representatives in executive and legislative offices, and to the holding of them to strict responsibility. But let us not, with a confession that we, the people, are incapable of selecting honest representatives, assume the still more difficult office and duty of directly discharging the delicate functions of government by the hasty action of a necessarily uninformed majority of the electorate, or, what is more likely, by a minority of an electorate, a majority of which declines to take part in the government through disgust at the impracticable and unwise burdens that are sought to be thrown upon them.

I have no doubt that this movement toward direct government, or, as it is called, toward pure democracy, with a view of giving absolute power to a majority of the voting class, will continue for some time to come. I am not blind at all to the strength of the movement for the initiative, referendum and recall. I am quite aware that I am swimming against the stream but this does not discourage me or make my conviction less strong. The impatience at constitutional restraints will grow with the longing for absolute power by the voting minority. But I am very hopeful that when the American people, after many humiliating experiences and difficulties of their own making, shall see that the ultimate issue is socialism and an unlimited control of the majority of the electorate on the one hand, or our present government on the other, they will make the wise choice and will give up this new solution of the problems of society. They will then return to an appreciation of the wisdom of our ancestors in the framing of a government of the people, for the people, by the people, in which the checks and balances secure deliberation and wisdom in ultimate popular action, and protect the individual in the enjoyment of those rights which have enabled him and his fellows to carry society and civilization to the high point which they have reached in the history of human kind.

As Mr. Lincoln said in his first inaugural:

> A majority held in restraint by constitutional checks and limitations and always changing easily with deliberate changes of popular opinion and sentiment is the only true sovereign of the people. Whoever rejects it, does of necessity fly to anarchy or despotism.

5

The Direct Primary

In the discussion of the expression, "We the people," set forth in the preamble of the Constitution, my remarks have taken the wide range of a consideration of the electorate, and the methods and procedure adopted for securing an expression of the will of the people, and the proper limitations and restraints in such procedure for the purpose of securing deliberation and the clear exercise of popular judgment after full information.

There is one other proposed reform that has been associated with the new methods of initiative, referendum and recall, though not necessarily involving them or involved in them. I mean the direct primary. That is a method of selecting the party candidates to be voted for in the election by a preliminary election of the members of the party. It is also usual and necessary to have a declaration of party principles so that the whole electorate may know what may be expected if the party succeeds in electing its candidates and controls the legislature and the executive. The direct primary itself cannot furnish this, and it is usually accompanied by some plan for securing such a declaration either from a party committee or a conference of candidates. The same evils which have prompted a resort to such radical methods as the initiative, the referendum and the recall, have also stimulated a wish to change the old methods of party government, of the selection of party candidates, and the declaration of party principles.

In many States until a few years ago the controlling element in a party was practically self-perpetuating. The qualifications of those whose votes or preferences were allowed to control the selection of the local committees and managers of the party, were so limited that it was an easy matter for the leaders of the party to continue their power. They became properly known as the bosses of a machine. The machine strengthened itself whenever the party was successful by distributing the patronage thus secured to create an organization of office-holders, or expectant office-holders, which was well-nigh invincible in the party councils and in determining party policy.

Of course, the managers of great corporations that entered into politics for the purpose of preventing raids upon them, or for the purpose of securing undue privilege from the public, found such machines and organizations ready tools for their hands to attain their purposes, and with the corruption fund which they were able to take from their profits, they supplemented the use of patronage to lubricate the machine and make it operate with certain efficiency for the achievement of their ends. When the people were aroused to the sense of their danger from corrupt corporate control in the government, they properly turned to the boss system and the political machine as the instrument which enabled the powers of evil and of corruption to control parties, and through parties to control governments. They, therefore, directed their energies toward legislation which would take away the means of support upon which bosses and machines had thrived. They found that the local political conventions and the caucuses of a limited membership which did not by any means admit or include the whole electorate of the party, selected the delegates to the local municipal, county and district conventions in which were nominated the municipal officers and the representatives to the State legislature and the members of Congress. In the same conventions were elected the delegates to the State conventions, which in turn selected the Governor and the other officers of state. Each caucus and each convention gave opportunity for manipulation by the machine, so that the real rank and file of the party except the comparatively few "insiders" had little voice in the preliminary selecting of candidates and declaring of party principles. The only modification of this absolute power which the machine maintained was through the vote of the people at the election upon the result of the machine's work. The healthy fear of a defeat at the polls frequently led to the nomination for those offices, which did not give the incumbents great political power, of good candidates in order to attract the support of the party and the independent voter. For offices of patronage and political power the agents of the machine were generally nominated.

I may stop a little to refer to this influence which we call the force of public opinion. It is the saving grace in the defects of popular government. It grows out of publicity and a free press. It is what has made government in communities possible and even tolerable under conditions that when stated seem necessarily to involve the most revolting and demoralizing corruption and tyrannical boss rule. It is what has enabled the great municipal community of New York City, the greatest city in this country and one of the greatest in the world, to live under such a control as that of Tammany and still have a useful government, effective in many ways, though with many faults. This public opinion is made up not by the views of the electorate alone, but by those of the whole people, including women, minors and residents ineligible to vote, reflected in the press and reaching those in power in a thousand different ways. It exists, of course, to some extent in every form of government, however tyrannical, but it has its full flower among an intelligent, active and enterprising people who support a free, courageous, alert and discriminating press, the individual members of which present different aspects of the facts and of the issues, but which united together present in composite form an evidence of the public will that places a most healthy restraint upon the otherwise irresponsible boss or machine manager. The distinction between a people capable of self-government and one that should be still in leading strings is shown more in the difference in the intelligence and effective power of public opinion of the two peoples than in any other way. I remember an incident in the Philippine Islands when I was Governor that made me dwell upon such a difference. I was waited on by a committee of respectable Filipino gentlemen, who asked permission to form and exploit a political party for the securing of independence by peaceable means. I told them they could do so without securing my permission, but I cautioned them that, as there were men then engaged in active and open revolt against the government, the organization and maintenance of such a party, before peace was restored, might subject them to annoying curiosity and suspicion of government agents and officers. They said that they and their people were used to securing direct authority from the governor-general in Spanish times for such a political movement and they did not wish to go into it unless I approved. They wished, therefore, to satisfy me that the Filipinos were capable of self-government, and they could do so in a paper they would leave me. The argument presented was based on the statistics as to education in the Islands and the number of offices to be filled in the central, provincial and municipal government. As these showed that there were twice as many educated people as there were offices, they considered their case established, because it gave the people of the Philippines the benefit of two shifts of public servants, and a people would be unreasonable that wanted more. I attempted to explain to them that it was the average intelligence of the whole people that constituted their governmental capacity, and this not only because a considerable part of them took part in elections, but because of this force of public opinion coming from the whole people and restraining public servants in every conceivable way. I don't think I convinced my petitioners but it made me formulate for my own benefit and future use a statement of that great saving force in a government of a free and intelligent people.

But to return to the party primary. A party is a voluntary organization, and originally the natural theory was that the members of the party should be left to themselves to determine how their party representatives were to be selected and their party principles were to be formulated; but the abuses to which completely voluntary organizations of this kind led, brought about a change of view as to the function of the government with reference to such party procedure.

The first step taken was to provide legal machinery and regulations for the holding of party primaries and a convention in the local divisions, which the party authorities might by proper legal notice make applicable to the selection of their candidates and the declaration of their principles before any election. It was voluntary. It was left to the committees of the parties to indicate their wish to act under the law by formal notice, and then it became binding, and penalties followed the breach of its provisions as declared in the law.

This legislation, however, did not prove to be enough, and so those who wished to bring about honest methods in politics determined to make a compulsory law for the government of parties who proposed to present candidates at any election. Parties thus came to be recognized as official entities and the laws for the holding of primaries and of conventions have become as specific in their provisions and as severe in their penalties for violations as the election law itself. The officers who are appointed as judges and clerks of regular elections are made to discharge similar functions in party primary elections, and the State bears the expense, on the theory that the whole public are interested, that each party should honestly select its candidates and declare its principles.

I fully concur in the critical importance that this character of legislation attaches to party action, and I do not hesitate to say that we have not yet arrived at a satisfactory solution of the problem presented.

It must be obvious to everyone that while all members of the party who can vote ought to have a voice in the selection of candidates and in the determination of principles, it is in the highest degree unfair for persons who are not members of the party, but members of some other party, to exercise any influence in the selection of the candidates or the declaring of the principles. So the most difficult question in all primary laws is the one which confronts the reforming legislator on the threshold. It is how to determine properly and certainly who are qualified electors at a party primary. The other question, which is its counterpart, is to discover who are not entitled to vote, so that if they do vote, they shall be punished and sent to prison for their violation of law and justice. Shall the party electorate be limited to those who are willing to swear that they voted for the party candidates who ran in the last election? Must they have voted for all the candidates? Would not a vote for a majority of the candidates entitle the voter to stand as a regular party man and to vote at the party primary? Or must the qualifications be determined not by what the voter has done in the past, but by what he intends to do in the future? Shall it be enough for him to say that he intends to vote for the party candidates and to follow what he understands to be the party's principles in the next election? The advantage of having the qualifications fixed by what the voter has done in the past is that the definite issue of his qualification then presented is dependent upon an ascertainable fact. If he has not voted as he says he has voted, then he is guilty of perjury and guilty of a plain attempt to defeat the law and secure a vote which is illegal. Prosecutions for frauds of this character would soon keep voters in primaries of their own party.

On the other hand, it is urged that if men have conscientiously reached the conclusion that they intend to be Republicans or Democrats thereafter, it would seem that they ought to have a right to partake in the selection of the candidates to represent them. But the objection to this is that when it comes to an oath as to what they are going to do, there is no means of determining, except in the mind of the man who is taking the oath, what the fact is. He is swearing as to a mental state, and he is the best witness of that state, and nobody can contradict him in any such way as to subject him to conviction for perjury, even if he never intended to support the party. The fact that he subsequently actually votes for some other candidate in the election than the candidate of the party in whose primary he has cast a vote, is not clinching evidence of the fraud he has committed, because he can say he changed his mind and he can hardly be contradicted.

The evil that has proceeded from this uncertainty as to the qualifications of party electors has become so great that I venture to think that the wiser and more practical rule will be to limit party electors for the purpose of selecting candidates in the future to those who supported the party at the last election. That is always or generally a large enough body to secure a disinterested vote, or at least secure a vote that is not under the control of any machine or any pernicious influence.

The reports leave no doubt whatever, indeed the statistics of the elections frequently conclusively confirm the conclusion, that in State and other primaries, thousands and tens of thousands of Democrats vote at Republican primaries, and vice versa. It often happens that in one party, a primary issue, like the selection of a candidate, is settled in advance by general agreement as to who the candidate shall be or what the principle shall be. In such a case the voters of that party feel entirely free to go into the primaries of the other party, and sometimes, with malice aforethought, to vote for the candidate in that party whom it will be most easy for the candidate of their own party to defeat at the general election.

Of course this is all wrong. This is not taking the voice of the party. It is taking the voice of men who are not interested that the party should succeed, and who do not intend to be genuine supporters of the men whom they put upon the party ticket.

In connection with this subject, I am reminded of an experience I had in local politics in Cincinnati, my home. Soon after I came to the Bar, I was living in the 5th Ward, which in those days included within its boundaries both a well-to-do quarter and one which was not. Our precinct had frequently been represented in local Republican conventions by a man named Martin Muldoon, who was reported to have made a modest competence in this service. Living in the same precinct with me was another reformer named Aaron Ferris. He had a most solemn countenance and a voice and bearing of the most monitory and minatory kind. He was a perfect Puritan in type. We agreed that something ought to be done to oust Martin from his representative functions. Accordingly we drummed up as many Republican voters as we could through the precinct and urged them to be alive to their political duties and attend the primary. But we found that we were likely to be swamped by many Democrats who had always voted for Martin in a Republican primary in honorable return for aid which Martin and his Republican voters gave some candidate of theirs in a Democratic primary. It was agreed that we could only escape this result by securing one of the judges and by energy in challenging. Ferris' qualifications fitted him exactly for the judgeship and my then somewhat formidable proportions seemed to make it appropriate for me to take the office of outside challenger. The plan was put through without awaking the suspicions of Martin to the extent of installing Ferris as judge. The first man who came to the polls was Michael Flannigan. I nearly created a riot by challenging his vote. Michael's attitude was that of indignant surprise and offended dignity, and his aspect became threatening, but I persisted in my challenge and stated as a ground that he was a Democrat and not entitled to vote in a Republican primary. Then was vindicated our choice of Ferris as a judge. Minos of Crete could not have seemed more forbidding as he produced a Bible and demanded, in deep tones, of the would-be voter that before he give true reply to the questions he was about to ask him, he should place his hand upon the Book, and repeat after him: "I solemnly swear, in the presence of Almighty God, as I shall answer at the last day of Judgment, that I am Republican"—Ferris had not gone further when

Flannigan jerked his hand away, retreated from the poll, muttering "To h—l with the vote." The effect was instantaneous and work as Martin would, he could bring only a few who would or could pass the examination. We had rallied enough of our own side to defeat Martin under these conditions and we sent a good man to act as delegate. But Martin advised me then that that would be the last time Aaron Ferris would be permitted to be a judge at a primary election in that precinct.

This story illustrates the difficulty in holding fair primaries, but I agree it does not suggest a means of avoiding it that would always succeed. Ferrises are not always to be had as judges and would-be voters are not always as afraid of an oath, however solemn.

It seems to have been the opinion in the Courts of some States that in carrying on an election of this sort, no citizen, whatever his party, could be deprived of the right to vote in either primary. Such a construction may turn upon peculiar language in a state constitution, but the result is so absurd in the provision for a party primary that it cannot for a moment be sustained on general principles and is utterly at war with fairness and honesty in party control.

Until some method has been devised successfully to prevent this fraud I have been describing, we cannot be said to have a successful primary law. Of course, it is helpful to have party primaries of all parties on the same day. In this way, if there is a real controversy in all parties, the voters are likely to divide themselves according to their real and sincere party affiliations, because one can only vote in one primary; but the case of a lively fight in one party and none in another is so frequent that the difficulty I have suggested is often a real one.

The first impulse, and a proper one, of the honest legislator, in dealing with this subject, is to give all the members of the party an equal voice in the selection of candidates and in the declaration of party principles. Therefore all the rules which limit the caucus to the active few, or which exclude regular members of the party, have been properly abolished under such primary statutes, and provision is made for every such member to cast his ballot.

The question upon which opinions differ vitally is whether these electors of the party shall cast their ballots directly for their candidates to be run at the general election, or whether they shall select delegates to local conventions, the candidates to be selected in the local conventions. The modern tendency is toward the direct selection of candidates by the party electors themselves, without the intervention of a convention. I am inclined to think that for a time at least this elimination of the party convention in local politics is a good thing.

Theoretically the convention would be better for reasons which can be very shortly stated. If all the electors, divided into wards and precincts, could select honest and intelligent delegates to represent them in a convention, and these delegates were to give their best thought and disinterested effort to the selection of candidates, I have no doubt that the candidates selected would be better for the party and better for the people than the candidates selected directly at a primary. And this is because the delegates can better inform themselves as to the qualifications of the party candidates than can the people at large. And, secondly, the delegates of a party have a sense of responsibility in selecting the party candidates to secure the support of the people at the general election which is utterly absent in the votes which are cast by the electors of the party at the direct primary polls. There the party electors vote for the men who have been brought favorably to their attention by the newspapers and other means of publicity which the candidates themselves are able to adopt and use. They cast their votes very much as the electors at a general election cast their votes, for the men whom they like, or the men whom they know, and frequently without much knowledge or preference at all. Whereas, in a convention, the leaders and the delegates have the keenest care with respect to what is going to happen at the general election.

In the selection of State and national candidates, this becomes a very important matter. One tendency in a direct election of candidates in a national party will be to select a popular partisan, while that of a convention system will be to take the more moderate man whose name will appeal to the independent voter. Thus a primary election in 1860 would certainly have nominated Seward, not Lincoln; in 1876 would have nominated Blaine, not Hayes.

A third objection to the direct election of candidates by the people is the obvious advantage which the men with wealth and of activity and of little modesty, but of great ambition to be candidates, without real qualification for office, have over the men who, having qualifications for office, are either without means or refuse to spend money for such a purpose, and are indisposed to press their own fitness upon the voters. In other words, the direct election of candidates very much reduces the probability that the office will seek the man.

Whenever I hear or see the phrase "the office seeking the man," I am reminded of a story I have frequently told, that I heard when I was on the Federal Bench and holding court in Kentucky. A Republican Governor had been selected for the first time in the history of the State. An old man, named Aleck Carter, from one of the mountain counties of the State, where live the great majority of such Republicans as there are in Kentucky, who had been voting the Republican ticket all his life, and apparently to no purpose, journeyed down on an old mare from the mountains to Frankfort, the capital. The Kingdom had come and he wished to be there to see, and also to get his reward. When he applied for an office, he was told that in contrast to Democratic methods, this was to be an administration in which the spirit of reform was strong and that the office was to seek the man. He put up at the Capitol Hotel for ten days; then he changed to a boarding house, and finally he merely hired a room and relied on his friends and free lunches for sustenance. But the hour came when neither money nor credit nor Kentucky hospitality could tide him over another day and he must go. As he went by the Capitol Hotel, where the politicians were gathered, an acquaintance called out to him: "Aleck, where are you going?" "I am going home," said he. "I've heard tell, since I've been here, a good mite about an office seeking a man, but I hain't met any office of that kind. My money's gin out and I'm bound for the mountains." Then a hopeful thought seemed to strike him and he continued, "But if any of 'youuns' see an office hunting a man, tell 'em that you just seen Aleck Carter on his old mare 'Jinny' going down the Versailles pike and he was going damn slow."

Were Aleck yearning for an office under the dispensation of direct primaries, he would not be embarrassed by any such newfangled fashion in official preferment, for it has no vogue in the days of the direct primary.

The direct primary puts a premium on self-seeking of an office. After men are nominated as party candidates, the party is behind them, and can elect them even though they modestly refrain from exploiting themselves. But in the stage previous to this, when the candidates are to be selected at a direct primary for a party, modest but qualified men are never selected. This substantially lessens the number of available candidates capable by reason of their intelligence and experience of filling the offices well.

I have thus stated three serious objections to the direct election of candidates by the people for local offices and for representatives in Congress and the legislature, and yet I do not think that they are sufficient to overcome the present necessity of avoiding the evils that have arisen from the delegate and convention systems so far as these local and district officers are concerned. The delegates selected for the local convention are many of them usually not of a character to resist the blandishments and the corrupt means which will in such cases be used by bosses and the principals of bosses. The local convention of local delegates offers such a rich opportunity for manipulation of those who are corruptible,—things are done so quickly by committees of credentials, and on resolutions,—that the opportunity of the unscrupulous boss in such a convention is very great. I sympathize, therefore, with the movement to abolish the local convention, at least until the exercise of the direct primary shall have broken up the local machines and shall have given an opportunity to the electors of the party, even with the disadvantage of inadequate information, to express their will.

When, however, the question is of the State convention and its continuance in politics, I am strongly inclined to a different opinion. The delegates who are sent to a state convention should be voted for directly by the same electorate that selects the representatives to the legislatures, and their character is likely to be very much higher than that of the delegates to a local convention. The circumstances offer as much reason for confidence in their honesty as in that of those who are selected for the legislature by the primary. The unit of a national party in a practical sense is the State party. That is the body that helps to formulate a political policy for the national party. If the party has a majority in the legislature, it ought to have a State policy, the determination and declaration of which can best be had in a convention. It is not indispensable that the parties in local controversies should announce principles at all, and, therefore, the necessity for a local convention on that account is really small. But when it comes to a party of the State, there ought to be some body having representative authority to declare what the party policies are to be. Now in some States there has been substituted for the party convention an assembly of party candidates, and in others of the elected party managers from each county, but none of these methods secures a reliable expression of what the party opinion really is as well as a State convention with delegates selected for the purpose.

I do not mean to say that there is not any opportunity in a State convention for political manipulation. I do not mean to say that corrupt politicians will not try to be influential, and will not succeed in some directions, as they will under any system, but I do mean to say that the opportunity for manipulation and the defeat of the will of the party electors is very much less in a state convention than it is in a local convention. It is the best means of securing an authoritative expression of the party, and offers comparatively little opportunity for boss control if the primaries at which the delegates are selected are conducted by the same method as in the direct selection of candidates for legislative representatives.

The holding of a State convention gives an opportunity for consultation among party leaders. Party leaders are not necessarily dishonest men. On the contrary, the great majority of them are honest and anxious for the party to succeed by serving the people well in the government with which the party may be entrusted. Consultation should not be tabooed. Conference and discussion lead to wise results, and conference and discussion and deliberation with reference to party policies are not possible at the polls. They are not possible when the electors number into the millions. The abolition of the State convention in my judgment, though it may be the result of the present movement, is an extreme measure which subsequent experience will show to have been a mistake.

I think it will be found—at least that has been the result of my experience in hunting for material for judicial appointments—that the method of selecting State candidates through direct vote, rather than by nomination of a convention, has not been as successful in securing as good judicial material as the old method of conventions. The result in such direct primaries is unduly affected by the fortuitous circumstance as to whose name is at the head of the list of candidates, or by the fact that he is the incumbent and his name but not his qualification is known.

The direct election of candidates for office by the people shows better results in small communities than it does with electorates like that of a state, because the character of local candidates can be very much more certainly and definitely known, and the choice made with more discrimination by the people of a local neighborhood.

What I have said with respect to a state convention applies even more forcibly to a national convention. There are public men of influence who contend that we ought to have a general national primary to settle upon candidates. I think this is carrying the direct action of the people in the selection of candidates far beyond what is practicable. The defects of the present primary system, especially that one which I have already pointed out, the impossibility of preventing voters of the opposition from voting in the party primary, would be emphasized to such a point that the selection of a candidate by popular vote would be much less satisfactory than the system of a convention attended by delegates selected by properly conducted primaries in congressional districts, or by a convention of a state. The necessity for a national convention ultimately to determine the national party policy, and to consider carefully the qualifications of candidates, I hope will always be recognized. There is not any objection—indeed there ought to be no hesitation about it—to making the representation in the convention proper and fair, so that the voters of the party may have an influence as nearly proportionate to the influence they wield in the election as is practicable. If there are rotten boroughs, as there are doubtless, under the present system, they ought to be eradicated, but to go to the other extreme of abolishing a convention which has always been the method of selecting a President, is, it seems to me, altogether unwise.

There is a tendency on the part of those who favor the direct election by the people at a party primary in all cases, to resort to loud declamation in favor of a method that gives all people their choice. I have commented on the fact that the electors are not all the people, and that others are interested in the government beside the electors; but I submit that the question is not to be governed by the general declaration that an expression of all the people at an election is necessarily better than the expression of their delegates in convention, and that the mere assertion is not proof. The real end that we have in view is a better government for each individual and for all the people, and if we can get better candidates, and if we can more surely secure the intelligent and deliberate consideration of party principle through conventions, then we should adopt conventions because what we are after is good results. The voting of all the people on an issue, or for a candidate, is not the end. It is a means, and if it is not the best means of securing good candidates and of accurately interpreting the deliberate judgment of the people, then it is not the means that ought to be adopted.

I close the discussion of this general primary, having pointed out the arguments for and against the features which are now forming the subject of discussion. While the general primary is always classed as part of the so-called reforms of the initiative, the referendum and the recall, I do not consider that they have any necessary relation. It is very essential that we should have party machinery which will prevent as far as practical corrupt bossing of the party and consequent corrupt bossing of the community, and the direct primary in local elections with certain limitations is a practical step to oust the boss and destroy the machine built of patronage and corruption. This all honest men are in favor of, if the means proposed is really effective.

We must have party government in this country. A popular government cannot be made efficient without parties, and as parties now include millions of voters, it is essential that some means should be determined by which the party will can be best interpreted into the selection of candidates and the declaration of principles.

I have described the machinery of old and the machinery at present, and that which is proposed. I have attempted to point out the defects in each, and I look forward to the next ten years as probably furnishing a composite system which shall give us the best practical result. Of course, no system can avoid the effect of corruption. None can be boss or machine proof, but some method can be adopted which will minimize these evils and bring about the healthy control of party agencies by the people who compose it.

6

"In Order to Form a More Perfect Union"

The first purpose stated in the preamble of the Constitution for its framing and adoption was "in order to form a more perfect union." The Articles of Confederation, under which the War of the Revolution had been conducted, were inadequate in many particulars. The Continental Congress really had but little power. It conducted the war through committees; it appointed the commanding generals, but its requisitions upon States for money and men were nothing but recommendations, sometimes followed and sometimes ignored, and its exercise of the function of law-making was very limited.

The condition of the colonies after the recognition of our independence by Great Britain was not encouraging. There was no authority anywhere sufficient to better conditions. Hamilton's description was not an exaggeration when he wrote in *The Federalist* in Paper XV:

> We may indeed, with propriety, be said to have reached almost the last stage of national humiliation. There is scarcely any thing that can wound the pride, or degrade the character, of an independent people, which we do not experience. Are there engagements, to the performance

of which we are held by every tie respectable among men? These are the subjects of constant and unblushing violation. Do we owe debts to foreigners, and to our own citizens, contracted in a time of imminent peril, for the preservation of our political existence? These remain without any proper or satisfactory provision for their discharge. Have we valuable territories and important posts in the possession of a foreign power, which, by express stipulations, ought long since to have been surrendered? These are still retained, to the prejudice of our interest not less than of our rights. Are we in a condition to resent, or to repel the aggression? We have neither troops, nor treasury, nor government. Are we even in a condition to remonstrate with dignity? The just imputations on our own faith, in respect to the same treaty, ought first to be removed. Are we entitled, by nature and compact, to a free participation in the navigation of the Mississippi? Spain excludes us from it. Is public credit an indispensable resource in time of public danger? We seem to have abandoned its cause as desperate and irretrievable. Is commerce of importance to national wealth? Ours is at the lowest point of declension. Is respectability in the eyes of foreign powers, a safeguard against foreign encroachments? The imbecility of our government even forbids them to treat with us. Our ambassadors abroad are the mere pageants of mimic sovereignty.

After speaking of the unnatural decrease in the value of land, and the absence of private credit, he said:

To shorten an enumeration of particulars which can afford neither pleasure nor instruction, it may in general be demanded what indication is there of national disorder, poverty, and insignificance, that could befall a community so peculiarly blessed with natural advantages as we are, which does not form a part of the dark catalogue of our public misfortunes?

He points out the cause as follows:

The great and radical vice, in the construction of the existing confederation, is in the principle of legislation for states or governments, in their corporate or collective capacities, and as contra-distinguished from the individuals of whom they consist.

He emphasizes the remedy in these words:

But if we are unwilling to be placed in this perilous situation; if we still adhere to the design of a national government, or, which is the same thing, of a superintending power, under the direction of a common council, we must resolve to incorporate into our plan those ingredients, which may be considered as forming the characteristic difference between a league and a government; we must extend the authority of the union to the persons of the citizens—the only proper objects of government.

Another and very important condition in the Confederacy which created the desire for a more perfect union is stated by Madison, in the forty-second number of *The Federalist,* where he comments on the power given Congress in the proposed new constitution to regulate commerce between the States. He says:

The defect of power in the existing confederacy, to regulate the commerce between its several members, is in the number of those which have been clearly pointed out by experience. . . . A very material object of this power was the relief of the states which import and export through other states, from the improper contributions levied on them by the latter. Were these at liberty to regulate the trade between state and state, it must be foreseen that ways would be found out to load the articles of import and export, during the passage through their jurisdiction, with duties which would fall on the makers of the latter, and the consumers of the former. We may be assured by past experience that such a practice would be introduced by future contrivances; and both by that and a common knowledge of human affairs, that it would nourish unceasing animosities and not improbably terminate in serious interruptions of the public tranquillity.

Thus we see that the use of the expression "more perfect union," if it was intended to imply that the union then existing was anything like perfect, was unjustified and inaccurate. The union was so lacking in a firm bond between its members that it really is wonderful that the fabric of a government, if it can be so called, did not come tumbling down before a change was made.

The Constitutional Convention was held behind closed doors and the several accounts of its proceedings and the debates are not complete or full. All students of the Constitution are greatly indebted to Prof. Max Farrand, of this university, for assembling the accounts into one work, where a comprehensive view of all that is known of the making of that wonderful instrument can be had, and for his excellent history on the subject.

After it was signed and reported to the Congress, Hamilton, Madison and Jay joined in the work of expounding and justifying it in *The Federalist.* There were many who opposed it with vigor, and that largely because it greatly reduced the power of the then independent States. Clinton of New York, Samuel Adams of Massachusetts, and Patrick Henry of Virginia, were among those who doubted and objected. The feeling which had roused opposition to the ratification by the States, at once upon its going into force led to a controversy over its construction, and to a movement for its amendment. Parties were formed on these issues. Mr. Jefferson and the strict constructionists who exalted the power of the States were the Republican party, which has now become the Democratic party. Hamilton, Adams, Marshall and others who favored a strong central government and a curtailing of the power of the several States, in order to make a Nation, were the Federalist party. Mr. Jefferson insisted that the Constitution did not contain a sufficient protection to the individual, and there were, therefore, proposed in Congress, at its first session, ten amendments, which were ratified on the fifth of December, 1791. The first eight of these were really a bill of rights to protect individuals against the aggression of Congress and Federal authority.

It may be as well to note at this point that the original bill of rights of the Federal Constitution was not a restraint of the State governments against the infraction of individual rights, but a restraint of the National Government. The Fourteenth Amendment was adopted July 20, 1868. It placed in the hands of the Federal Government the enforcement of the personal rights of every person in the United States. That section provides "No state shall make or enforce any law which shall abridge the privileges or immunities of citizens of the United States, nor shall any state deprive any person of life, liberty or property without due process of law, nor deny to any person within its jurisdiction the equal protection of the laws."

It is not necessary to go into a discussion of the full scope of this amendment and the various decisions construing it. It is sufficient to say that it vests in the National Government the power and duty to protect, against the aggression of a State, every person within the jurisdiction of the United States in most of the personal rights, violation of which by Congress is forbidden in the first eight amendments to the Constitution.

The ninth amendment provided that the enumeration in the Constitution of certain rights should not be construed to deny or disparage others retained by the people, and the tenth laid down the rule of interpretation that the powers not delegated to the United States by the Constitution and not prohibited by it to the States were to be considered as reserved to the States respectively or to the people. These two clauses were intended to avoid too wide a construction of the national powers under the Constitution and were proposed and insisted upon by the followers of Jefferson.

The eleventh article provided that the judicial power of the United States should not be construed to extend to any suit in law or equity commenced or prosecuted against one of the United States by citizens of another State or by citizens or subjects of any foreign State. This was proposed at the first session of the third Congress, also by the followers of Jefferson, and was adopted to avoid the effect of the decision of the Supreme Court in *Chisholm vs. Georgia* in 1793, that a State might be sued by a citizen of another State. This amendment exalted the sovereignty of the States. One of usual attributes of sovereignty in a government is immunity from suit in its courts. The amendment was, therefore, a victory for the States' rights men and for the narrower view of the Constitution.

From the first, then, the issue was as to what kind of "a more perfect union" had been established. Jefferson had not been a member of the Convention that made the Constitution and was doubtful of its wisdom. He finally carried Madison with him in his strict construction views, although the latter had been one of the principal agents in framing the instrument and in bringing about its adoption.

The Federalist party, of which Washington may be said to have been the leader, and of which Hamilton was the most able exponent, was in control of the administration for three presidential terms, the two terms of Washington and the one of Adams, and the Judges appointed to the Supreme Court were of that political complexion. The first Chief Justice was John Jay. It is interesting to note that Mr. Jay resigned the office of Chief

Justice to become an Ambassador of the United States to Great Britain, for the purpose of negotiating a treaty with Great Britain called "Jay's Treaty," which subjected him to the bitterest partisan denunciation. When Jay returned home, and the chief justiceship became vacant, he was offered a reappointment by President Adams. He declined it because he did not think the Supreme Court was sufficiently respected and did not have sufficient power. Considering the far-reaching influence of the man who took the place, Jay's reasons for declining now sound strange.

Upon Jay's refusal to take the office again, President John Adams appointed John Marshall, who was confirmed by the Senate, but who did not take his seat upon the Bench until after the installation of Mr. Jefferson in the Presidency. Until that time he acted as Secretary of State.

The transfer of the government from Adams to Jefferson was not accompanied by an excess of courtesy on either side. Mr. Adams refused to ride with Mr. Jefferson to the Capitol or to attend the inauguration. Indeed he left Washington the night before. On the other hand Mr. Marshall is said to have remarked of the manner of Mr. Madison, the new Secretary, in taking possession of the Department of State, that he, Marshall, was glad to escape with his hat.

Although the Federalist party died as the effect of the popular election of 1801, which brought Jefferson to the Presidency, and although its opponent was triumphant in its elections, and reigned supreme as the Democratic party for nearly forty years, the construction which was put upon the Constitution during that long period reflects Federalist views. They were embodied in the great judgments delivered by the greatest Judge that America or the World has produced—John Marshall.

Had the views of Jefferson prevailed in the construction of the Constitution, the effect of that instrument would have been determined by the independent and varying judgments of the several States, and our union would have been treated as a compact of sovereign members, rather than as a sovereign nation. From time to time, Jefferson and his successors appointed judges upon the Supreme Court with a view to neutralizing the influence and views of Marshall. But so strong was the personality of the great Chief Justice, so powerful his intellectual force, so clear his statesman-like conviction that this was and must be a nation, that enough of the new men put upon the Court were changed to his view to keep the States' rights men always in the minority, and the control of Marshall continued until his death in the administration of Andrew Jackson.

In the case of *Marbury vs. Madison,* Marshall laid down the proposition which insured the power of the Federal Supreme Court to declare invalid any law of Congress which was held by the Court to be in violation of the Constitution. This doctrine was denounced by Jefferson as a usurpation by the Court. In *Cohens vs. Virginia,* the Chief Justice announced the supremacy of the Federal Supreme Court in the consideration of Federal questions and its power to overrule the decisions of a Supreme Court of a State in such matters and to set aside the law of a State which was in conflict with the Federal Constitution. In *McCulloch vs. Maryland* and in *Osborn vs. the Bank,* the same great jurist, as the organ of the Court, settled for all time the liberal construction of the Constitution in conferring powers upon the National Government to be implied from the express powers. The Court refused to limit the implication of powers to those which were indispensable to the exercise of the express powers, but held that any method of carrying out the express powers which was reasonably proper and adapted to the purpose, was in the discretion of Congress.

When Jefferson and Madison as political factors were seeking to minimize the national powers under the Constitution, they were merely representing the spirit of state sovereignty which was strong in Jefferson, because he feared danger to individual rights and a monarchical tendency in a national construction of the Constitution. In communications to Congress, in published letters, and in every other way, he thundered against the power of the Supreme Court and the construction that it was putting upon the Constitution in exalting and broadening the national sovereignty and minimizing the power of the States. But it was all to no purpose, and he had the irritating disappointment of finding his own appointees, as I have already indicated, concurring in the views of Marshall and making the decisions of the Supreme Court consistent from the first in a Federalistic construction of the fundamental instrument of government. The school of Jefferson was continued by Calhoun, the great rival of Webster, one of the greatest statesmen of any time, and one of the strongest logicians and political writers. Calhoun attempted in South Carolina to set at naught the collection of customs duties, on the ground that the Federal customs law

violated the Constitution. In doing this, he encountered a vigorous assertion of national authority by Andrew Jackson. But, on the other hand,
Andrew Jackson denounced the construction of the Supreme Court, which
upheld the legislation establishing a United States Bank, and refused to
recognize the law as valid, or to follow the Court's decision. But the judgments of the Supreme Court were permanent, and while one President
nullified or disregarded them, others succeeded and ultimately the view of
the Court was established.

When Marshall died in 1835, the question of anti- and pro-slavery had
come to be the chief issue before the people of the United States. And the
tendency of the dominant Democratic party was toward the maintenance
of slavery as entitled to protection under the Constitution. The slave-
holding party was strong in its wish to extend slave-holding territory with
a view to spreading the doctrine and strengthening its influence. In Section
2, Article 4, the Constitution of the United States provides as follows: "No
person held to service or labor in one state under the laws thereof, escaping
into another, shall in consequence of any law or regulation therein be discharged from such service or labor, but shall be delivered up on claim of
the party to whom such service or labor may be due."

Under the authority of this provision Congress passed what was
known as the fugitive slave law.

It ought to be said that Jefferson and Madison were by no means pro-
slavery men. Jefferson was anxious that slavery should be abolished, and it
could almost be said that early in the constitutional and political history
of this country there was no tense issue in respect to slavery. The slave trade
in the United States, the Constitution provided, might be forbidden by
Congress after 1808. The States' rights attitude of neither Jefferson nor
Madison could be attributed to the influence of this issue. However, the
development of the cotton industry through the South through the invention of the cotton gin, and the supposed necessity for the use of slave labor
in raising cotton, gave to the South a strong interest in maintaining it as a
social institution, and made its preservation the chief feature in the Democratic party's doctrine.

When, therefore, the slave property became valuable, as it did in the
time of Jackson and later, the enforcement of the fugitive slave law became
most important to the pro-slavery party in Congress and in the nation.

Chief Justice Taney, who succeeded Marshall, and the other members of the Supreme Court, therefore, found no difficulty, Democrats as a majority of them were, in maintaining the supremacy of national authority upon State territory in the execution of laws passed in pursuance of the constitutional power and duty of Congress to provide for the return of fugitive slaves.

Decisions made on this subject strengthened the national construction of the Constitution by the Supreme Court in spite of the division in the Democratic party, and in spite of the contention by the southern branch of the party that secession was constitutional, and properly within the power of the States choosing to resort to it. Indeed the fugitive slave law put the abolitionists and those who sympathized with them in the attitude, temporary though it was, of opposition to the national authority on State soil.

Thus by a series of fortuitous circumstances, the construction of the Constitution has always been entrusted to a court that was naturally inclined to uphold the national power and not to emphasize unduly the sovereignty of the States.

When the war came on, the question submitted to the arbitrament of war was the right of secession, and that of course was decided in the negative by the result at Appomattox. Since then no question has been made by any party or school of politics as to the views that Marshall enforced—in respect to the national power.

This history is a striking tribute to the power of the Supreme Court in shaping the destinies of the nation and to the law-abiding character of the people of the country in that, however much political parties may have temporarily differed from the judgments of that Court, those judgments have ultimately prevailed.

Of course there was the Dred Scott decision, involving the status of a free Negro as to citizenship, which, delivered late in the fifties, aroused the indignation of the anti-slavery party against Chief Justice Taney and the majority of the Court, and called forth the careful but forcible criticism of Lincoln and the unmeasured abuse of the abolitionists. That question, however, was removed from judicial controversy by the war and the war amendments to the Constitution, and at any rate had only indirect bearing on the main question of the rights of the States and the powers of the general Government.

Circumstances in the growth of the country have served greatly to increase the volume of Federal power. This has not come from a new construction of the Constitution, but it has come from the fact that the Federal power has been enlarged by the expansion of the always conceded subjects of national activities. It is true that there was a judgment of the Supreme Court as far back as 1846, in the case of the Genesee Chief—Chief Justice Taney delivering the decision—which had the effect to increase largely the Federal jurisdiction in one direction. The maritime jurisdiction of the admiralty courts in England had been limited to tidal waters because in England no other waters were navigable. In the United States, however, there were thousands of miles of river navigation and lake navigation that were beyond the reach of ocean tides. The question was whether the maritime jurisdiction of the United States Government reached to navigable rivers and lakes. Congress passed a law extending the jurisdiction of the Federal Admiralty Courts to such waters and the Supreme Court sustained the law, reversing some decisions that tended to another view. This was one apparent enlargement of Federal jurisdiction in the history of the Supreme Court, but it was a natural and necessary application of the Constitution in the light of the common law and its proper adaptation to our circumstances. It is this power which now places all navigable rivers and harbors within the control of the United States, and leads to the passage of the rivers and harbors bills appropriating money for their improvement, with a view to their navigation.

A great increase in the volume of Federal jurisdiction not due to an enlargement of its defined limits, but due to the increase of business within those limits, arises from the power given to Congress by the Constitution to regulate commerce between the States, with the Indian tribes and with foreign nations. As I have stated, it was the interference with interstate commerce by State obstruction that was one of the chief reasons for bringing the people together into the formation of a Federal Constitution. Originally the business between the States was considerably less than the business done within the States, so that the national control of interstate commerce seemed less important than regulation by the States of their own commerce. But with the invention of steam navigation of waters, and with the construction of railroads, the interstate commerce of the country has increased from one-fourth of the entire country's commerce to three-fourths of it.

In 1887 a law was passed organizing the Interstate Commerce Commission, and delegating to it certain regulative powers in respect to railroad rates in traffic between the States. This law has been amended and re-amended and amended again until now the control exercised over interstate commerce by the Interstate Commerce Commission, when that commerce is carried by railroads, is rounded and complete in the regulation of rates, and in other matters affecting the interest of the public. Regulation of express companies and of telegraph and telephone companies in their interstate business has also been entrusted to the Commission.

Then again, the necessities of modern government and the tendency toward greater paternalism have induced Congress to vest, by statute, in the general Government, powers that under the Constitution were impliedly within congressional creation, but which had been allowed to lie dormant in view of the supposed lack of public necessity for their exercise. Thus, as an outgrowth of the power of regulating commerce, comes the anti-trust act, which forbids the organization of business combinations to do an interstate commerce business by combinations or conspiracies in restraint of interstate trade, or to establish monopolies therein. This has thrown into Federal jurisdiction a most important power, the exercise of which is now revolutionizing and purifying business methods and ridding them of unfair competition, of unjust suppression of fair competition, and of irresponsible but powerful monopolies and private despotisms in each large branch of industry. These colossal combinations are gradually being dissolved under the influence of the anti-trust law and the action of our Federal Courts.

Another great addition to the volume of Federal jurisdiction has arisen under the same clause of the Constitution in the adoption of the pure food act. The Federal Government has no power to interfere with the food products grown or made and used in a State, but it has the power to regulate commerce between the States and to say what are proper subjects of that commerce, and to prevent the use of interstate commerce for the circulation of that which may injure the people reached through such commerce. It, therefore, has the power to insist that shippers shall comply with the regulations looking to the purity of the food products and of the drugs and medicines which they make the subjects of interstate commerce.

Bills have been urged upon Congress to forbid interstate commerce in goods made by child labor. Such proposed legislation has failed chiefly because it was thought beyond the Federal power. The distinction between the power exercised in enacting the pure food bill and that which would have been necessary in the case of the child labor bill is that Congress in the former is only preventing interstate commerce from being a vehicle for conveyance of something which would be injurious to people at its destination, and it might properly decline to permit the use of interstate commerce for that detrimental result. In the latter case, Congress would be using its regulative power of interstate commerce not to effect any result of interstate commerce. Articles made by child labor are presumably as good and useful as articles made by adults. The proposed law is to be enforced to discourage the making of articles by child labor in the State from which the articles were shipped. In other words, it seeks indirectly and by duress, to compel the States to pass a certain kind of legislation that is completely within their discretion to enact or not. Child labor in the State of the shipment has no legitimate or germane relation to the interstate commerce of which the goods thus made are to form a part, to its character or to its effect. Such an attempt of Congress to use its power of regulating such commerce to suppress the use of child labor in the State of shipment would be a clear usurpation of that State's rights.

Another recent increase in the volume of Federal business is due to an application of the same clause of the Constitution to what is known as the white slave business, that is, the transfer of women from one State to another for purposes of prostitution and the spread of vice.

Take another instance under another head of Federal jurisdiction. The post office has proved a most convenient means of perpetrating fraud by sending letters to people who, influenced by false pretenses contained in the letters, part with their money. This has led to a statute punishing those who use the post office to defraud. Acts of this sort are generally cognizable in the State as the crime of obtaining money under false pretenses. The fact, however, that the scheme is usually a conspiracy that covers many States, and that there is difficulty in securing the necessary witnesses in a

State court has brought into the Federal Court a large volume of business of this kind.

Then within the last Administration, the functions of the Post Office Department have been extended to include the maintenance of Postal Savings Banks and a Parcels Post. These new enterprises are bound to involve wider Federal usefulness and greater manifestation of Federal authority.

The addition to the business of the National Government in its executive and judicial branches, due to the enforcement of all these statutes, is enormous and is an explanation of why the central Government seems to have grown at the expense of the States.

Moreover, the Spanish War thrust on the Government at Washington the full care and supervision of the Philippines and Puerto Rico, and their population of nine million of people. The Platt Amendment gives a quasi-governmental responsibility in Cuba. Then the construction and maintenance of the Panama Canal and the government of the Canal Zone increase greatly the volume of our strictly national affairs.

This great expansion of Federal activities has been almost within the present generation and within the recollection, and by the agency, of living men; but it has not changed the form of our government, nor has it lessened our obligation to respect the sovereign rights of the State.

This brings me to a consideration of the importance of maintaining the constitutional autonomy of our States. Our Federal system is the only form of popular government that would be possible in a country like ours, with an enormous territory and 100,000,000 population. There is a great homogeneity among the people, greater indeed than many of us suppose, but, on the other hand, not only the mere geographical differences, but the differing interests of the people in different localities, require that a certain part of their government should be clearly within their own local control and not subject to the interference of people living at a great distance from them. But for this safety valve by which people of one State can have such State government as they choose, we would never be able to keep the union of all the people so harmonious as we now have. The friction that would occur between different parts of the country under any other system is well illustrated by the working out of the issue of national conservation.

The public domain in lands west of the Mississippi and Missouri rivers was changed into private ownership through the homestead law, the pre-emption acts, the grants to the Pacific Railroads, the stone and timber act, the reclamation act and other land legislation. The administration of these acts was not rigid, but lax in accord with the public sentiment of the people who were pioneering and forgot everything in the zeal for expanding the settlement of the country. About seven years ago the whole country woke up to the fact that vast areas had passed to private and corporate ownership without compliance with law and that much of the valuable land of the government had gone. The necessity for preserving the forests pressed itself upon the minds of all the people and there came a public demand for stricter enforcement of the land laws, for recovery of those lands lost through fraud that could be recovered and the punishment of the conspirators in the fraud. The cry was for national conservation and a very necessary and useful doctrine it has proved to be.

Now that the sharpness of the public attention in the East has been somewhat abated, there has come from the West a complaint that finds support in all the public land States that a certain rigidity and delay in making patents under the land laws have created a halt in development wherever the public domain is found, and that the withdrawal of coal lands, oil and gas lands, phosphate lands, water power sites, with a view to the passage of a conservation law for leasing rather than selling outright these sources of national wealth, growing more valuable every day, is a wrong policy and that the people of the States where these lands are should now be given an opportunity quickly to acquire the necessary title to them and to develop them and expand the productiveness of those States. The feeling is becoming more acute and the politics of whole States are turning upon it. Some reasonable adjustment of the trouble will have to be reached. The case is an exception because generally matters having such an immediate local importance are within the control of the people of the State. But the asperity and vigor of the complaints illustrate very well the inevitable result if everything were regulated from Washington and the State governments were reduced to nothing but agencies of the National Government.

Again, the great financial resources available to the Federal Government by use of its taxing power offer a temptation to those who would spend for local purposes without the burden of paying heavy taxes at home.

The South with its natural political tendencies and as the result of its political history would be naturally in favor of a strict view as to what are proper objects of national expenditure, but since the abolition of slavery and since the disappearance of the political issue as to the voting of the Negroes in the South, in other words, since the practical nullification of the fifteenth amendment in those States, there has been a revolution of feeling and a strong impulse on the part of southern politicians to favor national legislation to accomplish many purposes which had been denounced as unconstitutional in earlier days. In other words, we find from the South and from the West a willingness to have the National Government spend a large part of its receipts in enterprises that will inure to the benefit of the State communities and will be paid for more largely by people living in States not benefited than by the people of the States which are.

This has been one of the criticisms directed against the river and harbor bills and against public buildings bills. They have been called the "pork barrel" bills. They have been usually attacked in those parts of the country that had to furnish most of the "pork" and got little of it, that is, the populous Eastern and Middle States. There are now organizations in the older part of the country whose purpose is to devise plans for Federal improvements there which will give the people of that section what is regarded as their share.

Criticism of public improvement bills is not, however, always just. There are enterprises so national in their character and effect that people remote from them geographically are still very beneficially affected. Such I conceive to be a comprehensive plan for keeping the Mississippi within its banks, to be contributed to by the States but to be executed under Federal authority.

In the reclamation law for the irrigation of arid public lands in Western States, the money expended was to be expended from a fund to be made up of the proceeds of sales of public lands in those States, and from the water rents and assessments upon the irrigated lands. Thus the burden on the general Government was localized and confined to government lands in the States benefited. These proceeds have been anticipated by issuing $20,000,000 bonds, but as they are to be paid out of funds raised as above described, the fairness of the reclamation plan can hardly be questioned.

Other expenditures now proposed cannot be so justified, however.

There is now being agitated and advocated a plan to build good roads in all the States of the United States, the fund for the purpose to be contributed to by the general Government and the States. Under the plan, the State of New York would receive from the fund just about one-half the sum to be awarded to Nevada, while New York's contribution would be many times that of Nevada. This is unjust and is dangerous. While there is probably no doubt of the power of the National Government to build wagon roads from one State to another, roads of this character are so much a matter of local concern, and the interstate traffic is so largely taken care of by railroads and river and sea navigation, that I believe it to be most unwise for the general Government to indulge in road building. The States should do it. The older States have already taken up the work and the rest should follow them. The evils of "pork barrel" bills in rivers and harbors appropriations, and in public buildings bills will seem small and inconsiderable in the mad chase for a share in the good roads bills which the imaginations of many Congressmen have already made into law.

The same proposal is being made in respect to the draining of the swamp lands of the various States. Most of these lands were given by the central Government to the States and much profit has been made out of them. If what remain unsold are to be drained, let the States do it, who own them; or let them reconvey them to the United States Government which may then drain them as a profitable investment in improving its own property if it is found to be such.

It is to be remembered that in the expenditure of the people's money in the United States Treasury, Congress is a law unto itself in that it exercises complete discretion to say what is a proper national purpose. Such a question can never come before the Supreme Court. This is very different from the exercise of Congress of the power of taxation. That affects individual right directly. Any complaining tax-payer may, therefore, at once invoke the judgment of the courts on the validity of a tax law. The distinction gives additional importance to public scrutiny of the purposes to which the Nation's funds are applied.

In the pursuit of home popularity by Congressional representatives by securing national appropriations for local purposes, and in the effort to avoid legitimate State expenditure by loading undue burdens on the general Government, there is danger that the States will lose their dignity and power. Such dangerous proposals, however, find much support in the present temper of pseudo-reformers and demagogues who would rejoice in any governmental effort, however unfair, to take from those who have, and give to those who have not.

It is essential, therefore, in the life of our dual government that the power and functions of the State governments be maintained in all the fullness that they were intended to have by the framers of the Constitution. This is true not only for reasons I have given, but because the tendency to enlarge the constitutional authority and duties of the National Government has gone far beyond the mere expenditure of money.

A school has arisen called the New Nationalist School that proposes to put into operation a great many new remedies through the National Government, basing the national authority on the failure or unfitness of the States to discharge their proper and exclusive duties under the Constitution. This school is one which is closely associated with that which is trying to enforce new doctrines as to the direct rule of the people and an unsettling of the security of individual rights. Its members are generally impatient with the suggestion that certain reforms can only be effected through the State governments. They are in favor of national "hair trigger" legislation, and anything that has to depend upon the action of the forty-eight different States can never be of that kind.

To one opposed to the adoption of such remedies as I have been commenting on, the existence of the State governments is one of the chief grounds for hope that the tendency to error in the weakening of constitutional guaranties that is now going on in some States may be halted by the conservatism of other States, and that the errors from actual experience in departing from representative government in the more radical States will ultimately bring back the whole nation to sounder views.

I favor the principle of a graduated income tax. I urged the sixteenth amendment upon Congress in order to add to the nation's tax resources. But the present law was avowedly passed only to reduce the fortunes of the rich. It will not do so materially. There is a power in the State governments of reducing or dividing these fortunes in a practical way. Each State has complete control over the testamentary privilege given to any owner of property and may take away the power of leaving it all to one child or require that it be left in some other way, and this without the violation of any of the guaranties of the Constitution. Now, if this be true, why has it not been proposed in some State? First, because the "hair trigger" reformer desires to reform the entire country at one and wishes to seem to do it in a way to attract attention and support a national party. Second, because no State, however bitter against its own rich men, would wish to deprive itself of their residence and of their tax-producing quality by passing a law which would drive them into some other State where the devolution of property is more in accordance with previous tradition and custom. Therefore, while this power to reduce the possibility of the accumulation of great fortunes and their maintenance through two or three generations is completely within the action of the States, not a single State has attempted it.

The experience of Kansas and some of the other States, where populism ran riot for a time, is instructive. Then everyone was against the creditor and in favor of the debtor and wished to put obstacles in the path of the former in seeking to recover his money when due. To gratify the popular demand, the legislature passed stay laws which introduce many delays in the legal procedure of the State for the collection of mortgages. The people of Kansas learned a lesson from the result of such legislation that has not yet been forgotten. Capital fled the State of Kansas as men flee from a contagious disease and business became as dead in Kansas as if it had no population at all. The blight that followed taught the statesmen of that State the utilitarian doctrine that honesty is the best policy, and that laws that drove creditors from a State and frightened away all capital, helped neither those who owed money nor those who did not owe money in the State. These so-called remedial laws were very soon repealed and since then other States have not made exactly the same mistake, though there are similar lessons in store for many of them.

There is a great advantage in having different State governments try different experiments in the enactment of laws and in governmental policies, so that a State less prone to accept novel and untried remedies may await their development by States more enterprising and more courageous. The end is that the diversity of opinion in State governments enforces a wise deliberation and creates a *locus pænitenti;ae* which may constitute the salvation of the Republic.

7

"To Establish Justice," Part I

The next reason for ordaining the Constitution as stated in the preamble was "to establish justice." There were courts in each State exercising general jurisdiction under its authority. The establishment of justice referred to in the preamble was the creation of courts under the authority of the new National Government to hear causes that involved its laws, and also to supplement the work of the courts of the various States by providing tribunals for ordinary litigation which should be indifferent as between citizens of different States. The Constitution could not properly remit to State tribunals the exercise of all judicial power. Such an arrangement would make the new government lack dignity and the usual functions of a sovereign, and more than that, there would be no final and supreme tribunal to settle questions of Federal law where the Supreme Courts of the State might differ.

The Constitution provides that there shall be one Supreme Court, and such inferior courts as Congress may from time to time ordain and establish. It also defines what the judicial power of the United States is or may extend to, thus giving the limitations of the jurisdiction that Congress may confer upon courts it creates. Under the Constitution, except in suits be-tween States and in suits by Ambassadors, the Supreme Court cannot hear suits as brought, but has jurisdiction only to review the decisions of other courts.

While the Constitution provided for one Supreme Court, it did not limit the number of Judges. It was, therefore, for Congress to provide what number of Supreme Court Judges there might be. This very important power Congress has, at times, threatened with partisan zeal to abuse. It has been once or twice proposed to change the supposed political complexion of the Court by creating additional judgeships. Every patriot sincerely hopes that Congress may never be moved to adopt such a course. The number of Judges originally was seven. It was then reduced to five. The number has been changed from time to time, and now the number is nine.

The original judiciary act was drafted by Oliver Ellsworth. He was a member of the Constitutional Convention and of the United States Senate from Connecticut. Upon the committee with him were three or four other members of the Constitutional Convention, from which it is to be inferred that the act properly carried out the purposes of that framing body. Mr. Ellsworth subsequently became Chief Justice of the United States, but his greatest public service for which he is chiefly remembered was his judiciary act. While the judiciary act has been amended from time to time, it still retains much of its original language and form. It established, as inferior courts, in each of the circuits, now numbering nine, a district court and a circuit court and defined their jurisdictions, and provided for the appellate jurisdiction of the Supreme Court. In 1892, an intermediate appellate court, called the Circuit Court of Appeals, was created in each circuit. In 1911, the jurisdiction of the circuit courts was transferred to the district courts and the circuit courts were abolished.

The Constitution makes the tenure of office of a judge during good behavior, which means during his life, provided he be not impeached. It provides that his compensation shall never be diminished during his term of office, and in this way he is made as independent as possible of the legislative or executive power after he has once been appointed and con-firmed by the Senate. I shall comment on the beneficial effect of these provisions in a later chapter.

Congress has passed a law providing that all Federal Judges may retire after a service of ten years upon attaining the age of seventy. The law is in form not compulsory because I presume it was thought doubtful whether Congress had any power to retire Judges, even though they continue the full salary as a life pension. I think the absence of power in Congress to do this is a defect. There is no doubt that there are Judges at seventy who have ripe judgments, active minds, and much physical vigor, and that they are able to perform their judicial duties in a very satisfactory way. Yet in a majority of cases when men come to be seventy, they have lost vigor, their minds are not as active, their senses not as acute, and their willingness to undertake great labor is not so great as in younger men, and as we ought to have in Judges who are to perform the enormous task which falls to the lot of Supreme Court Justices. In the public interest, therefore, it is better that we lose the services of the exceptions who are good Judges after they are seventy and avoid the presence on the Bench of men who are not able to keep up with the work, or to perform it satisfactorily. The duty of a Supreme Judge is more than merely taking in the point at issue between the parties, and deciding it. It frequently involves a heavy task in reading records and writing opinions. It thus is a substantial drain upon one's energy. When most men reach seventy, they are loath thoroughly to investigate cases where such work involves real physical endurance.

I don't know that there is any method, except by a change of the Constitution, for remedying the defect that I have suggested. It has sometimes been proposed that, as the retirement pension is optional with Congress, it be granted on condition that the Judge retires at seventy, and if he does not then retire, but delays his retirement until after he has become somewhat older, he shall not have the privilege of retirement on a pension. This it is thought would frighten Judges into an acceptance of the Congressional pension at the right age. I doubt if anything could be accomplished by such legislation.

I would certainly not agitate now the question of amending the Constitution in respect to the tenure of the Federal Judges, because it would be dangerous in the present hysterical condition of many people, and a movement would at once be set on foot not only to retire Judges at seventy, but to make them elective and to give them short terms. Hence, for the present, we can afford to continue to leave the matter to the good sense of the Judges themselves. I ought to add, however, that the experience of men, close to the Court, in respect to the willingness of the Judges to retire after they have become seventy, has not been very different from that of Gil Blas with the Bishop.

I shall not read at length the article defining the judicial power. It is sufficient to say for our purposes that it extends to all cases involving the construction of the Constitution of the United States and the statutes and treaties of the United States, in other words, to the enforcement of Federal law as distinguished from State law; and, secondly, that it includes the consideration of all kinds of litigation between citizens of different States.

It is difficult for us who have been born and brought up in an atmosphere of the Federal and State courts to realize how complicated and almost unintelligible our judicial system is to foreigners. They find it difficult to understand dual governmental authority in which, over the same territory, courts may exercise the same kind of jurisdiction concurrently, and yet act under different sovereignties. I have already stated the reasons for the establishment of a Federal judicial system. I need not further refer to the necessity for a national tribunal to settle finally national questions. The other reason requires a little further comment. Those who framed and adopted the Constitution feared that the citizen of one State seeking to assert his rights in another State before the courts of that other State, might find himself prejudicially affected by the local feeling in favor of a resident and against a non-resident—in favor of a citizen against a non-citizen. It was, therefore, given to Congress to establish inferior courts in every State so that in each State a citizen of another State might have his cause heard before a tribunal whose Judge, bearing the commission of the President of the nation and exercising the authority of the National Government, would be presumed to be free from any local feeling and to administer justice with entire impartiality between litigants, whatever their residence or citizenship. The effectiveness of this provision and its wisdom have been fully vindicated by 125 years of actual experience.

The greatest function of the Federal Courts, and especially of the Supreme Court, is the power to declare void the laws either of Congress or of the legislatures of the States which are found to conflict with the provisions of the Constitution.

In England there had been some intimation by Lord Chief Justice Holt and by Lord Chief Justice Coke that Courts had the right to disregard acts of Parliament. Coke said that the common law controlled acts of Parliament and adjudged them void when against common right and reason, and Holt adopted this dictum of Coke which he found to be supported by Lord Chief Justice Hobart, who, in a reported case, insisted that an act of Parliament made against natural equity so as to make a man judge in his own cause was void. But England is without a written constitution, and the generally accepted rule in English law is that Parliament is omnipotent and that the acts of Parliament must be enforced by the Courts and are beyond any criticism on their part or any power of theirs to declare the acts void.

In the United States, however, we have a written Constitution. It declares the fundamental law and it imposes limitations upon the powers of all branches of the Government. Now if any branch of the Government exceeds those powers to which it is thus limited, the act is without authority and must be void. The question is who is to determine whether the act does exceed the authority given. The action of the Supreme Court is confined to the hearing and decision of real litigated cases and the exercise of judicial power between parties. It is essential to the carrying out of this jurisdiction that the Court should determine what the law is governing the issue between the litigants. Therefore, when a statute is relied upon by one party, and it is claimed by the other that the statute can have no effect because in violation of the fundamental law, the Court must decide whether the statute was within the power of the legislature which passed it or not. That process of reasoning is the one pursued by Chief Justice Marshall in the case of *Marbury vs. Madison*. The reasoning has been accepted as sound in practice for 125 years and courts have exercised this authority, both the Supreme Court of the United States and the Supreme Court of States, for all that time.

The other theory is that it is for the branch of the Government exercising authority to determine whether it is acting within its authority or not, that its judgment on the subject is conclusive, and that any other branch of the Government having to investigate the validity of its act must accept the fact of its action as proof of its validity.

Experience has shown that the obligation to keep within the Constitution sits very lightly upon State legislatures and it is not always regarded by Congress. The people are temporarily moved to demand something which the Constitution forbids. It is argued with some force that if there were no method of resorting to the Courts to declare the invalidity of laws, the members of Congress or of the legislatures would be as careful to follow closely the limitations of their power as the British Parliament has been to follow the unwritten constitution of that country. The assumption that the Courts are the real arbiters as to the issue of the validity of a legislative act, it is said, lifts the responsibility from legislators and they, therefore, vote for the measures they favor without regard to constitutional restriction. I concede the force of this argument to the extent of admitting that both legislatures and Congress are not as sensitive to their constitutional obligations as they ought to be, and they are quite willing to shift the burden of defeating popular measures to the judicial tribunals. But we cannot safely assume that if the decision of the legislatures or Congress were final as to validity of laws, and there could be no resort to the Courts, temporary but powerful pressure in favor of infringements of the Constitution contained in legislation pleasing to the constituencies would not prevail.

To contend that the Courts have no power whatever to consider the validity of laws passed by a legislature or Congress under a written Constitution is much too extreme a doctrine. We may admit that some courts have gone too far in the exercise of this power. They ought not to exercise it, except when the conflict between the Constitution and the act whose validity is in question are irreconcilable. The violation of the constitutional limitation must be plainly beyond the permissible discretion of the legislature in interpreting its own powers under the Constitution. Courts ought not to set aside a law when there is room for difference of opinion as to its validity, and though the Court, in passing on the matter as an original question, might think it crosses the line, it must accept the view of the legislature as most persuasive of the view that what it has done is within the permissive limits of its discretion. In other words, the invalidity of a law solemnly adopted by the legislature given authority to enact laws should not be declared, unless the want of power appears to be beyond reasonable doubt.

The modern argument against the action of the Courts in holding laws to be invalid is that it gives to them a political and legislative power and deprives the people of that which should be theirs. One enthusiast in the crusade against the Courts has pointed out that 458 acts of legislatures had been declared invalid by the State and Federal Courts during a recent year, and has concluded that the Courts are thus exercising enormous political and legislative power. He insists that such power ought to rest with the people and, therefore, that such decisions of the courts should be referred to the electorate at the next election.

An argument like this does not appeal to anyone who understands the facts. The general run of cases presenting the issue of validity or non-validity, under a fundamental law, does not involve politics at all or any-thing like legislative discretion. It involves only a lawyer-like construction of the Constitution and the law in question to decide whether they are in conflict. I doubt not that of the 458 cases, nearly all were cases of palpable violation of the fundamental law which it was a purely non-political, judi-cial function for the Courts to recognize and declare. In the remainder, there may have been questions which were economical or political in the larger sense. I mean by this, political in the general view of the powers of the National Government and not political in the sense of partisan politics of a temporary color. They may have involved the extent of the police power of government and its proper curtailment of individual rights.

If, in the latter very small class of cases, the people differ from the construction put by the Courts upon such a question, they still have the authority to amend the Constitution and make it so plain that no court can ignore it.

Checks upon the action of the people in amending their constitutions have been imposed with a view to secure full information and deliberation on the part of the people, and certainly both those things are essential to a safe amendment of the fundamental law. It only means delay in a radical change and when we consider how short a period a decade is in the life of a nation, a delay of two or three years is not only tolerable but ought to be necessary. I shall consider the general attack on so-called judge-made law later on in this volume.

I now come to consider two new remedies for supposed evils growing out of our judicial system, State and national. I refer to the popular recall of judicial officers and the popular recall of judicial decisions. I shall discuss these in their order.

The popular recall of judges has been put into effect in several States and it was made part of the constitution of Arizona tendered for approval, when her people in convention asked for admission to statehood. I vetoed the bill admitting her on the ground that the proposed constitution contained this provision. Congress then made the admission conditional on the people's striking out this clause of the constitution and the people did so. Promptly upon admission, however, the clause was restored to their constitution by the people of the State. I do not think I can better state my views on this subject than by an extended quotation from my message to Congress vetoing the Arizona bill, in which I said:

> The Constitution distributes the functions of government into three branches—the legislative, to make the laws; the executive, to execute them; and the judicial, to decide in cases arising before it the rights of the individual as between him and others and as between him and the government. This division of government into three separate branches has always been regarded as a great security for the maintenance of free institutions, and the security is only firm and assured when the judicial branch is independent and impartial. The executive and legislative branches are representative of the majority of the people which elected them in guiding the course of the government within the limits of the Constitution. They must act for the whole people, of course; but they may properly follow, and usually ought to follow, the views of the majority which elected them in respect to the governmental policy best adapted to secure the welfare of the whole people.
>
> But the judicial branch of the government is not representative of a majority of the people in any such sense, even if the mode of selecting judges is by popular election. In a proper sense, judges are servants of the people; that is, they are doing work which must be done for the government, and in the interest of all the people, but it is not work in the doing of which they are to follow the will of the majority, except as that is embodied in statutes lawfully enacted according to constitutional limitations. They are not popular representatives. On the contrary, to fill their office properly, they must be independent. They must decide every question which comes before them according to law and justice. If this question is between individuals, they will follow the statute, or the unwritten law, if no statute applies, and they take the unwritten law growing out of tradition and custom from previous judicial decisions. If a statute or ordinance affecting a cause before them is not lawfully enacted, because it violates the Constitution adopted by the people,

then they must ignore the seeming statute and decide the question as if the statute had never been passed.

What I have said has been to little purpose if it has not shown that judges to fulfill their functions properly in our popular government must be more independent than in any other form of government, and that need of independence is greatest where the individual is one litigant, and the State, guided by the successful and governing majority, is the other. In order to maintain the rights of the minority and the individual and to preserve our constitutional balance we must have judges with courage to decide against the majority when justice and law require.

By the recall in the Arizona Constitution, it is proposed to give to the majority power to remove arbitrarily and without delay any judge who may have the courage to render an unpopular decision. By the recall it is proposed to enable a minority of 25 percent of the voters of the district or State, for no prescribed cause, after the judge has been in office six months, to submit the question of his retention in office to the electorate. The petitioning minority must say in their petition what they can against him in 200 words, and he must defend as best he can in the same space. Other candidates are permitted to present themselves and have their names printed on the ballot, so that the recall is not based solely on the record or the acts of the judge, but also on the question whether some other and more popular candidate has been found to unseat him. Could there be a system more ingeniously devised to subject judges to momentary gusts of popular passion than this?

We can not be blind to the fact that often an intelligent and respectable electorate may be so roused upon an issue that it will visit with condemnation the decision of a just judge, though exactly in accord with the law governing the case, merely because it affects unfavorably their contest. Controversies over elections, labor troubles, racial or religious issues, issues as to the construction or constitutionality of liquor laws, criminal trials of popular or unpopular defendants, the removal of county seats, suits by individuals to maintain their constitutional rights in obstruction of some popular improvement—these and many other cases could be cited in which a majority of a district electorate would be tempted by hasty anger to recall a conscientious judge if the opportunity were open all the time.

No period of delay is interposed for the abatement of popular feeling.

The recall is devised to encourage quick action, and to lead the people to strike while the iron is hot. The judge is treated as the instrument and servant of a majority of the people and subject to their momentary will. Not after a long term in which his qualities as judge and his character as a man have been subjected to a test of all the varieties of judicial work and duty so as to furnish a proper means of measuring his fitness for continuance in another term, but on the instant of an unpopular ruling, while the spirit of protest has not had time to cool and even while an appeal may be pending from his ruling in which he may be sustained, he is to be haled before the electorate as a tribunal, with no judicial hearing, evidence or defence, and thrown out of office and disgraced for life because he has failed, in a single decision, it may be, to satisfy the popular demand.

Attempt is made to defend the principle of judicial recall by reference to States in which judges are said to have shown themselves to be under corrupt corporate influence, and in which it is claimed that nothing but a desperate remedy will suffice. If the political control in such States is sufficiently wrested from corrupting corporations to permit the enactment of a radical Constitutional amendment, like that of judicial recall, it would seem possible to make provision, in its stead, for an effective remedy by impeachment in which the cumbrous features of the present remedy might be avoided, but the opportunity for judicial hearing and defence before an impartial tribunal might be retained. Real reforms are not to be effected by patent shortcuts, or by abolishing those requirements which the experience of ages has shown to be essential in dealing justly with everyone. Such innovations are certain in the long run to plague the inventor or first user, and will come readily to the hand of the enemies and corrupters of society after the passing of the just popular indignation that prompted their adoption.

Again judicial recall is advocated on the ground that it will bring the judges more into sympathy with the popular will and the progress of ideas among the people. It is said that now judges are out of touch with movements toward a wider democracy, and a greater control of governmental agencies in the interest and for the benefit of the people. The righteous and just course for a judge to pursue is ordinarily fixed by statute or clear principles of law, and the cases in which his judgment may be affected by his political, economic, or social views are infrequent. But even in such cases, judges are not removed from the people's influence. Surround the judiciary with all the safeguards possible, create judges by appointment, make their tenure for life, forbid diminution of salary during their term, and still it is impossible to prevent the influence of popular opinion from coloring judgments in the long run. Judges are men, intelligent, sympathetic men, patriotic men, and in these fields of the law in which the personal equation unavoidably plays a part, there will be found a response to sober popular opinion as it changes to meet the exigency of social, political and economic changes.

Recall of Judicial Decisions

The proposition for a recall of judicial decisions by a popular vote is so utterly at variance with any procedure that ever was suggested in respect to civilized government that it is hard to deal with it. It had its origin in the impatience felt by some reformers in the economic views of judges who held that a law imposing limitations upon the hours of work of people engaged in certain industries was an infringement upon their individual right of free labor. The reformers contend that the law should be sustained as a legitimate exercise of the police power of the Government. The suggestion that such a question should be ultimately left to a popular election is now sought to be bolstered up by a phrase in an opinion of Mr. Justice Holmes, in *Noble State Bank vs. Haskell*, 219 U.S. 104, in which he says: "It may be said in a general way that the police power extends to all the great public needs. . . . It may be put forth in aid of what is sanctioned by usage or held by the prevailing morality or strong and preponderant opinion to be greatly and immediately necessary to the public welfare." Again he says: "With regard to the police power, as elsewhere in the law, lines are pricked out by the gradual approach and contact of decisions on the opposing sides." I fancy that Mr. Justice Holmes was the most surprised man in the United States when he learned that this language of his had been used to justify the anomalous, I had almost said absurd, proposal that the decision of the Supreme Court of a State or of the United States, in a case between litigants involving the question of the validity of the exercise of the police power, should be submitted by referendum to the reviewing judgment of a single popular election.

This was the last thing which Mr. Justice Holmes or the Supreme Court, for whom he spoke, had in mind when he referred to a strong and preponderant public opinion. Such an election would indeed be a most ephemeral and unstable guide to determine how far a man's personal rights were to be modified in the interest of the public police power. If we can judge by actual experience under referendums of this general character, the election, if carried at all in favor of the police power, would be carried by a small minority of the electorate in the very probable failure of a majority of the electorate to go to the polls, and by a still smaller minority of the whole people whose settled view constitutes public opinion. It would be influenced by all kinds of irrelevant considerations and by campaign mis-representations as to the facts and the real issue. Every circumstance, whether the unpopularity of a party litigant or the supposed pecuniary benefit to the people of the particular locality, or any other upon which an appeal to prejudice or selfish interest could be based, would be used to influence the election. It is difficult to state a fact less conclusive of "a strong and preponderant public opinion" than a single vote upon such an issue. What was in the mind of the learned Justice and of the Court for whom he spoke was a view entertained by most people, and evidenced by expressions of popular will in the press, in the pulpit, in juridical writings, as well as by legislative action and popular elections. All of these evidences should cover a period long enough to leave no doubt about the clarity of the opinion or its deliberate character. Such an opinion is not expressed in election controversy where the losing vote is substantial, but it is the result of a general and continued acquiescence that does not suggest a party division or a heated campaign.

The main argument used to sustain the recall of judicial decisions is that if the people are competent to establish a constitution, they are competent to interpret it and that this recall of decisions is nothing but the exercise of the power of interpretation. The fallacy of this argument should be manifest. The approval of general principles in a constitution, on the one hand, and the interpretation of a statute and consideration of its probable operation in a particular case and its possible infringement of a general principle, on the other, are very different things. The one is simple, the latter complex; and the latter, when submitted to a popular vote, is much more likely to be turned into an issue of general approval or disapproval of the act on its merits for the special purpose of its enactment and in its application to the particular case than upon its violation of the Constitution. Moreover, a popular majority does not generally ratify a constitution, or any principle of it, or amend its terms until after it has been adopted by a constitutional convention or a legislature, and the final approval is, and ought to be, surrounded with such checks and delays as to secure full information and deliberation. In other words, the course of procedure in the adoption of a constitution or amendment is radically different from that proposed in the hasty vote of a majority in recalling a particular judgment of a Court and is hedged about to avoid the very dangers that I have pointed out as likely to ensue were this inconceivable and outlandish plan incorporated in our judicial system.

The proper and reasonable method of avoiding the effect of a decision of the Supreme Court construing the Constitution, which the considerate judgment of the people holds to be contrary to the public good, is to treat the Constitution as construed in existing force, and to amend the Constitution according to the provisions of the Constitution itself. That involves an ultimate submission to the people after full discussion and deliberation. Why is it necessary, therefore, to suggest such a clumsy, unsatisfactory and impracticable method?

How could uniformity of fundamental or any other kind of law be possible under such a system? No one would claim that uniformity would be the result from successive elections held in different years. Instead of a constitution, consistent in its construction and uniform in its application, it would be a government by special instances, a government that in the end necessarily leads to despotism.

When this remarkable device of recalling judicial decisions was first advanced, it was carefully limited in its application to the decisions of State Courts and to issues concerning the extent of the police power, but so well received have been the demagogic attacks upon our Courts made upon the political platform that now this novel invention has been extended to include the judgments of the Supreme Court of the United States and to embrace all of those which hold laws to be invalid because in violation of the Constitution.

Many of these judgments concern and enforce the guaranties of personal rights contained in the Constitution and nullify statutes which infringe them. It follows that many of the decisions to be submitted under this plan to the learned and discriminating judicial judgment of a majority of the voters who take the trouble to vote, would present the issue as between the people in whose avowed interest the law in question was passed and the individual whose property rights are said to be unjustly affected by the law. On such an issue, with the opportunities for demagogic appeals to popular prejudice against the defendant who might be a corporation or a rich man, and in the confusion of an excited campaign, is there not great danger that individual property right would be ignored and the law in question which infringed it would be sustained? To what would this all necessarily lead? To confiscation and then to socialism. Indeed it is difficult to tell whether the recall of judicial decisions is not as socialistic as it is anarchistic.

In the first chapter I commented on the fact that popular government was only a means to an end, to wit, that of the happiness of all classes and individuals, that this end could best be reached by the rule of a majority of a large representative electorate restrained by a constitution, defining the authority of the branches of the Government and restricting the invasion by the electorate of certain declared individual rights necessary to preserve and protect individual effort, with a view to the progress and happiness of society and its members. We have seen that to enforce and secure these constitutional rights an independent judiciary was established as an instrument through which, on his own initiative, each individual could invoke adequate protection to his rights. This method of uniting popular control with self-imposed restraint through a constitution and an independent judiciary to enforce it, is the secret of the strength of our nation, and it explains why we have lived and grown stronger under the same Constitution in the face of all kinds of obstacles, including the greatest civil war in history, and the difficulties of a material expansion and growth of population beyond the dreams of the most imaginative statesman. This is what called forth the encomium of Lord Acton, the great historian, in the memorable sentences I quoted from him.

Now what do we have in the initiative, referendum, and the two recalls urged by a school of men who profess to be friends of popular government and most concerned to promote the people's happiness? We have a system by which it is proposed not only to weaken and render nugatory the declared guaranties of personal rights and the constitutional restraints upon the electorate and its majority, but also to take away the power and independence of that branch of the Government, the judiciary, without which such guaranties and restraints would be written in water. It is not alone the popular control of laws and executive action that gives a Democracy strength and long life. It is its capacity to do justice to the individual and the minority. Lack of this is what destroyed ancient democracies. What preserves ours are those self-imposed popular restraints and practical means for enforcing them that keep the course of the majority of the controlling electorate just to all and each of the people.

There are real grounds for criticizing our judicial system as a whole which the politicians and demagogues do not find so profitable to dwell upon, or to suggest remedies for. I concede that our judicial system is not perfect or as good as it can be, and ought to be made. I have been preaching reform in our judicial procedure for years, especially in the enforcement of the criminal law. In addresses and in presidential messages I have pointed out the great need for cheapening the cost of civil litigation and for expediting it so as to put as little a burden on the poor litigant as possible.

The ultra reformers, the "hair trigger" gentlemen, pay little attention to the tedious detail of reforming procedure so as to reduce the cost of litigation and to speed final judgments. This is really one of the greatest reforms now needed; and it will do the poor man more good ten times than the shining nostrums held out to him as a ground for electing their inventors. But the work of amending procedure and cutting down cost bills and of cutting out useless forms and delays in the law is not spectacular. It does not attract votes. Still the much-abused lawyers have through their Bar Associations made many useful recommendations of changes in procedure and are knocking at the door of Congress and legislatures to secure their adoption.

I do not think we need to be discouraged by the charges and threats made against our Courts, especially if we remedy their real defects by the reforms already pointed out. There have been many attacks upon Courts in the past. Jefferson and Jackson were both most severe in their criticisms of the Federal Judiciary, and both were as popular and influential with the people as any Presidents we have had. And yet the Courts survived their attacks and lived to maintain principles which they both held to be abhorrent, and subversive of the liberties of the people. The Dred Scott decision, the legal tender cases, the income tax decision and the Insular cases, in all of which the judgment was carried by a bare majority, subjected the Court to the bitter attack of those who sympathized with the minority decisions, and in each period of agitation and conflict people shook their heads and said that the authority of the Supreme Court had been much shaken. Yet the tribunal has gone on its way discharging its high function in the Government with patriotic purpose to maintain its authority, and to preserve the constitutional rights of the individual and the form of government as prescribed by our fathers. The Court lives today, strong, virile, patriotic and able and willing to recognize progress, to treat the Constitution as elastic enough to permit a construction which will conform to the growth and necessities of the country, to view constitutional restrictions with reasonable regard to the changes which have taken place in our business and in our society, and yet determined to enforce the principles of individual right and the essential limitations upon the branches of the Government which are provided for in our fundamental law. The greatest advantage of our plan of government over every other is the character of the judicial power vested in the Supreme Court. The statesmen and historians of Europe look upon it with wonder and amazement, speak of it with profound approval, and regard it as the chief instrument in the maintenance of that self-restraint which the people of the United States have placed upon themselves and which has made this Government the admiration of intelligent critics the world over.

8

"To Establish Justice," Part II

The Selection and Tenure of Judges

The most conspicuous feature of the new government under the Federal Constitution was its division into three parts—the legislative, the executive, and the judicial. Experience has vindicated that division, except, it may be, that some lack of efficiency has shown itself in the absence of more useful co-operation between the executive and the legislative branches. The wisdom of keeping the executive and the legislative branches apart from the judiciary has, however, been confirmed by the event, not only under the American Constitution, but in England and in all the states under her flag. In the United States, where judicial systems have different degrees of this quality, permitting comparison, the greater the independence of the Courts the stronger their influence, and the more satisfactory their jurisdiction and administration of justice.

In a popular government, the most difficult problem is to determine a satisfactory method of selecting the members of its judicial branch. Where ought such power to be placed? It is a great one. It is said it ought not to be entrusted to irresponsible men. If this means that judges should not be men who do not understand the importance of the function they are exercising, or the gravity of the results their decision may involve, or do not exert energy and sincere intellectual effort to decide according to law and justice, everyone must concur. But if it means that judges must be responsible for their judgments to some higher authority, so that for errors made in good faith they incur a personal liability, then we know from centuries of actual experience that the interest of justice, pure and unde- filed, requires their immunity. Finality of decision is essential in every branch of the Government, or else government cannot go on. This is as true of its judiciary branch as of other branches. Therefore, somebody must have the final word in judicial matters, and the only question is who can best exercise this power. The answer to the question must be found in the real character of the function which the judges are to perform.

There is a school of political philosophers today who say that there are no positive standards of right and justice, but that these vary with the pop- ular will, and that we are to learn what they are from its expression.

If right and justice are dependent on the votes of the electorate, and if what are known as individual rights are merely privileges held at the will of a majority, then the proposition that the judicial officer represents the people in the same sense as the executive officer, so that when the electoral majority differs from his judgment he ought to be removed, has some logi- cal foundation. So, too, in this view, the proposition that the final decision of the courts shall be submitted on review to a popular election has reason in it.

But I shall assume, for the purposes of this discussion, that principles of right and justice and honesty and morality are not merely conventional and have a higher source than a plebiscite.

There is a broad field for the proper exercise of legislative power in prescribing rules of human conduct, and it is the function of courts to interpret them. This is the work of trained lawyers who know the theory and purpose of government, who are familiar with previous statutes, and who understand legislative methods of expression so that they can put themselves in the attitude of the legislature when it acted. When it is the duty of a court to say whether what was enacted by the legislature under the forms of law is within its power, it must discharge a delicate duty and one requiring in its members ability, learning, and experience properly to interpret both the seeming law and the Constitution, and properly to measure what was within the permissible discretion of the legislature in construing its own authority. The majority of questions before our Courts, however, are neither statutory nor constitutional, but are dependent for decision upon the common or customary law handed down from one generation to another, adjusted to new conditions of society, and declared from time to time by courts as cases arise. Thorough study is required to enable a judge to know and understand the whole range of legal principles that have thus to be discriminatingly adapted and applied. Work of this kind requires professional experts of the highest proficiency, who have mastered the law as a science and in practice.

Where are we to get such experts? When a man of high character, ability and intelligence is to be selected for the chief executive office, the electorate can be safely charged with electing one from the necessarily few candidates who are sufficiently prominent. But what of the searching out in a large profession the best expert, the man with real learning, with judicial temperament, with keenness of perception, with power of analysis and nice distinction, with large technical experience? Can he be found better by election or by appointment? There can be but one answer to this query. The selection can be really popular without resorting to an election. The Chief Executive elected by the people to represent them in executive work does, in appointing a judge, execute the popular will. He can search among the members of the Bar and can inform himself thoroughly as to the one best qualified. Generally he has sources of information, both of an open and a confidential character, and if he is not himself a lawyer or personally familiar with the qualifications of the candidates, he has an Attorney-General and other competent advisers to aid him in the task.

For these reasons, in every country of the world, except in the Cantons of Switzerland and the United States, judges are appointed and not elected. With us, in the decade between 1845 and 1855, when new constitutions were being adopted in many States, a change was made to the elective system. It was not an improvement. In some States the change was not made. A comparison between the work of the appointed judges and of the elected judges shows that appointment secures in the long run a higher average of experts for the Bench. The principle of the short ballot, which is much put forward nowadays by reformers, and which thus far is much more honored by them in the breach than in the observance, really limits the election by the people to the Chief Executive and to legislators, and delegates to the elected Executive the appointment of all other officers, including the judiciary. The Executive who makes the appointments is properly held responsible to the public for the character of his selections.

We have had many able judges by popular election. These have owed their preferment to several circumstances. The effect of the old method of appointment was visible in the working of the new system for a decade or more, and good judges were continued by general acquiescence. In some States, indeed, the practice of re-electing judges without contest obtained until within recent years. Moreover, able judges have been nominated often through the influence of leading members of the Bar upon the politicians who controlled the nominations. Shrewd political leaders have not infrequently treated a judgeship as a non-political place, because the office has had comparatively little patronage. If the nominee has been a man of high quality, conspicuously fit, commanding the support of the professional and intelligent non-partisan votes, it has tended to help the rest of the ticket to success. The instances of great and able judges who have been placed on the Bench by election are instances of the adaptability of the American people and their genius for making the best out of bad methods, and are not a vindication of the system. That has resulted in the promotion to the judicial office of other judges who have impaired the authority of the courts by their lack of strength, clearness, and courage, and who have shown neither a thorough knowledge of the customary law, nor a constructive faculty in the application of it. Great judges and great courts distinguish between the fundamental and the casual. They make the law to grow not by changing it, but by adapting it, with an understanding of the progress in our civilization, to new social conditions. It is the judges who are not grounded in the science of the law, and who have not the broad statesmanlike view that comes from its wide study, that are staggered by narrow precedent and frightened by technical difficulty. The decisions of courts criticized for a failure to respond to that progress in settled public opinion which should affect the limitations upon the police power, or the meaning of due process of law, have generally been rendered by elected courts. Paradox as it may seem, the appointed judges are more discriminatingly responsive to the needs of a community and to its settled views than judges chosen directly by the electorate, and this because the Executive is better qualified to select greater experts.

More than half a century's experience with the election of judges has not, therefore, commended it as the best method, though, for the reasons stated, its results up to this time are better than might have been expected. But with the changes proposed in the manner of making nominations and of conducting elections of judges the system is certain to become less satisfactory. Now we are to have no state or county or district conventions, and the judges are to be nominated by a plurality in a popular primary, and to be voted for at the election on a non-partisan ticket, without party emblems, or anything else to guide the voter. Like all the candidates for office to be elected under such conditions, they are expected to conduct their own canvass for their nomination, to pay the expenses of their own candidacy in the primary, and in so far as any special effort is to be made in favor of their nomination and election, they are to make it themselves. They are necessarily put in the attitude of supplicants before the people for preferment to judicial places. Under the convention system it happened not infrequently, for reasons I have explained, that men who were not candidates were nominated for the Bench, but now in no case can the office seek the man. Nothing could more impair the quality of lawyers available as candidates or depreciate the standard of the judiciary. It has been my official duty to look into the judiciary of each State in my search for candidates to be appointed to Federal judgeships, and I affirm without hesitation that in States where many of the elected judges in the past have had high rank, the introduction of nomination by direct primary has distinctly injured the character of the Bench for learning, courage, and ability. The nomination and election of a judge are now to be the result of his own activity and of fortuitous circumstances. If the judge's name happens to be the first on the list, either at the primary or the election, he is apt to get more votes than others lower down on the list. The incumbent in office, because he happens to be more widely known, has a great advantage. Newspaper prominence plays a most important part, though founded on circumstances quite irrelevant in considering judicial qualities.

The result of the present tendency is seen in the disgraceful exhibitions of men campaigning for the place of State Supreme Judge and asking votes, on the ground that their decisions will have a particular class flavor. This is the logical development of the view that a popular election is the only basis for determining right and justice: but it is so shocking, and so out of keeping with the fixedness of moral principles which we learned at our mother's knee, and which find recognition in the conscience of every man who has grown up under proper influence, that we ought to condemn without stint a system which can encourage or permit such demagogic methods of securing judicial position. Through the class antagonism unjustly stirred up against the Courts, fiery faction is now to be introduced into the popular election of judges. Men are to be made judges not because they are impartial, but because they are advocates; not because they are judicial, but because they are partisan.

It is true that politics have played a part even when judges have been appointed. They have usually been taken from the lawyers of the prevailing party. The President or a Governor appointing them has been elected on a partisan ticket, is the titular head of his party, and is expected to give preferment to those who supported him. This has not, however, resulted in political courts, because the control of the Government has naturally changed from one party to another in the course of a generation and has normally brought to the Bench judges selected from both parties; and then, if the judges are made independent by the character of their tenure, the continued exercise of the judicial function entirely neutralizes in them any possible partisan tendency arising from the nature of their appointment.

More than this, there is a noticeable disposition on the part of some Chief Executives to disregard party in making judicial appointments, and this ought to be so. In the early history of our country, and indeed down to the Civil War, the construction of the Constitution as to the powers of the Federal Government was a party question, and doubtless affected the selection of Federal Judges. Yet the effect of the judgments of Marshall and his Court was not weakened by Taney and his Democratic associates when they came to consider the Constitution. The Federalist party died in 1800, but its national view of our Government was vitalized by John Marshall, and preserved by the Supreme Court in unchanged form until the Civil War robbed the States' rights issue of its political and sectional importance. Today a sound and eminent lawyer of either party, who can conscientiously take the oath to support the Constitution, may be appointed by a conscientious Executive. What is true of the National Government is true of the

State governments, and there is not the slightest reason why an Executive should not appoint to the judiciary of his State qualified persons from either party.

I come now to consider what should be the judicial tenure of office. In our Federal and State constitutions the rights of the individual as against the aggression of a majority of the electorate, and, therefore, against the Government itself, are declared and secured in a way peculiar to our Anglo-Saxon ancestors. The abstract declarations in favor of personal liberty and the right of property in the fundamental law of the continental countries were often as ample as in ours, but it was in the provision for the specific procedure to secure them that the early English charters of freedom, the Magna Charta, the Petition of Right and the Bill of Rights, were remarkable. This procedure is preserved in our constitutions and, upon the initiative of the individual who conceives his rights infringed, is to be invoked in the courts. Therefore, the first requisite of the judiciary is independence of those branches through the aggression of which the rights of the individual may be impaired. The choice of the judges must always rest either in a majority of the electorate of the people, or in a popular agent whom that majority selects, and so must be directly or indirectly in control of the party to be charged in such controversies with the infringement of individual rights. How, therefore, can we secure a tribunal impartial in recognizing such infringements and courageous enough to nullify them? It is only by hedging around the tenure of the judges after their selection with an immunity from the control of a temporary majority in the electorate and from the influence of a partisan Executive or legislature.

Our forefathers who made the Federal Constitution had this idea in their minds as clear as the noonday sun, and it is to be regretted that in some of their descendants and of the successors in their political trust this sound conception has been clouded. They provided that the salaries of the judges should not be reduced during their terms of office, and that they should hold office during good behavior, and that they should only be removed from office through impeachment by the House of Representatives and a trial by the Senate. The inability of Congress or of the Executive, after judges have been appointed and confirmed, to affect their tenure has given to the Federal judiciary an independence that has made it a bulwark of the liberty of the individual. On the other hand, this immunity has had some effect in making Congress grudge any betterment of the compensation to these great officers of the law. Congress has failed to recognize the increased cost of living as a reason for increasing judicial salaries, although this fact has furnished the ground for much other legislation. They have declined to conform the income of the judges to the dignity and station in life which they ought to maintain, and have kept them at so low a figure as to require from that class of lawyers who are likely to furnish the best candidates for judicial career a great pecuniary sell-sacrifice in accepting appointment. I presume, therefore, that in spite of the efforts of the Bar and of men of affairs to increase judicial salaries, and in spite of the confession as to the cost of living in Washington that actual service in the Government wrings from the advocates of a simple life who happen to get into office, we must continue to require from those who have the honor, the responsibility and the labor of the exercise of judicial functions under the Federal Government, mean living and high thinking, and we must endure the indignation that is justly stirred in us when widows and children of men, able and patriotic, who have served their country faithfully and have done enormous labor for two or three decades on the Bench, are left without sufficient means to live. Nothing but the life tenure of the Federal judiciary, its independence and its power of usefulness have made it possible, with such inadequate salaries, to secure judges of a high average in learning, ability, and character.

When judges were only agents of the King to do his work, it was logical that they should hold office at his pleasure. Now, when there is a recrudescence of the idea that the judge is a mere agent of the sovereign to enforce his views as the only standards of justice and right, we naturally recur to the theory that judges should hold their office at the will of the present sovereign, to wit, the controlling majority or minority of the electorate. The judicial recall is a case of atavism and is a retrogression to the same sort of tenure that existed in the time of James I, Charles I, Charles II and James II, until its abuses led to the act of settlement securing to judges a tenure during their good behavior. It is argued that there is no reason to object to a recall of judges that does not apply to judges elected for a term of years. The answer is that the conceded objections to an elective judiciary holding for a short term of years are doubled in force in their application to judicial recall. The States which have elective judges have gotten along somehow through the political capacity of the American people and the force of public opinion to make almost any system work. Under the present system a judge is certain to retain his position for a few years, and during that time at least he is free from interruption or the threat of popular disapproval. This certainty of tenure, though short, conduces to the independent administration of his office. As he draws near another election and hopes to have another term, it is true that his courage and his impartial attitude toward issues that have any political bearing are likely to be severely tested. Because the country has survived a judiciary largely selected in this manner does not seem to be a very strong reason why we should proceed to increase the evil effect of the short tenure by making it merely at the will of the plurality of those of the electorate who choose to vote.

I have stated my reasons for thinking that appointment of judges results in the selection of better experts in the science of law than the elective system. But even if the qualifications of the two incumbents under the two systems were equal upon their accession to office, the longer experience afforded by the life tenure and the greater opportunity it gives to learn the judicial duties make the better average judges. It matters not how experienced a man may be in the learning of the law, and in its practice, there are still lessons before him which he must learn before he can become of the greatest public service.

Other benefits from the life tenure in its effect upon the judges who enjoy it are that it makes the incumbents give their whole mind to their work, to order their household with a view to always being judges, and to take vows, so to speak, as to their future conduct. They must put aside all political ambition. One of the great debts which the American people owe to Mr. Justice Hughes is the example that he set in the last presidential election when the most serious consideration was being given to making him the candidate of the Republican party. He announced his irrevocable determination not to enter the political field because he had assumed the judicial ermine.

What, now, are the objections urged to a life tenure? The first is that it makes judges irresponsible, in the sense that they are so freed from the effect of what people think of them that they are likely to do unjust and arbitrary things. The immunity of life tenure does make some judges forget that it is nearly as essential to give the appearance of doing justice as it is to do substantial justice. They forget that the public must have confidence in, and respect for, the Courts in order that they achieve their highest usefulness in composing dangerous differences and securing tranquillity and voluntary acquiescence in the existing order. Still, the life judges in whom these faults really exist are comparatively few. The criticism is apt to be made in many cases where it is not deserved, because of the contrast that lawyers and litigants find in dealing with courts under the two systems. The Federal Judges have the power which the English judges have. They are so far removed from politics or the fear of election that the counsel before them receive only the consideration which their eminence as lawyers justifies. Under State statutes, following the tendency to minimize the power of the Court, the judge is greatly restricted in the exercise of discretion to free the issue before the Court from irrelevant and confusing considerations. The jury trial given by the Federal Constitution is the trial at common law given by a court and jury, in which the court exercises the proper authority in the management of the trial and assists the jury in a useful analysis and summing up of the evidence, and an expression of such opinions as will help the jury to reach right conclusions. All this tends to eliminate much of what almost might be called demagogic discussion, which counsel are prone to resort to in many of the local State Courts, and which the State judge fears to limit lest it be made the basis of error and a ground for new trial under some statute narrowing his useful power. We must, therefore, weigh the frequent characterization of the Federal Judge as a petty tyrant in the light of the contrast between proper authority exercised by him and the control exercised by judges in State Courts, where opportunity is too frequently given to the jury to ignore the charge of the court, to yield to the histrionic eloquence of counsel, and to give a verdict according to their emotions instead of their reason and their oaths. Why is it that every lawbreaker prefers to be tried in a State Court? Why is it that the Federal Courts are the terror of evildoers? One of the reasons may be found in the better organization of the Federal prosecuting system. But is it not chiefly because the judge retains his traditional control of the manner of the trial and of the counsel and really helps, but does not constrain, the jury to a just verdict? Is it not because law and justice more certainly prevail there rather than buncombe and mere sentiment?

But it is said that the unpopularity of the Federal Courts among the lawyers as a whole shows that the life tenure has a bad effect upon their character as judges. I agree that when a judge is thoroughly disliked by the Bar, who are his ministers and assistants, it is generally his fault, because he has much opportunity properly to cultivate their good will and respect. Still, much must be allowed for in the impatience of the general Bar at Federal Judges, because there are many lawyers who appear but rarely in United States Courts, are embarrassed by their unfamiliarity with the mode of practice, and feel themselves in a strange and alien forum.

There are substantial causes for the local unpopularity of Federal Courts, and these exist without any fault of the judges. The chief reason for creating local courts under the Federal authority was to give to non-residents an opportunity to have their cases tried in a court free from local prejudice before a judge who had the commission of the President of the whole country, rather than a judge whose mandate was that of the Governor of the State where the case was tried, or of the people of the county in which the court was held. In other words, the very office which they serve, that of neutralizing local prejudice, necessarily brings them more or less into antagonism with the people among whom such local prejudice exists.

A similar answer may be made to the charge against the Federal Courts, that they are biased in favor of corporations. This has grown naturally out of their peculiar jurisdiction. Throughout the Western and Southern States, foreign capital has been expended for the purpose of development and in the interest of the people of those sections. They have been able to secure these investments on reasonable terms by the presence in their communities of the Federal Courts, where the owners of foreign capital think themselves secure in the maintenance of their just rights when they are obliged to resort to litigation. While this has been of inestimable benefit in rapid settlement and progress, it has not conduced to the popularity of the Federal Courts. Men borrow with avidity, but pay with reluctance, and do not look upon the tribunal that forces them to pay with any degree of love or approval.

Then, an important part of the litigation in the Federal Courts on the civil side consists of suits brought to prevent infringement by State action of the right of property secured by the Fourteenth Amendment to the Constitution. Such action is usually directed against large corporations, who thus become complainants. If any such suits are successful, and State action is enjoined, it is easy for the demagogue and the muckraker to arouse popular feeling by assertion that the Federal Courts are prone to favor corporate interests. It is not the bias of the judges, but the nature of their jurisdiction, that properly leads litigants of this kind to seek the Federal forum. The unsuccessful suits of this kind are never considered by the critics of the Federal judiciary. Hence the plausibility of the charge. But it is unjust. In no other courts have the prosecution of great corporations by the Government been carried on with such success and such certainty of judgment for the wrongdoer, and the influence of powerful financial interests has had no weight with the Federal Judges to prevent the enforcement of law against them.

Again, the litigation between non-resident railway and other corporations and their employees in damage suits has usually been removed from the State Courts to the Federal Courts, where a more rigid rule of law limiting the liability of the employer has been enforced. This has created a sense of injustice and friction in local communities that is entirely natural, and has given further support to the charge that the Federal Courts are the refuge of great corporations from just obligation. It was the business of Congress to remove this by adopting an interstate commerce employers' liability act like that which is now on the statute book, giving the employees much fairer treatment, and by passing the workman's compensation bill which is pending in Congress and will, I hope, soon be enacted into law.

But it is said, "When you get a bad judge you cannot get rid of him under the life system." That is true unless he shows his unworthiness in such a way as to permit his removal by impeachment. Under the authoritative construction by the highest court of impeachment, the Senate of the United States, a high misdemeanor for which a judge may be removed is misconduct involving bad faith or wantonness or recklessness in his judicial action or in the use of his judicial influence for ulterior purpose. The last impeachment and removal of a Federal Judge, that of Judge Archbald, was on the ground that he sought sales of property from railroad companies, or their subsidiary corporations, which were likely to be litigants in his courts, and indicated clearly by a series of transactions of this sort his hope and purpose that such companies would be moved to comply with his request because of his judicial position. The trial and the judgment were most useful in demonstrating to all incumbents of the Federal Bench that they must be careful in their conduct outside of Court as well as in the Court itself, and that they must not use the prestige of their judicial position, directly or indirectly, to secure personal benefit. Mr. Justice Chase was tried in Jefferson's time for gross improprieties of a partisan political character calculated to cast discredit on his Court. It would seem in this day and generation that he ought to have been removed, but the spirit of the impeachers was so partisan and political that it frightened many of the Senators and neutralized the improprieties that were made the subject of the impeachment articles. It was this case which evoked from Thomas Jefferson the comment that impeachment was "the scarecrow" of the Constitution, and that it was impracticable as a means of disciplining judges. Under the ruling in the *Archbald* case and the evident tendency of the Senate, the criticism of Jefferson has lost much of its force.

The procedure in impeachment is faulty, because it takes up the time of the Senate in long-drawn-out trials. This fact is apt to discourage resort to the remedy and has lessened its proper admonitory and disciplinary influence. The pressure upon both Houses for legislation is so great that the time needed for inquest and trial is grudgingly given. An impeachment court of judges has been suggested, but the public would fear in it lenity toward old associates. The wisdom of having the trial by the higher branch of the Congress, entirely free from the spirit of the guild, commended itself to the framers of the Constitution and is manifest. A change in the mode of impeachment, however, so as to reduce materially the time required of the Senate in the proceeding, would be of the greatest advantage. If the whole Senate were not required to sit in the actual trial, and the duty were remitted to a committee like the judiciary committee of that body, whose decision could be carried on review to the Senate in full session, the procedure might be much shortened. The Judicial Committee of the English Privy Council is now a supreme court for colonial appeals, probably having its origin in the difficulty of assembling the whole Council to attend to litigated causes. The English House of Lords is a court, but sits only with the Law Lords, who are really a judiciary committee of the Peers to act as such.

It has been proposed that instead of impeachment, judges should be removed by a joint resolution of the House and the Senate, in analogy to the method of removing judges in England through an address of both Houses to the King. This provision occurs in the Constitution of Massachusetts and in that of some other States, but it is very clear that this can only be justly done after full defense, hearing and argument. Professor McIlwain of Harvard has written a very instructive article on the subject of removal by address in England, in which he points out that this is a most formal method, and that in the only case of actual removal of a judge by this method a hearing was had before both Houses of Parliament quite as full, quite as time-consuming, and quite as judicial as in the proceeding by impeachment. Advocates of the preposterous innovation of judicial recall have relied upon the method of removal of judges as a precedent, but the reference only shows a failure on the part of those who make it to understand what was the removal by address.

By the liberal interpretation of the term "high misdemeanor," which the Senate has given it, there is now no difficulty in securing the removal of a judge for any reason that shows him unfit, and if the machinery for holding the trial could be changed from the full Senate to a judicial committee, with the possible appeal to the whole body, impeachment would become a remedy entirely practical and effective.

One who is convinced that the Federal judiciary, both supreme and inferior, because they are appointed and hold office for life, are the greatest bulwark in the protection of individual right and individual liberty and the permanent maintenance of just popular government, must have a strong personal resentment against any member of that body who in any way brings discredit on the Federal judiciary and weakens its claim to public confidence. I feel, therefore, no leniency or disposition to save the Federal Judges from just criticism and I am far from making light of serious charges against them or of defects that have cropped out from time to time.

Some local Federal Judges are not sufficiently careful to avoid arousing local antagonism in cases where they have a choice as to the method of granting a suitor relief. Congress has taken steps in this direction so that one judge is not enough to authorize an injunction where it is sought to prevent the enforcement of a State statute claimed to violate individual rights.

Again, the patronage that judges have exercised has disclosed a weakness that can be prevented by changing the system. Judges now appoint clerks and the relation established between the judge and the clerk is so close and confidential that it is often difficult to secure from the judge the proper attitude of criticism toward the clerk's misconduct. I am convinced that the clerks ought to be appointed by the Executive, be brought within the classified civil service, and be subject to removal for cause either by the Executive or by the judge.

Abuses have grown out of court appointments to receiverships and to other temporary lucrative positions. It would be well if possible to relieve the judges of such duties. In the case of national banks, the receivers are appointed, not by the Courts, but by the Comptroller of the Currency. I think it might be well in the case of interstate railroads, the creditors of which seek relief in the Federal Court, to have the receivers appointed by the Interstate Commerce Commission. Patronage is very difficult to dispense. It gives to the Court a meretricious power and casts upon it a duty that is quite likely to involve the Court in controversies adding neither to its dignity nor its hold upon the confidence of the public. Some great English judges have tarnished their reputation in its use. A receiver appointed by another authority would be quite sufficiently under control of the Court if the Court could remove him for cause and punish him for contempt of its orders.

Again, the judges in the Federal Courts have not shown as strong a disposition as they should to cut down the expenses of litigation; but this is completely in the control of Congress, which would help the people much more by enacting a proper fee bill than by such attempts as we have seen, to impair the power of Courts to enforce their lawful decrees. The attitude of the Federal Courts as to the cost of litigation was originally brought about by the increase in litigation and the hope that heavy costs would operate as a limitation, but this works great injustice and is an improper means to the end.

The great defects in the administration of justice in our country are in the failure to enforce the criminal laws through delay and ineffectiveness of prosecution in the criminal courts, and in the cost and lack of dispatch in civil suits. In the enforcement of the criminal laws of the United States in the Federal Courts there is little to criticize. They might well serve as models to the State Courts. On the civil side, the same cannot be said. The costs may be and ought to be greatly reduced. The procedure in equity causes has been greatly simplified by the new equity rules just issued by the Supreme Court. A bill to authorize that Court to effect the same result in cases at law is likely soon to pass. Then we may hope that the Federal Courts will furnish a complete object lesson to State legislatures in cheap, speedy, and impartial judgment.

I have thus taxed your patience with the reasons that convince me that appointment and a life tenure are essential to a satisfactory judicial system. They may seem trite and obvious, but I have thought in the present disposition to question every principle of popular government that has prevailed for more than a century, that it might be well, at the risk of being commonplace, to review them.

In the present attitude of many of the electorate toward the Courts, it is perhaps hopeless to expect the States, in which judges are elected for short terms, to return to the appointment of judges for life. But it is not in vain to urge its advantages. The Federal Judges are still appointed for life, and it will be a sad day for our country if a change be made either in the mode of their selection or the character of their tenure. These are what enable the Federal Courts to secure the liberty of the individual and to preserve just popular government.

9

"To Establish Justice," Part III

Public Need of Educated Lawyers and Judges—The Necessity and Advantage of Judge-Made Laws

A great French judge truly said that the profession of the law was "as old as the Magistrate, as noble as Virtue, and as necessary as Justice." The importance of having a Bar, the members of which are sufficiently skilled in the principles of law and the procedure of the Courts, properly to advise laymen as to their rights and the method of asserting or defending them, and to represent them in judicial controversies, I need not dwell upon. It has been the habit in many States to regard the practice of the law as a natural right, and one of which no one of moral character can be deprived. Such a view of course ignores the importance of the profession to society and looks at its practice only as a means of earning a living. Laymen can readily be made to see that society should be protected against the malpractice of the medical profession and surgery by men who know nothing of disease, or the effect of medicine, or the handling of a surgical instrument. It is, therefore, comparatively free from difficulty to secure laws prescribing proper educational qualifications for those holding themselves out as physicians or surgeons. The danger to society of the misuse of the power which a lawyer's profession enables him to exercise is not so acutely impressed upon the layman until he has had some experience in following bad advice. A legal adviser cannot ordinarily injure his client's bodily health, but he can lead him into great pecuniary loss and subject him and his family to suffering and want. The more thorough the general education of one who proposes to be a lawyer, the more certainly his mind will be disciplined to possess himself of the principles of law and properly to apply them. There is a spirit of hostility manifested by some courts and lawyers, and some who are not lawyers, to the suggestion that a fundamental general education is necessary to the making of a qualified member of the legal profession. In Indiana the constitution impliedly forbids the imposition of examination for admission to the Bar. The argument is: "Look at Abraham Lincoln. He never had any education of any sort. He educated himself, and note his greatness both as a lawyer, a statesman and a man." Such an argument would do away not only with the necessity for education at the Bar, but the necessity for school or colleges of any kind. The question is not whether exceptional men have made themselves learned men, educated men and great lawyers without the use of schools, academies, colleges or law schools, but the question is by what means are we likely to produce the best average members of the profession. By what means are we most likely to make them skilled and able and useful in the office for which the profession is created? Certain law schools in the country have imposed the necessity for a collegiate education upon intending lawyers before they shall begin the study of their profession. In the medical profession, schools of a similar standard require, after the Bachelor's degree, a study of four years. In the law schools a study of three years is now generally required, and in many States the same period has been fixed as the necessary period of preparation for the Bar examinations. It is said this will exclude many worthy young men who would aspire to the law. As the reason of the profession for being is to serve society, the interest of society is the point from which we must approach the question, and but little consideration should be given to the welfare of those who would like to practice law and are not fitted to do it well. The graduates of colleges are in number greatly more than sufficient to supply the needs of the clerical, the medical and the legal professions, and there is no danger that there will be any dearth of lawyers of good material because a heavier burden of preparation is required of them. The view that the profession exists solely as a livelihood creates a demand for law schools furnishing the easiest and shortest way for their students to acquire the temporary information needed to pass the required examinations. Such schools are cramming factories with no thought to the broad legal education which students should bring to the practice after they are admitted to the Bar. They confer only a smattering of the law and only a transient familiarity with the subjects upon which they are examined. Men who are thus prepared may become good lawyers, but if they do, it will be because of their natural mental capacity and the education that they give themselves afterwards, and not because of any basis of legal learning they acquired in such schools. For the good of society, the standards of legal education ought to be made higher and a broad collegiate education before the study of the law should be insisted upon as the *sine qua non.*

In most States the question of the admission to the Bar is given to the Supreme Courts. It should be possible, therefore, to secure, through such good and eminent lawyers, a proper standard for the making of new lawyers. They ought, of all men, to appreciate in the highest degree the benefit in the administration of justice of requiring the most thorough preparation for the practice of the profession. They could impose a standard for preliminary and fundamental education, and then for the education in law. Of course the judges do not generally prepare the questions for examination, or mark them. They delegate this to a committee of lawyers. When we find in one of the great States of the Union a committee of examination that imposed questions based on cases taken from reports of its own State, some of doubtful authority, and gave no credit for answers which differed from the decisions of the Courts, however good the reasons, we are not surprised to learn that some of the best prepared students from first-class law schools were rejected, and that applicants with education in the law much less thorough were admitted. The latter pursued the course of studying the special character of previous questions and "cramming" the answers to them from a book prepared by one of the committee. This book shows not a few instances in which the answers required were hardly sustained by good authority, even in the particular State. Some features of this bad system have been changed. The reform should be more radical. No court that knowingly permits such a system to remain in vogue can escape criticism. Examinations of this kind commercialize the practice of the law more than any other one. Those who come to the Bar by a mere trick of memory, and without thorough absorption of legal principles, are not likely to improve the tone of the practice to which they have succeeded by such means.

What I wish to dwell upon especially here is the influence of a proper standard for admission to the Bar on another function of lawyers than that of advising and representing clients. We get our judges from the Bar, and we add to the education of our judges when they are on the Bench by the Bar. It is the tone of the Bar, therefore, and the ability and learning of the Bar that necessarily affect the learning and standards of the Bench. The influence of a great Bar to make a great court and to secure a series of great decisions, everyone familiar with judicial history knows.

The function of judges is to interpret constitutions and statutes, and apply and enforce them, and also to declare and apply that great body of customary law known as common law which we received from past generations. According to the view and theory of one who does not understand the practical administration of justice, judges should interpret the exact intention of those who established the Constitution, or who enacted the legislation, and should apply the common law exactly as it came to them. But frequently new conditions arise which those who were responsible for the written law could not have had in view, and to which existing common law principles have never before been applied, and it becomes necessary for the Court to make new applications of both. The power which the Court thus exercises is said to be a legislative power, and it is urged that it ought to be left to the people. That it is more than a mere interpretation of the legislative or popular will, and in the case of the common law that it is more than a mere investigation and declaration of traditional law is undoubtedly true. But it is not the exercise of legislative power as that phrase is used. It is the exercise of a sound judicial discretion in supplementing the provisions of constitutions and laws and custom, which are necessarily incomplete or lacking in detail essential to their proper application, especially to new facts and situations constantly arising. Then, too, legislation is frequently so faulty in proper provision for contingencies which ought to have been anticipated that courts cannot enforce the law without supplying the defects and implying legislative intention, although everyone may recognize that the legislative body never thought anything about the operation of the law in such cases and never had any intention in regard to them. Neither constitutional convention nor legislature nor popular referendum can make constitutions or laws that will fit with certainty of specification the varying phrases of the subject matter sought to be regulated, and it has been the office of courts to do this from time immemorial. Indeed, it is one of the highest and most useful functions that courts have to perform in making a government of law practical and uniformly just. You can call it a legislative power if you will, but that does not put you one bit nearer a sufficient reason for denying the utility and necessity of its exercise by courts.

Of all the people in the world who ought not to be heard in objection are the advocates of the initiative and referendum as a means of legislation. Legislatures and constitutional conventions have been bad enough in the enactment of measures inconsistent in themselves, and full of difficulty for those charged with their enforcement; but now it is proposed to leave the drafting of laws to individual initiative and to submit them to popular adoption without any possibility of correction and needed amendment after discussion, which is always afforded in the representative system. The puzzles in legislation now presented to courts by this new method of making laws can be better understood by reading some of the perspiring efforts of the Supreme Court of Oregon. Instead of dispensing with courts, this purer and directer democracy is going to force upon judicial tribunals greater so-called legislative duties than ever. Of course legislatures and the people have always the power to negative the future application of any judicial construction of a constitution, or a law, or any declaration of a common law principle, by amendment or new law.

The practical impossibility of making laws that are universally applicable to every case has thrown upon the Courts the duty of supplying the deficiency either by construction of written laws or constructive application of the common law. This discretion of courts is guided and limited by judicial precedents. The precedents form a body of law called judge-made law by those who would attack it; but it is better to have judge-made law than no law at all. Indeed the curative and lubricating effect of this kind of law is what has made our popular governmental machinery work so smoothly and well. I cannot refer at length to the now much-mooted question of the power of the Courts to refuse to recognize legislative acts which are beyond the permissible discretion of the legislature in construing its own constitutional authority. I can only say that the power has been exercised for one hundred and twenty-five years and unless the Courts continue to retain it, individual rights and every interest of all the people will come under the arbitrary discretion of a constantly changing plurality of the electorate to be exercised by varying and inconsistent decisions of successive elections.

But however necessary it is to entrust such discretion to the Courts, we must recognize that its existence is made the basis for a general attack, by professed reformers of society, upon our judicial system, and that this attack is finding much sympathy among the people. There are good grounds for criticising our present administration of justice in the lax enforcement of the criminal law and in the high cost and lack of dispatch in civil litigation.

These defects are not all chargeable to the Courts themselves, by any means. The lax administration of the criminal law is due in a marked degree to the prevalence of maudlin sentiment among the people, and the alluring limelight in which the criminal walks if only he can give a little sensational coloring to his mean or sordid offense. Then the State legislatures, responding perhaps to a popular demand, and too often influenced by shallow but for the time being politically influential members of our own profession, devise every means to deprive the Court of its power at common law to control the manner of trial and to assist the juries, but not to constrain them, to right conclusions. Codes of procedure of immense volume and exasperating detail keep litigants "pawing in the vestibule of justice" while the chance of doing real justice fades away. Then, too, unnecessary opportunity for appeals and writs of error and new trials is afforded by statute, and the litigant with the longest purse is given a great advantage. More than this, many questions that ought to be settled by administrative tribunals with proper authority have been thrust upon the Courts. This has had two effects. It involves the Courts in quasi-political and economic controversies which they ought not to be burdened with, and which necessarily expose them to criticism as being prejudiced. Second, it takes up the time of the Courts in executive matters and delays dispatch of legitimate judicial work. The creation of the interstate commerce commission, of State public utilities commissions, of boards of conciliation and arbitration in labor controversies, of commissions for fixing compensation for injured workmen, and of other executive agencies for the determination of issues involved in proper governmental regulation and exercise of the police power, is lifting much from the Courts. Then the American Bar Association and many State associations are zealously and successfully working to induce legislatures and courts by statute and rules to simplify procedure and make it a vehicle of quick justice at little cost.

But the lax administration of the criminal law and the cost and delay of civil litigation are not the special objects of attack by social reformers. Their fire is directed against what they call the legislative power of the Courts that I have described. This they contend is now being exercised to defeat measures essential to true social progress by reactionary judges. Let us trace out the reasons for this antagonism and perhaps in them we can find the true solution of the difficulty so far as there is any real substance in their complaint.

In the Federal Constitution there were embodied two great principles, first, that the Government should be a representative popular government, in which every class in society, the members of which have intelligence to know what will benefit them, is given a voice in selecting the representatives who are to carry on the Government and in determining its general policy. On the other hand, the same Constitution exalts the personal rights and opportunities of the individual and prescribes the judicial machinery for their preservation, against the infringement by the majority of the electorate in whose hands was placed the direction of the executive and legislative branches of the Government. The common law rule was followed, by which each individual was given independence in his action, so long as that independence did not infringe the independence of another. This has given the motive for labor, industry, saving and the sharpening of intellect and skill in the production of wealth and its re-use as capital to increase itself. The material expansion of our country, unprecedented in history, would have been utterly impossible without it. When the Constitution was adopted, there was not only legal independence of the individual, but actual independence in his method of life, because he could and did produce almost everything that was needed for his comfort in the then standard of living. We have now become a people with an immense urban population, far from the sources of necessary supply, and, therefore, we have become far more dependent on each other that life may go on and be enjoyed. While it is undoubtedly true that the living of the average individual is far more comfortable than it ever was, we have now reached a point in the progress of our material development when we are stopping to take breath and to make more account of those who are behind in the race. We are more sensitive to the inequality of conditions that exist among the people and the enjoyment of the comforts of life. We are pausing to inquire whether, by governmental action, some changes cannot be made in the legal relations between the social classes, and in the amelioration of oppressive conditions affecting those who in the competition between individuals under existing institutions are receiving least advantage from the general material advance. It is essential that our material expansion should continue, in order to meet the demands of the growing population and to increase the general comfort. Were we to take away the selfish motive involved in private property we would halt, stagnate and then retrograde, the average comfort and happiness in society would be diminished, and those who are now in want would be poorer than ever. The trend of those who would improve society by collectivist legislation is toward increasing the functions of government, and one of the great difficulties they have to meet is provision for the rapidly increasing pecuniary burden thus entailed. Municipalities and States which have attempted something of this kind are finding that their credit is exhausted and their tax resources insufficient. Whatever the changes, therefore, we must maintain, for the sake of society, our institutional system of individual reward, or little of the progress so enthusiastically sought can be attained. It is not alone constitutional restraints which limit thoughtless, unjust, and arbitrary popular excesses, but also those of economic laws and the character of human nature, and these latter work with seemingly cruel inevitableness which ought to carry its useful lesson home.

The social reformers contend that the old legal justice consisted chiefly in securing to each individual his rights in property or contracts, but that the new social justice must consider how it can secure for each individual a standard of living and such a share in the values of civilization as shall make possible a full moral life. They say that legal justice is the removal of all those restrictions on the free action of an individual which are not necessary for securing the like freedom on the part of his neighbors, while social justice is the satisfaction of everyone's wants so far as they are not outweighed by others' wants. The change advocated by the social reformers is really that the object of law should be social interests and not individual interests. They unjustly assume that individual rights are held inviolate only in the interest of the individual to whom such rights are selfishly important and not because their preservation benefits the community. On the contrary, personal liberty, including the right of property, is insisted upon because it conduces to the expansion of material resources which are plainly essential to the interests of society and its progress. We must continue to maintain it whether our aim is individualistic or social. As long as human nature is constituted as it is, this will be true. When only altruistic motives actuate men, it may be different.

But we must recognize the strong popular interest in the sociological movement and realize the importance of giving it a practical and successful issue. We are not tied to the defects of the past, or present, and we ought to be anxious to guide the proposed reforms so that we shall secure all the good possible from them without ignoring the inestimable boon of experience we have inherited from centuries of struggle toward better things.

The Supreme Court of the United States has given many evidences of its appreciation of the changes in settled public opinion in respect to the qualification of individual rights by the needs of society. Its definition or rather lack of definition of the police power, and its proposed method of pricking out its limitations in accord with predominant public opinion, is an example. Indeed, many other instances of the infusion of social ideas into the law by construction of remedial statutes and by adjustment of common law principles to cases of social justice could be cited. It is noteworthy that this is most evident in the highest of our Courts with judges of greatest experience, ability and learning in fundamental jurisprudence and of statesmanlike constructive faculty. It is through discrimination and farsighted legislators and through great and learned judges that we can safely and surely achieve the social changes and reforms within the practical range of enforceable law. It must be remembered that with men as they are, government and law cannot make every change in society however desirable. Law which is unenforceable or ineffective is worse than none. There are zones in the field of social relations in which progress can only be made by the moral uplift of the individual members of society, and in which the use of legal compulsion is worse than futile.

Nevertheless, many who are infused with the new ideas are prone to look askance upon what they call the individualistic system and are quite willing to do away with the constitutional restraints and the teachings and influence of the common law upon which such a system must rest. Relying upon the willingness of an inflamed majority to possess themselves of advantages over a minority, or the individual, they advocate remedies that tend toward confiscation.

Attempts made to carry out such ideas have, of course, startled the owners of property and capital to measures of defense, and leading members of the Bar have ranged themselves in support of these measures. Indeed, in the enormous material development, the services of the profession have been invoked and often to protect methods that were indefensible. The profession has suffered from not having that independence of clients, enjoyed by English barristers, in which the relation between the two is temporary and but for a single cause. Such a relation does not produce that widespread, popular impression of complete identity of the professional advocate and adviser with the client, especially the corporate client and all its interests and plans. For these reasons our profession at present is under suspicion of being subsidized by our relation to the property of our clients, and of not being able to discuss without prejudice the betterment of present conditions in society. Those who are advocating these reforms propose, therefore, in the future largely to dispense with lawyers, largely to dispense with constitutional restraints and to place their whole confidence in the direct action of the people, not only in the enactment of laws, not only in their execution and enforcement, but also in the judicial function of determining justice in individual cases. This hostility to our profession, while it is natural and can be explained, is unjust. We are as intelligent, generous, patriotic, self-sacrificing, and sympathetic a class as there is in society. We are not opposed to progress, real progress. Moreover, we know how to do things, and in the end no successful legal step forward will be made without our aid and shaping. We are far from lacking in a desire to improve social conditions. We recognize the inequalities existing between social classes in our communities, and agree to the necessity of new legal conceptions of their duties toward each other. But we have been driven by circumstances into an attitude of opposition. The proposals made for progress have been so radical, so entirely a departure from all the lessons of the past and so dangerous to what we regard as essential in preserving the inestimable social advances we have made since the Christian era, that we have been forced to protest. The result is that at present the militant social reformers and the lawyers are far apart. We don't talk exactly the same language. It is enough to answer our expressed opinions for them to say that we think and talk as lawyers.

What, then, is it necessary for us to do in this coming crisis; for it is a crisis in the life of courts and administration of justice. Many of the social reformers are oblivious of the lessons to be derived from experience in enforcement and operation of laws upon society. They do not realize the necessity for making the many different rules of law fit a system that shall work. They bring to the repair of a mechanism of interlocking parts, rude and unsuitable instruments. Nothing could more reflect upon their crude conception of judicial procedure than the proposition of a recall of judicial decisions. Social changes are not to be successfully made by a cataclysm, unless present conditions are as oppressive as those which caused the French Revolution. To be valuable they must come slowly and with deliberation. They are to be brought about by discriminating legislation proceeding on practical lines and construed by courts having an attitude of favor to the object in view.

I have spoken little to my purpose if I have not made clear the necessity for broadening much the qualification of the general body of our judiciary to meet the important and responsible requirements that the present crisis in our community has thrust upon them. Their coming duties call for a basic knowledge of general and sociological jurisprudence, an intimate familiarity with the law as a science, and with its history, an ability to distinguish in it the fundamental from the casual, and constructive talent to enable them to reconcile the practical aspirations of social reformers with the priceless lessons of experience from the history of government and of law in practical operation. How can this be brought about? Only by broadening the knowledge and studies of the members of the legal profession. It is they who make the judges, who contribute to their education, and who help them to just, broad, and safe conclusions.

What we lawyers need now is to rouse our profession to speak out. We must be heard in defense of the good there is in our present society and in pointing out the social injury which a retrograde step may involve. But we must also put ourselves more in touch with the present thinking of the

people who are being led in foolish paths. We must study sociological jurisprudence. We must be able to understand the attitude of the sociological
reformer. We must show our sympathy with every sincere effort to better
things. What the people need in respect to this matter is light, and the
profession engaged in administering law, and in promoting just judicial
conclusions, must contribute their valuable assistance in giving it. In so far
as the conditions in society are new, in so far as its needs are different from
what they seemed to be at the time of the adoption of the Constitution,
or as they were recognized under the common law, embodied in a century
of our judicial decisions, they should be studied by the profession. We
should seek to know exactly what are the conditions that are sought to be
remedied. We should be willing to meet them in seeking to remedy every
condition that is possible to remedy consistently with the maintenance of
those principles that are essential to the pursuit of material progress and the
consequent attainment of spiritual progress in society and to permanent
popular and peaceful government of law.

The working of the problem presented is not the task of a year. It may
require a generation or more. We must prepare our successors, the future
American Bar, to meet the demand.

Every law school should require those who are to be admitted to its
halls to have a general education furnishing a sufficiently broad foundation
upon which to base a thorough legal education. That general education
ought to include a study of economics and a study of sociology, and the
curriculum of every law school should include a close study of the science
of general and sociological jurisprudence as a basis for the study of the
various branches of our law; and this raising of law school standards should
meet a sympathetic response from Supreme Courts in requirements for
admission to the Bar. Then the members of the Bar will come to the discussion of social remedies in courts, in the halls of Congress and in legislatures,
and in appeals to the people, properly equipped, and will bring the controversy down to a practical issue and the fight can be fought out on a common ground. The valuable lessons of the past will be given proper weight
and real and enduring social progress will be attained. We shall avoid, then,
radical and impractical changes in law and government by which we might
easily lose what we have gained in the struggle of mankind for better things.

10

"To Insure Domestic Tranquility,
Provide for the Common Defence"

The next two purposes stated in the preamble for ordaining and establishing the Constitution were to "insure domestic tranquility" and "provide for the common defense."

The Constitution gives to Congress the power to provide for calling forth the militia to execute the laws of the Union, suppress insurrections, and repel invasions; to raise and support armies; to provide and maintain a navy.

Power is vested in the President, on application of the legislature of a State, or of the executive (when the legislature cannot be convened), to protect it against domestic violence.

The President has direction of the foreign policy of the country, except when treaties are to be made, in which case the Senate, by a vote of two-thirds present, must concur in them, and except when foreign war is to be the policy, when Congress must declare it.

I shall devote this chapter to the consideration of the necessity for the maintenance of a national militia, an army and navy, and to the questions arising in respect to them, together with the possibility of avoiding war and securing peace and thus maintaining a common defense through our treaty-making power.

Save in the District of Columbia, and in the territories, under the exclusive jurisdiction of the Federal Government, domestic tranquillity is secured by the State authorities, and this by the municipal police in cities, by the sheriffs and constables in counties, and if these local arms are insufficient, by the State militia, acting under the direction of the Governor. The State authorities, as we have seen, may, however, invoke the assistance of the President of the United States through a formal notice to him that domestic violence prevails to such an extent that with their available forces they cannot suppress it. Thereupon, the President of the United States in the discharge of his duty should order the army of the United States to the assistance of the State authorities in the maintenance of order.

But it is not essential for the use of the army of the United States to maintain order anywhere within the United States that the Governor or the legislature of the State should call upon the President for assistance. There is "a peace of the state," and there is "a peace of the United States." Obstruction to the laws of the State by force violates the peace of that State. Obstruction by force to the laws of the United States violates the peace of the United States, and the Supreme Court has specifically declared, in a number of cases, that there is a peace of the United States which it is the business of the President to preserve by all the force at his disposal. For instance, it is the duty of the Government, under the Constitution and the laws of the United States passed in accordance therewith, to circulate the mails. Now, if those mails are obstructed by violence, it is the duty of the President, by the United States marshal and his deputies, if they have sufficient force, to clear the obstructions and see to it that the agents of the Government in the mail service have freedom to discharge their functions. The same thing is true as to the enforcement of the orders and judgments of the United States Courts. Should the marshals and their deputies and the *posse comitatus,* whom the marshal is able to summon, be insufficient, then the President, pursuing certain preliminaries required under the statute, may direct the army to preserve the peace of the United States by enforcing the law of the United States.

This last phase of the Federal power was more often in evidence when there were Federal election laws regulating the holding of Congressional elections. It then became the duty of the President to direct the marshals to assist in the enforcement of those laws whenever their operation was obstructed, and even the army was at times called in for this purpose, until there was a rider on an appropriation bill, passed in the days of President Hayes, by which it was forbidden to use the army as a *posse comitatus*. I have always thought that this was a congressional limitation upon the executive power of doubtful constitutional validity.

This suggests the controversy between President Cleveland and Governor Altgeld as to the President's right to send troops to Chicago at the time of the so-called Debs strike and attempted rebellion against organized government. There the orders of the Federal Courts enjoining interference by large bodies of men with the operation of railways, and the obstruction of mails, were held for naught and were violently resisted by rioters, and President Cleveland, under the advice of Attorney-General Olney, and through the orders of Lieutenant-General Schofield, sent out Federal troops to Chicago under General Miles to see to it that these obstructions ceased. They were sent to preserve not the peace of Illinois but the peace of the United States. Governor Altgeld insisted that he had control of the situation, and that it was a usurpation on the part of President Cleveland to attempt to send Federal forces into his State. President Cleveland declined to recognize Governor Altgeld's right to object to his sending the troops of the Government in the United States wherever he might choose. He told the Governor that he did not have to wait for a request by the legislature of Illinois or by Governor Altgeld before he could, by use of the army, suppress unlawful obstruction to the laws of the United States or the process of its Courts.

The injunctions issued in the case against Debs were sustained as valid by the Supreme Court of the United States in a *habeas corpus* suit brought to release Debs from his imprisonment for contempt for defying those injunctions. In that case the Supreme Court, by unanimous judgment, left no doubt whatever that President Cleveland was entirely right in his action and that Governor Altgeld was much too narrow in his view of the power of the Federal Government in such a case.

The army of the United States is theoretically composed of three branches. First, there is the regular army of the United States. That today cannot by law exceed 100,000 men, and its number is fixed by executive order of the President. Practically Congress must consent to the number because it appropriates money for the pay of the army. Its exact number, exclusive of about 4,000 Philippine Scouts, on June 30, 1913, was 4,665 officers and 75,321 men. This is an army raised by voluntary enlistment, in which the term of enlistment is for seven years, with an obligation on the part of the enlisted man to serve four years with the colors and three years in the reserve, during which in time of exigency he may be summoned to active service. Second, in addition to the regular army of the United States, the statutes provide for a so-called volunteer army of the United States, an army raised only in time of war. It was the volunteer army that made up the bulk of our great army during the Civil War. Strictly speaking, this is no more a volunteer army than is the regular army, because both are the result of voluntary enlistments, but as the volunteer army is only used in time of war and the term is generally for a period limited by the end of the war, it is supposed to embrace those who but for the war would not enlist, while the men of the regular army enlisted in time of peace are considered professional or regular soldiers.

The present volunteer law is an old one, quite inadequate to modern needs and especially defective in its provision that the officers of the volunteer army shall be appointed by the State Governors rather than by the President of the United States. When it became necessary to raise additional troops to secure tranquillity in the Philippine Islands, and a volunteer army of 30,000 men had to be raised, a special law was passed which placed the appointing power in the hands of the President. The men under this special act were enlisted for two years, and at the end of the two years, the regiments were as well trained as those of the regular army; but the special law expired by its own limitation, and now the old law remains in force. Effort after effort has been made to pass a new one, which would be ready for use should war threaten, so that the Executive, without waiting for new legislation, might at once raise a volunteer force. But the lingering States' rights prejudice in Congress and the apparent indisposition to part with the State political power, which the transfer of the appointment of officers in the volunteer force from the Governors to the President would involve, have thus far blocked the adoption of the new law.

Colonel Upton, an officer of the United States Army, and a great military authority, who wrote a very valuable book on the military policy of the United States, denounced the feature of our policy by which the State authorities are given power to appoint officers in the volunteer force as producing some of the most lamentable results in our military campaigns.

The third national force is the militia, called the National Guard. The militia is a military force raised under the State laws which the National Constitution recognizes. It gives Congress authority to aid in the organization of the militia, and to provide rules for its discipline and drill. The President is its Commander-in-Chief when it is acting under his call. Its function as a national force is limited to the resistance to invasions of the national territory and it could not be employed as a national force beyond the limits of the United States in a foreign expedition.

This limit upon the national use of the National Guard was made prominent in the Spanish War when the question arose as to whether the famous Seventh Regiment of New York should go to Cuba. It very properly declined to tender its organization for foreign service because the contract of enlistment by its men embraced only domestic service; but every one of its members was given full permission to enter any regular or volunteer regiment for the war and many of them went.

The chief function and the most frequent use of the militia are in the maintenance of order in the State under whose authority it is organized. Unlike the volunteer army of the United States, its officers should, therefore, be appointed by the Governor, and so the Federal Constitution requires.

The people of the United States on the whole are a shrewd, enterprising and provident people, but they have not proven it by their military policy. Anyone who is at all interested may have the utter foolishness and stupidity of that policy shown to them as clearly as the light of day by reading what I have already referred to, Colonel Upton's *History of the Military Policy of the United States*. He shows from the beginning how, through the interference of political theories and the variation of different administrations, we have been ludicrously unprepared for wars into which we entered with all the confidence and nonchalance of a nation with a thoroughly equipped and adequate army. In the War of 1812 our regular army amounted to 6,000 troops. There were 5,000 British troops in Canada. Had we had an army of 25,000 at the time, we could have taken Canada without difficulty. Instead of that we suffered a number of humiliating defeats in the outset of the war and, before we finished it, we had upon paper enlisted in the army and paid for at one time or at another 500,000 troops. We have expended $50,000,000 in pensions paid for service in that war. The same thing is true of all of our wars, and Congress continues to be as reluctant as possible to maintain an adequate army to accomplish the legitimate purposes of such a force. So far as our military policy is concerned, it would seem as if the maxim that "The Lord looks after children and drunken men" ought to be extended to the United States, for by hook or crook, through mistakes of the enemy or through luck and by the expenditure of far greater treasure and many more lives than were necessary, we have generally been successful. This result is always used as an argument to resist a reasonable addition to the army and to incurring reasonable expense in time of peace that we may be better prepared in time of war. Men rise in their seats in Congress and pay deserved tributes to the bravery and efficiency of that volunteer army of half a million men who marched down Pennsylvania Avenue in the spring of '65 after the Civil War, and then point to them as a proof that we could organize an army of citizen soldiers in any emergency entirely adequate to meet foreign attack. They seem oblivious to the fact that it took three solid years of the hardest kind of practical training in actual warfare to make those citizen soldiers what they were—the best-trained army that ever trod in shoe leather. No standing army ever had a better training than they had. To use them as evidence that citizen soldiery can be whipped into an effective military force in the time in which effective and well-equipped European armies could be mobilized for action is to fly in the face of all reason and experience. Of course, our separation by oceans from possible enemies gives us the greatest good reason for avoiding the burdens and inconveniences of a large standing army, but we ought not for that reason to be helpless. We are very much nearer to Europe and Asia by many days than we were in Washington's time.

We are now policing the Philippines with about 12,000 of our troops. We are policing Hawaii with about 2,500 of our troops. We shall police the Isthmus with perhaps 3,000 of our troops. A force is necessary in Alaska, and in addition to these territories, we have between the oceans forty-eight States with a population of 90,000,000 people.

You may remember the controversy between Great Britain and this country over the boundary between Venezuela and British Guyana when President Cleveland demanded that the issue be arbitrated and Secretary Olney as Secretary of State asserted with startling abruptness the Monroe Doctrine and the intention of the Government of the United States to enforce it. The only other time when we came nearer to a breach with Great Britain in the century of peace that has followed the War of 1812 was during the Civil War over the Trent affair. When we were taking this defiant position on the Venezuelan question, there was not on our whole coast a single fortification that could resist the guns of a modern navy. The then English fleet could have sailed into every important port of the United States and subjected every coast city to a ransom and been exposed to no danger except from one modern gun at Sandy Hook. The result of this informing experience was that the nation proceeded to defend itself by coastwise fortifications. And now as against a naval invasion, the country is very heavily fortified, but the guns of these fortifications need a force of some forty thousand men in order that every gun may be equipped with one complement of men.

We have spent upon these fortifications much more than $100,000,000. We are also fortifying the Philippine Islands by making Corregidor Island, which guards the entrance to Manila Bay, impregnable. We are fortifying Honolulu as a naval base and the defenses there will soon be formidable. We are fortifying the entrances to the Panama Canal and they soon will be swept by our guns in such a way that no naval attack can be made upon the canal. It is true that the coast fortifications in the United States proper are constructed with a view to resisting only a sea attack by navy and not a land attack by an army which might disembark at an unprotected point somewhere and march around to take the forts. This was a policy deliberately adopted in Mr. Cleveland's time, because it was not supposed that the prospect of the landing of a military force so far away from Europe, or so far away from Asia was a danger to be apprehended; but there is now being agitated the question whether this was not an error, and whether the fortifications ought not now to be supplemented in such a way that resistance could be made to land forces.

Today the coast artillery, who are coast defense men, embrace upwards of 24,000 men. If you take this number from the 75,000 men we have in our army today, it leaves not more than 51,000 as a mobile army, and if you take from that number the 17,000 men that we use in the Philippines, Alaska, Hawaii and on the Isthmus of Panama, it leaves us in this country as the mobile army consisting of infantry, cavalry and light artillery, but 34,000 men. It is this force, amounting to about one in every 2,600 persons, that constitutes our regular army for use in the insurance of domestic tranquillity and the common defense of 90,000,000 people between the oceans.

This is not adequate for present legitimate purposes. If the mobile army in the United States were increased to 65,000, it would not be an excessive provision. That would require an addition to the army of 36,000. The passage of a proper volunteer law is a crying need. I am glad to say that the law with respect to the militia is a modern law and has been improved by amendment from time to time, and that the Federal Government is intelligently spending money and exercising disciplinary authority to make a militia of 100,000 that could be called into requisition in time of a war of defense.

One of the great difficulties that Presidents and Secretaries of War now have in a proper management of the War Department is in the economical and strategical housing of the troops in the United States proper. An army of the size of ours should be stationed at posts properly distributed with a view to rapid concentration anywhere, but few enough in number and large enough in capacity to permit the assembling at each post under general officers, a large enough body of troops to give the officers and men experience in drilling and maneuvering with brigades and divisions instead of with companies and battalions. In the Indian Wars and for other reasons, the posts were increased in number properly to meet the then strategical necessities. Now four-fifths of them ought to be abandoned to carry out the plan suited to our present needs, and this is resisted for political reasons by members of Congress and the Senate. A military post helps the neighborhood because much government money is spent there and the whole military policy of the United States has to suffer from this political cause.

We may well take pride in such an army as we have, for we have a body of army officers that are brave, efficient and skilled, lacking in experience possibly in the mobilization and conduct of great bodies of troops but as well educated in military science as any officers in the world, and as full of expedients and as adaptable to circumstances as any I know. We now have a general staff of army experts to advise the Secretary of War. It is impersonal and it insures the continuity of military policy so far as the War Department is concerned which makes for good. Nevertheless, there is much to be done in order to fit our army for its proper place in the discharge of its constitutional functions and as a nucleus and skeleton for the organization of an adequate force, should war come upon us.

Now with respect to the navy, I only have to say that until within recent times we had a navy that made us third in the weight of our armament and possibly second to Great Britain, but that now, with the number of keels laid down by other nations for new vessels, our rank is gradually being reduced. The laying down of two battleships a year would possibly have enabled us to keep a better position, but the failure of the last Congress and of this one to give us more than one battleship affects our future armament and of course our naval prestige. Farragut said that the best defense was well-directed fire against the enemy, and by the same reasoning a navy which is efficient to make your enemy fear its attack is one of the surest means of keeping your enemy's force out of your country.

The great objection to the maintenance of such an army and navy, as I have suggested, is the burden of its cost. Two hundred and fifty million dollars a year are necessary for this purpose, and this does not include the $150,000,000 or more that are devoted to pensions for those who were injured in the Civil War. Those pensions are not properly a part of the expense of the present military system of the United States, and ought not to play a part in determining the expenditures for our present army and navy. They are due to our not having had an adequate army ready in the past. Certain it is that the larger army and navy we maintain, the less in size will be our pension list after another war, should we have one, because the more adequate provision we make for a prompt and active campaign, the less men we shall enlist and the less their loss of life and limb.

When we compare our expenditures with those of the armies abroad, we see that the maintenance of a navy and an army is much more expensive to us per man than it is to the nations abroad. They have a conscription system while we depend on voluntary enlistment. We have to pay in money and support a living wage. They compel service practically without a wage in money. I have not the comparative figures for the cost of the European armies and our own this year, but in 1906 this statement which I made as Secretary of War was true:

> Our regular army today amounts in effective force to about 60,000 men, and it costs us in round numbers about $72,000,000 to sustain our military establishment. France maintains an army on the active list of 546,000 men, and it costs her $133,000,000. Germany maintains an army which has upon its active list 640,000 men, and it costs her $144,000,000 a year to maintain it. In other words, France has an army about nine times the size of ours which it costs her substantially less than twice the sum to maintain, while Germany has an army more than ten times as large which it costs her just about double our sum to maintain.

But you may say all this has a very military and warlike sound, coming from a man whose voice has been supposed to be for international peace, and if you charge me with inconsistency in this, you will only be repeating what has often been said against me for my advocacy of a more effective army and the maintenance of an adequate navy.

I am strongly in favor of bringing about a condition of securing international peace in which armies and navies may either be dispensed with or be maintained at a minimum size and cost; but I am not in favor of putting my country at a disadvantage by assuming a condition in respect to international peace that does not now exist and I am opposed to injuring the useful prestige and weight of her international influence which, under present conditions, an adequate army and an adequate navy are required to maintain.

I am as strongly in favor as anyone can be of prosecuting every plan that will make war less and less probable. I believe there are practical plans that can accomplish much in this direction. I do not believe the plan of common disarmament is a practical plan. It has been tried and has failed. All Europe is an armed camp, and every time that any nation adds to its armament, the others with whom conflict is possible add to their respective armaments. Nothing but bankruptcy is going to stop these additions, and bankruptcy does not come as soon as we might properly welcome it.

The only thing that will bring about a disarmament is the certainty on the part of the nations, whose disarmament is important, that by some other means than war, they can secure the just and effective settlement of disputed questions that must arise between nations. When such a method is established and the nations are certain that it will accomplish its purpose, then they ought to have no motive for the maintenance of anything but a force sufficient to contribute to an international police force to carry out the decrees of the international tribunals in which international questions are settled.

I am an optimist, but I am not a dreamer, or an insane enthusiast on the subject of international peace. I realize the valuable uses to which wars have been just in the past and the progress that has been made through war in the civilization of the world. Resistance to tyrannical authority and despotism and the assertion of freedom have been possible only by revolution and the use of an armed force. Without such armed force, freedom would not have been won and beneficent governments would not have been established.

We can count on peace as a result of the establishment of international tribunals only in as far as the world is, or shall be, divided into nations and countries under well-ordered and just governments which can enforce peace within their own respective borders and prevent war of an internecine or civil character. As between nations, with proper authority established within their own borders, supported by the moral strength of their own peoples, we can assume a proper basis for the establishment of such international agreements as may ultimately prevent international war. Every treaty that is made between two nations of this established character, for the settlement of differences between them, by reference to an impartial tribunal, is a step toward international peace.

But there is a long way before us in the accomplishment of our purposes upon this head. And meantime our country is occasionally subject to the dangers that arise from the hostility of other countries. Since we have been a nation we have been at war for one-fourth of the time, and, therefore, those who are responsible for the policy of our Government have no right to assume that the possibility of future wars has altogether ceased.

And this leads me to the question of the fortification of the Panama Canal. We built the Panama Canal to make another great avenue of trade for the world and to shorten the passage around Cape Horn and through the Straits of Magellan; but we also built it for our own national profit, first, in bringing the Pacific and Atlantic Coasts nearer together for the coastwise trade, and second, in developing the strategic efficiency of our navy in protection of our country, by offering a means of transferring the navy quickly from one seaboard to the other.

The proposition to neutralize the canal so that it shall always be open to every nation, whether we are at war with that nation or not, is to deprive us of that one very great advantage in using our navy to which I have referred, because while we could transfer our navy from one side to the other quickly through the canal, our enemy would enjoy the same strategical opportunity. Thus we would share with our enemy the advantage which we had planned and so lose it.

More than this, the canal is a very valuable property and the locks and machinery may be easily destroyed. Treaties of neutralization would not prevent a lawless nation from violating them and rendering useless to us the canal at a time of emergency when it is most necessary. We have the right to fortify the canal, given us by Panama and acquiesced in by England, and there is not the slightest reason why we should not insure ourselves by fortifications against any injury which other nations may do.

The presence of fortifications does not lead us into war, and we don't have to use them unless there is some hostile threat against the canal. But it seems to me that we would be foolish in the extreme and utterly wanting in national prudence if we did not make it certain by our preparations that no nation can injure that work which has cost us $400,000,000 and which in time of national stress we shall certainly need. This is not at all inconsistent with the sincere desire never to have a war and to bring about peace as quickly as possible when we do have a war. It does not invite or approve a war any more than provision for a water supply invites or approves a conflagration. It is not at all inconsistent with the advocacy of treaties of arbitration and of general arbitration with all countries until those treaties are signed and until they embrace all nations of the earth, so that we can count on their effectiveness to prevent war.

We are thus naturally brought to the final topic of this chapter, and that is the treaties of general arbitration. We negotiated two of those treaties, one with France and the other with England. We then had so-called arbitration treaties with nearly all the nations of the world, but they excepted from their operation all questions of national honor or vital interest, and they provided that before they could become effective the Executive and the Senate of this country should make a special agreement with the country with whom we had the controversy for the special submission of the issues to the peace tribunal. These treaties, therefore, are practically nothing more than a general statement that we are in favor of arbitration of an issue when we agree to arbitrate it or, in other words, when we think it will be to our advantage to arbitrate it. Questions of national honor and of vital interest include all those questions, the agitation of which is likely to lead to war, and, therefore, arbitration treaties which except such questions may be said to be treaties for the settlement of those questions that never would involve war in their settlement anyhow. This clearly shows that they are not adapted at all to the purpose of preventing war.

The two treaties of peace we negotiated with France and Great Britain, however, took a decided step forward. First, they contained a formal agreement to submit either to The Hague, or to some other tribunal, all questions of difference arising between the two countries of a justiciable character, and then they proceeded to define what justiciable was by saying that it meant all questions that could be settled on principles of law or equity. That certainly included questions of vital interest and national honor, because they could both be settled on such principles. Under the second section, whenever a difference arose, whether it was justiciable or not, of whatever kind, and negotiation could not settle it, either party might delay final action for a year by demanding an investigation of the difference by a commission consisting of three persons selected by one government and three persons by the other to investigate and make a recommendation. If five of the commissioners decided that the question was justiciable, in accordance with the treaty, then both nations were bound to submit it to its arbitration. It seems to me that the negotiation of such a treaty between France and the United States, and between England and the United States, and between the other nations of Europe and the United States, would finally lead to the negotiation of such treaties between European countries themselves, and ultimately that we might have an interlacing and interlocking series of treaties comprehending so many countries as to lead to the formation of an international court of judicature. Before this court, any nation being aggrieved might bring any other nation to answer its complaint, the case might be heard upon proper pleadings, and the judgment of the court might be enforced either through the public opinion of the nations, or, if that failed, through an international police force. This may seem an ambitious project and, as I have said, it is essential to its carrying out that it be made between well-ordered governments which maintain peace at home and within their own borders, and which are sufficiently responsive to international public opinion to fear its criticism and yield to its demands. However remote such a court may be, each treaty of this kind made would diminish the chances of war, and when the system embraced all governments, it would certainly make them more willing to reduce armament and rely upon the international court of judicature.

The treaties were defeated in the Senate. They were defeated by amendments. One amendment put in so many saving clauses as to the causes which were to be arbitrated that it hardly seemed worth while to offer such a truncated and narrowed clause for reconsideration by the countries with whom we had negotiated the treaties.

The Senators from the South were very sensitive lest some of the repudiated debts of the Southern States should be made the basis of international arbitration by bondholders living in other countries. If these debts were just, they ought to be paid. If not, the tribunal would probably so decide. As a matter of fact, however, the treaties would not have included them because the language of the treaties only covered issues arising in the future, not past questions as these were.

The second and the chief objection to the treaty was that under its terms not only the Executive but the Senate was bound to arbitrate any difference which should be held, by five out of six of the commission established under the second clause, to be a justiciable one and therefore subject to arbitration. In other words, the Senate insisted that it could not agree to abide the decision of an international tribunal as to whether a treaty which it had entered into, bound it to submit to arbitration a certain question.

I never have been able to understand the force and weight of this argument. The Senate is not any more limited in its powers of agreeing to a treaty than the Executive. Both represent the Government. Now to say that this Government may not agree in advance with another government to arbitrate any of a class of questions that arises in the future, and to submit the question whether that issue is within the description of arbitrable questions as defined in the treaty, is to say that this Government has not any right to agree to do anything in the future. Such a limitation upon the treaty-making power of the Government and upon the treaty-making confirmation of the Senate is a limitation which would prevent this Government from entering into any useful arbitration treaty. It grows out of an exalted and unfounded idea by those who have for a long time been in the Senate, of the sacred nature of the Senate's function in treaty making as distinguished from the function of the Executive in making the same treaty which it has to confirm. A treaty binds the Government to some future action or else it is not a treaty at all. If a branch and agency of government has the treaty-making power, it has the right to bind the Government to something, and one of the commonest things that history has frequently illustrated as the subject of agreement is the submission of the construction of a treaty to an impartial tribunal. That is all this was. It was an agreement to submit to a tribunal the question whether the word "justiciable," as defined in the treaty, included an issue when that issue should arise.

But the treaties were defeated. Sometimes I have been very much disappointed, because I thought that their defeat was a retrograde step. Here we had two countries willing to go into a very comprehensive peace treaty with us of general arbitration, and after they were made, the Senate defeated the plan. If those nations could afford to make such treaties, why couldn't we do so? Have we any interests that could be prejudicially affected by such treaties more important to us than their interests could be to them? Is not the real objection to be found in the feeling on the part of many Senators that they are only in favor of arbitration when we can win and not when we may lose? That is not sincere support of the principle of arbitration.

Still I think the making of the general arbitration treaties and the discussion of them before the people have been useful, and that sometime in the future some other Executive may have the good fortune to negotiate another such treaty and to find a Senate not so sensitive as to its prerogative.

THE ANTI-TRUST ACT AND
THE SUPREME COURT

The Anti-trust Act and the Supreme Court

Commentary

Donald F. Anderson

In the late nineteenth and early twentieth centuries, the Republican Party was generally known as a high-tariff party committed to protecting American industries and labor from foreign competition. Whatever the original justification for maintaining high tariffs, a marketplace protected from foreign competition spawned many large corporations that came to dominate the American economy and, through their political and economic influence, to threaten both the free-enterprise system and the basic principles of popular government. Although the conventional political wisdom of the period placed great value on nineteenth-century liberal notions of "laissez-faire" and limited government regulation of business, those ideas were never left unchallenged in the public arena. Initially the Populist Movement, and later the Progressive Movement, challenged many of these assumptions and provoked a sharp national debate over the role of the national government in regulating the marketplace and controlling monopolies.

A rising tide of protest against the predatory practices of monopolies or so-called "trusts" led Congress in 1890 to enact the Sherman Antitrust Act. The language of the act was breathtaking in its comprehensive simplicity, if not its precision:

> Section 1. Every contract, combination in the form of trust or otherwise; or conspiracy, in restraint of trade or commerce among the several States, or with foreign nations, is hereby declared to be illegal. . . .
>
> Section 2. Every person who shall monopolize, or attempt to monopolize, or combine or conspire with any other person or persons, to monopolize any part of the trade or commerce among the several States, or with foreign nations, shall be deemed guilty of a misdemeanor.

Over the next thirty years, during the administrations of William McKinley (1897–1901), Theodore Roosevelt (1901–1909), William Howard Taft (1909–1913), and Woodrow Wilson (1913–1921), national debate on antitrust policy would focus on three closely related questions:

> 1) What did the Sherman Act mean, and what was it intended to accomplish?
>
> 2) Should the act be enforced vigorously and comprehensively against both capital and labor, or not?
>
> 3) Should the act be strengthened, weakened, or left to the courts to interpret and apply?

Enacting a vague, comprehensive law that apparently prohibited *every* restraint on trade created the illusion of comprehensive reform and raised popular expectations about the national government's willingness and power to control monopolies. Those expectations were soon dashed in *United States v. E. C. Knight Co.* (1895), the *Sugar Trust* case, when the Supreme Court refused to recognize federal power under the Sherman Act to control the Sugar Trust. The federal government lost its bid to enforce the act against the American Sugar Refining Company, which had acquired a number of local sugar refining companies, thereby capturing almost 98 percent of the sugar refining capacity in the nation. In a five to four decision, the Court held that the act, which was based on Congress's power to regulate "commerce among the states," could not reach the refining of sugar because that activity was *intrastate*, not interstate, commerce. As Chief Justice Melville Fuller indicated, "Commerce succeeds to manufacture and is not part of it." "Manufacturing," "production," or the refining of sugar were local commercial activities that had only an "indirect" effect on interstate commerce. Only activities that had a "direct" effect on interstate commerce could be regulated. The states could attempt to regulate such activities through their police powers, but the federal government could not. In short, unless the *Knight* case was overruled, the national government appeared helpless to deal effectively with monopolies under the existing Constitution and antitrust law.

Taft and other critics of the decision maintained that the federal government had mishandled the case by failing to offer adequate proof of the American Sugar Refining Company's *intent* to control the market and price of sugar. The government had *assumed* what needed to be proved—that such a total concentration of power in one corporation was designed to restrain trade. Taft never challenged the underlying constitutional theory of the *Knight* decision, just the flawed factual record upon which it rested.

The *Knight* decision exacerbated an already intense national debate over antitrust policy and forced subsequent Republican administrations to confront the antitrust issue in a serious manner. President Theodore Roosevelt responded to public pressures to control trusts by first distinguishing between "good" trusts and "bad" trusts. The Sherman Act should be enforced against "bad" trusts, he argued, but a blanket enforcement of the law against all large corporations would only adversely affect business and general prosperity in America.

Prior to joining the Roosevelt cabinet, Taft had also been associated with progressive views on the antitrust issue and had been a strong proponent of vigorous antitrust law enforcement. While a member of the Roosevelt cabinet, he had agreed completely with the president's antitrust policy, and as Roosevelt's handpicked successor, he vowed to continue those policies in his own administration. Both presidents were aggressive in bringing suits against violators of the Antitrust Act. Roosevelt, for example, brought a total of fifty-four suits, earning in the process a national reputation as a "trust buster." Letting his deeds speak for themselves, Taft brought ninety suits, almost twice as many in four years as Roosevelt had brought in seven.

Vigorous antitrust enforcement was only one of the shared goals of the Roosevelt and Taft administrations. Winning those suits at the Supreme Court level was a second, more important, long-term goal. Effective antitrust policy depended ultimately on reversing or neutralizing the *Knight* decision and reinvigorating the Sherman Act and the Constitution. These ends could be achieved permanently only by "packing" the Court with judges with a more sympathetic nationalist philosophy of federal power.

Both presidents were presented with opportunities to fill vacancies and change the direction of the Court. In fact, Roosevelt twice offered Taft a seat on the Court, only to have him decline each time. However, Roosevelt did appoint three Republicans to the Court—Oliver Wendell Holmes Jr. (1902), William Rufus Day (1903), and William H. Moody (1906)—all of whom reflected his nationalist Republican views of federal power. By themselves, these appointments were not enough to transform dramatically the direction of the Court. But combined with public and presidential pressures, they moved the Court steadily away from the *Knight* decision. In the *Northern Securities* case (1904), for example, the Court sustained the federal government's antitrust suit against the Northern Securities Company, which had purchased the Northern Pacific and Great Northern Railroads. The Court held that when three great railroads attempted to combine into a larger system to control rail traffic in a significant portion of the nation, courts could imply illegal intent and purpose to monopolize rail transportation from the combination. The decision resurrected hope that the Sherman Act could be interpreted broadly enough to reach at least the monopolistic practices of the railroad industry, if not those of other combinations.

The "packing" of the Court continued with greater force during the Taft administration. Presented with a windfall of five Supreme Court vacancies, Taft took great care to appoint judges whose political and jurisprudential views coincided with his own. By the end of 1911, he had appointed five Supreme Court judges—Horace Lurton, Charles Evans Hughes, Edward White (as Chief Justice), Joseph Rucker Lamar, and Willis VanDevanter—all of whom were, at least for the times, "pragmatic practical conservatives." Taft's efforts bore fruit in the spring of 1912, when the White Court upheld the convictions of the Standard Oil Trust and the American Tobacco Trust under a reinvigorated interpretation of the Sherman Act.

The *Standard Oil Trust* and *Tobacco Trust* cases appeared

to have infused new life into the Sherman Act, but not without igniting additional controversy over the novel "rule of reason" advanced by Chief Justice White. Writing for an overwhelming majority, White concluded that the words of the act, although apparently unequivocal and universal in character, had been intended to codify both existing common-law doctrines prohibiting restraints on trade and "reasonable" exceptions long recognized in the common law. By recognizing the existence of "reasonable" exceptions which were nowhere mentioned in the original Sherman Act or recognized by previous Supreme Court decisions, the Court appeared to be expanding its own power to determine whether or not trusts were behaving reasonably. The immediate effect of the new rule was to create a loophole for corporations being sued for antitrust violations that could demonstrate that their behavior was "reasonable" and conformed to responsible business practices. The "rule of reason" also had the immediate effect of decreasing convictions under the antitrust law and placing the judiciary in the position of determining what was "reasonable" corporate behavior and what was not.

When Woodrow Wilson and the Democrats captured the White House and both houses of Congress in 1912, one of their immediate goals was to strengthen the Sherman Act. As Kent Professor of Constitutional Law at Yale University, Taft interjected himself into the national debate by speaking out on antitrust issues. His extended essay *The Anti-trust Law and the Supreme Court* was published at the height of national debate over antitrust policy, a debate which culminated in the passage of the Clayton Antitrust Act and the Federal Trade Commission Act in the fall of 1914. Although touted by Taft as a dispassionate analysis of the abstruse issues of constitutional and antitrust law, *The Anti-trust Law and the Supreme Court* was, in fact, an unapologetic defense of the Supreme Court's recent interpretations of the Sherman Act and an attack upon the critics of the Court whose arguments, Taft argued, were "born of ignorance or demagoguery."

Taft's argument in this essay was clear and straightforward. There was, he maintained, significant popular misunderstanding of the Sherman Act, which had surfaced in the congressional debate over antitrust policy. To dispel that misunderstanding, Taft chronicled the evolution of antitrust law from its initial passage in 1890 to the *Knight* decision to the *Northern Securities, Standard Oil Trust,* and *Tobacco Trust* cases. His conclusion: the *Knight* decision, although never specifically overruled, had been seriously undermined by these decisions and was no longer supported by the contemporary Supreme Court.

The most significant aspect of Taft's essay, however, was his total support of Chief Justice White's interpretation of the Sherman Act and the "rule of reason." Departing from his earlier public pronouncements on the Sherman Act, Taft accepted White's argument that the original act was designed to codify common-law prohibitions on monopolistic practices, as well as five "reasonable" exceptions to those prohibitions long recognized in the common law. The "rule of reason" is, therefore, not an innovation at all, he argued, but a traditional part of the common law and of the Sherman Act itself. Critics of the rule, including Justice John Harlan Sr., were simply mistaken in their claim that the Court had authorized itself to engage in "judicial legislation" under the guise of determining what business practices were "reasonable." That the Court was now arbitrarily engaged in choosing between "good" trusts and "bad" trusts was a simplistic popular misconception based on ignorance of the law. In Taft's mind, the "rule of reason" was not a usurpation of legislative power or the arbitrary picking of winners and losers in antitrust suits by uncontrolled judges, but the application of principles long established in the common law which are best left to the judiciary to apply in a principled, flexible, and evolutionary manner. Taft's distinction between blatant judicial law making and judicial application of common-law principles is a subtle one and not easily understood by those uninitiated in the law and jurisprudence. However, it was easily rejected by those who disagreed with the consequences of the "rule of reason" and who were eager to simplify and exploit the issue for political purposes.

Taft concluded his essay by emphatically asserting that the Sherman Act was designed only to suppress certain business abuses. "It was not to interfere with a great volume of capital which, concentrated under one organization, reduced the cost of production and made its profits thereby and took no advantage of its size by methods akin to duress to stifle competition with it." The Sherman Act did not need to be amended to make it easier to attack and dismantle large corporations. The best policy was the current policy, which left the Court free to interpret and illuminate the law through case-by-case litigation. "A statute which is rendered more and more certain in its meaning by a series of decisions of the Supreme Court is more and more valuable," Taft maintained. "This furnishes a strong reason for leaving the act as it is." "If the law interpreted by the Supreme Court remains on the statute book as it is," he concluded, "it will continue to free business from its real burdens." In short, if the law is not broken, there is no need to fix it. The Democratic Congress, therefore, was trying to reform a law which, properly understood, provided a reasonable and workable approach to controlling culpable monopolies.

Taft's defense of the existing antitrust law and of the Supreme Court's dominant role in elaborating its meaning failed to forestall the passage of the Clayton Antitrust Act or the Federal Trade Commission Act. The Clayton Act attempted to provide more specific guidance to the courts regarding what business practices were illegal, but failed to exempt labor unions from the antitrust laws. The Federal Trade Commission Act set up an independent regulatory commission to define unfair business practices, but left significant room for subsequent judicial interpretations of FTC powers. Despite the president's loss in the political battles over antitrust policy to the Democrats in Congress, Taft's defense of a benevolent antitrust policy that distinguished between predatory monopolistic practices and the reasonable business practices of well-behaved corporations is one that echoes loudly to this day in the chambers of Congress and the courts whenever antitrust policy is debated.

1

Limitations upon Rights of Contract as to Property, Business, and Labor at Common Law

The prospect of legislation at this session of Congress amendatory of the Sherman law has again brought before the public the whole question of anti-trust legislation. A great deal of misunderstanding concerning the effectiveness of that law has been displayed in such discussion as has already arisen.

The decisions of the Supreme Court interpreting the statute have not been clearly understood by many of those who have taken part in that discussion. The proposals for further legislation do not take into account the progress of those decisions in making the statute effective.

In what follows I shall try to set forth in a summary way the present legal status of trusts and combinations in this country. I shall not attempt to discuss in any detail the proposals to amend and supplement the existing statute against trusts now pending in Congress. I shall confine myself to making clear the law against trusts and monopolies as it grew up under the common law, as it was changed by statute, as it has been enforced by the courts, and as it is today.

The federal anti-trust law is one of the most important statutes ever passed in this country. It was a step taken by Congress to meet what the public had found to be a growing and intolerable evil in combinations between many who had capital employed in a branch of trade, industry, or transportation, to obtain control of it, regulate prices, and make unlimited profit. Whether Congress intended it or not, it used language that necessarily forbade the combinations of laborers to restrain and obstruct interstate trade.

The statute, therefore, qualified three important phases of what we include in the general term "individual liberty"—the right of property, freedom to contract, and freedom of labor.

In this law Congress used general expressions, "restraint of trade," "monopoly," "combinations," and "conspiracy." It was passed in a country which recognizes as controlling the customary law handed down to us from England and known as the common law. It was drafted by great lawyers who may be presumed to have used those expressions with the intention that they should be interpreted in the light of common law, just as it has been frequently decided that the terms used in our federal Constitution are to be so construed.

It is of the highest importance, therefore, to consider, as a preliminary basis for our discussion of the statute, what the common law was in respect to restraints of trade—that is, its limitation upon the right of property and the right of free contract, and upon the right of one to dispose of his labor. Just what use should be made of the common-law rules on these subjects in giving effect to the statute we can determine later.

The statute made unlawful a great number of business methods and plans, all directed to the same purpose of suppressing competition and controlling prices, which until the passage of the act had been regarded merely as shrewd and effective, and as justified in the struggle for success. Such methods had resulted in the building of great and powerful corporations which had, many of them, intervened in politics and through use of corrupt machines and bosses threatened us with a plutocracy.

Combinations of labor also in the field of interstate commerce had grown to most formidable proportions. A few years after the passage of the anti-trust statute, Debs and the American Railway Union attempted to take the country by the throat and to stop the arterial circulation of interstate commerce in order to win a victory in the matter of better terms of employment for employees of a particular industrial company.

The statute was passed in 1890. It has, therefore, been nearly a quarter of a century on the statute-book. It has had the benefit of construction by the Supreme Court of the United States in a series of most important cases which presented issues that have in their decision searched its meaning; and, in spite of a great deal of assertion and intimation to the contrary, the effect of those years of litigation has been to give us a valuable and workable interpretation which any one who gives it sincere attention can understand and can follow in the methods of his business, in the use of his capital, or in the organization and rules of action of his trade-union.

One difficulty in giving the public a clear understanding of the meaning and effect of the statute is that it has been made a football of party politics, that shibboleths have been fabricated out of it without any clear understanding of the distinctions which the Court has made, that results have been misrepresented, and the superlatives of stump oratory have been substituted for a clear statement of the scope and operation of the law. Politicians have seized upon phrases that would attract the public eye, the meaning of which in the law they have not themselves understood, and have proposed amendments to accomplish purposes of a most indefinite character, without knowing or caring how they were to operate, if only the pressing of the amendment gave them a ground for appeal for votes and for a claim to the gratitude of their constituents.

The statute dealt with a most difficult subject. The members of Congress who passed it knew that it was a difficult subject. They made plain the object that they had in mind, and they used general expressions to accomplish it, which they thought had had definition in the existing law. The evil to be remedied was manifest, and they pursued the legislative course, so often pursued before, of trusting to the learned, just, and equitable construction of the courts to effect their legislative intention.

As early as the second year of Henry V, a restraint which any man put upon himself by contract not to engage in any branch of trade or labor was not legally binding on him and was unenforceable. This was in 1415. There is no authority that goes so far as to indicate that the making of such a contract was indictable, but the rule that it was void was without exception for two centuries. An effort to make an exception appears in the eighteenth year of James I, where it was held that a contract not to use a certain trade in a particular place was an exception to the general rule.

It was regarded as against the general interest of freedom of labor and trade to enforce a man's agreement to disable himself to earn his own livelihood, and so to become a charge upon the community. Probably that was the sole purpose at first. Later on the kings exercised the power to grant the privilege to individuals of exclusive dealing in particular trades, and they did this by patents for monopolies. Naturally, such an exclusion of all others from any particular business or trade by arbitrary royal act stirred the indignation of the people, and the abolition of those statutory monopolies followed.

Meantime there had arisen abuses growing out of the attempt on the part of traders to exclude others from the sale of foodstuffs and other necessities of life by what was called engrossing or regrating—that is, by cornering the market and enabling them to raise and exact exorbitant prices. These were made the subject of statutes punishing them as crimes. As the results of the royal monopoly and of the cornering by engrossing and regrating were in more or less degree the same, there came to be a confusion of the terms, and the word "monopoly" came to be applied also to the result of the cornering of the market.

The history and growth of the exceptions to the at first absolute rule avoiding all restraints of trade are interesting and important, and their development has continued down to very recent years. The absolute restriction proved in some ways to be embarrassing to trade rather than in the interest of its freedom. If a man had a business and wished to sell it, with its good will, he could get a better price if he might lawfully bind himself not to interfere with that business which he was selling by engaging in the same business within the same territory. This was in the interest of the purchaser, because he wished to secure the benefit of his bargain and make legitimate profit out of it, and it was not contrary to the public interest, because it did not affect the public. The condition of trade was not changed by the transfer from the one to the other, and the *status quo* was maintained by the agreement.

Of course, if the restraint upon the seller's going into business was larger in its scope than the business which he sold, either in the matter of territory or in the character of the business, it was beyond the proper and legitimate purpose of such a restraining term of the contract. Therefore it was held to exceed the just limits of the exception to the old rule and to be unreasonable and unenforceable. It was not punishable as an offense; it was merely a term of the contract for the breach of which the other party could not recover damages and in respect to which a court of equity would not aid him.

The instance of sale of a business with its good will is only one of a number of analogous cases in which a contract restraining the contractor in his future trade or business was deemed to be germane and legitimately adopted to the lawful purpose of the principal contract, and, therefore, enforceable as part of it if the restraint was limited in its terms to the needs of the main transaction. Another instance was that of an agreement by a retiring partner not to compete with the firm which he had just left, which was quite analogous to the sale of a business and its good will to a stranger.

A third instance was that of one entering a partnership stipulating that while he was a member of it he would not do anything to interfere by competition or otherwise with the business of the firm, which presents an exact analogy to the two previous cases. A fourth was where one sold property to another, and that other agreed not to use the property in competition with the business retained by the seller. In this case it was held proper for the owner of the property, who had full liberty either to sell or not to sell, to prevent injury to himself and his business by taking a contract from the buyer not to use it for such purpose.

A fifth instance was where an assistant or servant or agent entering upon a contract of service agreed as an incidental term not to compete with his master or employer after the expiration of his time of service. This was to protect the employer in his business from damage or loss caused by the unjust use on the part of the employee of the confidential knowledge he might acquire in such business.

It is conceivable that other analogous instances might arise in which exceptions would be made at common law to the general rule preventing the enforcement of contractual restraints upon the contractor's trade, though after a thorough search of the authorities I do not find any other instance suggested.

These exceptions were made because it was said that they were reasonable restraints of trade. Now, they were reasonable not because in a general way the judges thought they would not hurt anybody under the particular circumstances, but they were held to be reasonable as measured by the lawful purpose of the principal contract to which they were subsidiary and ancillary.

This gave a definition for judicial guidance. It laid down the purposes to which such a contract must be confined, and it was not open to the criticism that it enlarged judicial discretion into legislative action. I do not think that any well-reasoned and well-supported case can be found in which an agreement has been enforced by the courts of England or of this country where the main object was either to get or to keep another man out of business or to restrict his business in quantity, prices, or territory. When no other purpose than one of these has been manifested in the contract it has always been unenforceable at common law.

It used to be said that partial restraints of trade would be enforced if they were reasonable. The expression "partial" was not a happy one, and it was rejected later on because there came before the courts instances in which ancillary contracts of this character had to be, not partial, but general, and had to include the whole realm, or it might be the whole world. For instance, where a man was engaged in the manufacture of large ammunition, great guns, or war material, which to be profitable must be sold chiefly to sovereign governments and in which he had established a good will that was worldwide, and he wished to sell his business to another. If the seller was to secure a good price, and the purchaser was to receive and enjoy the good will and worldwide business which he was paying for, it was reasonable for the seller to stipulate in the contract of sale, as a term of it or as ancillary to it, that he would not go into the same business at all or anywhere.

What I wish to insist upon and emphasize as much as I can is that when it is said that a contract in restraint of trade was reasonable at common law, it was not a contract in which the restraint was the sole or chief object of the contract. The restraint was a mere instrument to carry out a different and lawful purpose of the main contract.

Fear of monopoly was one of the reasons why such restraints were not enforceable at common law. We see this clearly set forth by Chief Justice Parker in 1711, in the leading case of *Mitchel vs. Reynolds,* I. P. Williams, 181, 190, where he stated the objections to a contract in the restraint of trade of one of the contracting parties as follows:

First. The mischief which may arise from them: (1) to the party by the loss of his livelihood and the subsistence of his family; (2) to the public, by depriving it of a useful member. Another reason is the great abuses these voluntary restraints are liable to; as, for instance, from corporations who are perpetually laboring for exclusive advantages in trade and to reduce it into as few hands as possible.

The reasons were stated at length in *Alger vs. Thacher*, 19 Pick, 51, 54, by the Supreme Judicial Court of Massachusetts when Chief Justice Shaw was at its head, and when Putnam, Wild, Morton, and Dewey were associates. Referring to the rule as stated by Chief Justice Parker in 1711, the Court through Justice Morton said: "That the law under consideration has been adopted and practised upon in this country, and in this State, is abundantly evident from the cases cited from our own reports. It is reasonable, salutary, and suited to the genius of our government and the nature of our institutions. It is founded on great principles of public policy and carries out our constitutional prohibition of monopolies and exclusive privileges."

The unreasonableness of contracts in restraint of trade and business is very apparent from several obvious considerations: (1) Such contracts injure the parties making them, because they diminish their means of procuring livelihoods and a competency for their families. They tempt improvident persons, for the sake of present gain, to deprive themselves of the power to make future acquisitions; and they expose such persons to imposition and oppression. (2) They tend to deprive the public of the services of men in the employments and capacities in which they may be most useful to the community as well as themselves. (3) They discourage industry and enterprise and diminish the products of ingenuity and skill. (4) They prevent competition and enhance prices. (5) They expose the public to all the evils of monopoly; and this especially is applicable to wealthy companies and large corporations, who have the means, unless restrained by law, to exclude rivalry, monopolize business, and engross the market. Against evils like these, wise laws protect individuals and the public by declaring all such contracts void.

The changed conditions under which men have ceased to be so entirely dependent for a livelihood on pursuing one trade have rendered the first and second considerations stated by Chief Justice Parker, for this rule against the restraints of trade, less important to the community than they were in the seventeenth and eighteenth centuries; but the disposition to use every means to reduce competition and create monopolies has grown so much of late that the considerations last stated by the learned judge have lost nothing in weight as time has passed.

It will be observed, however, that the restraints in contracts in which the question of reasonableness or unreasonableness played any part at the common law were contracts in which one of the contracting parties disabled himself, and that constituted the restraint. Contracts or combinations between persons to restrain the trade of a third person were at common law voided by the statute against engrossing, and certainly never at the common law did the question arise whether such contracts were reasonable or unreasonable. They were always void and were never enforced. Early in the nineteenth century a contract restraining the trade of others came before Lord Chancellor Eldon in a case of this kind.

A combination of wholesale grocers formed what was called a fruit club and appointed a select committee to act for them. Their purpose was to purchase all imported fruits that came into the market in order that they might control the trade and compel all the other wholesale dealers to apply to them for a supply. They sold to their own members at a small price and to the outsiders at advanced prices and in such quantities as they thought proper. If any importer sold to any other wholesale dealer without making an offer to the club its committee refused to have any further dealings with the importer, and thus the club obtained complete control over the price of fruit.

The plaintiff had been a member of this club and then withdrew from it, but subsequently entered into an agreement with it to buy two cargoes of fruit, the club agreeing to let him have a quarter of the purchase at the price the club paid. The club purchased the two cargoes and furnished one-quarter of the whole lot to the plaintiff. He paid part of the price the club charged, but then declined to pay the rest on the ground that the price charged him exceeded what the club paid. In order to make his complete defense and to elicit the facts he applied to Lord Eldon in a bill of discovery to compel the club to show what its dealings were with respect to these two cargoes of fruit, and Lord Eldon declined to give him any relief on the ground that the association to which he originally belonged, and with which he was then seeking to enforce a partnership agreement, was contrary to public policy.

In the early part of the nineteenth century the regrating and engrossing statutes were repealed with a recital by Parliament that they interfered with the freedom of business instead of promoting it. There was thereafter no penalty for those acts which would have constituted engrossing or regrating, even though they resulted in monopolies. As Lord Justice Fry says in *Mogul Steamship Company vs. McGregor,* L. R. 23, O. B. D. 598, 629, referring to the recital of the act: "This statement is very noteworthy. It contains a confession of failure in the past, the indication of a new policy in the future." But in spite of this change in the statutory law of England it is perfectly clear that such engrossing or regrating combinations or contracts to interfere with and restrain the trade of third persons, though no longer criminal, continued to be unenforceable as between those who combined.

In *Hilton vs. Eckersly,* tried in the Court of Queen's Bench about 1863, a number of employers entered into a bond that they would carry on their works for a year in the matter of wages, employing workmen, and maintaining the rate of wages and the terms of the employment in accordance with the vote of the majority. One member violated the agreement, and this was a suit against him on the bond for his breach of the agreement.

One of the judges in the Queen's Bench, Mr. Justice Crompton, expressed the opinion that the contract was not only unenforceable, but that it gave a right of civil action to any one who was injured thereby, and that it was indictable as a common-law misdemeanor. The two other judges, Lord Campbell being one, agreed that the bond was unenforceable, but did not think that it was criminal. The Court of Exchequer Chamber on error held that the bond was unenforceable, but declined to pass on the question whether such a combination gave an action for damages or was indictable.

The *Mogul Steamship Company* case, decided by the highest courts in England in 1892, has figured very largely in the question of trusts and monopolies in this country, and has frequently been misunderstood. The facts were that a number of ship-owners who were regular carriers of tea entered into a combination to drive out of business an outsider who was in the habit of coming into the harbor of Hankow and lowering prices. The combiners agreed to conduct a year's steady and persistent campaign of underbidding against his ships and thus end his competition. Then the outsider brought suit for damages against the combiners for the injury they had done him.

This case turned on the question whether the combination was affirmatively illegal in such a sense that it was indictable at common law. Lord Coleridge held that it was not. In the Court of Appeals, two justices, Lord Justice Bowen and Lord Justice Fry, held that it was not, while the Master of the Rolls, Lord Esher, held that it was, following the authority of Justice Crompton in *Hilton vs. Eckersly*. In the House of Lords there was a unanimous judgment that the combination was not illegal in the sense of being actionable or indictable.

This case has been quoted frequently as indicating that such a combination as that was a reasonable contract of restraint at common law. It has no such effect. It will be found in nearly every one of the judgments that a clear distinction is made by the judges between an illegal contract and one which is unenforceable, and that the combination in that case was conceded to be unenforceable as a contract between the parties to it and to be void at common law.

Therefore we find that the state of the common law when Congress passed the anti-trust statute was that contracts in restraint of trade, in so far as they restrained a party to the contract, were void, unless they were reasonable in the sense that they were merely ancillary to a main contract which was lawful in its purpose, and were reasonably adapted and limited to that purpose, and that all contracts or combinations in which the contracting parties agreed to combine to restrain the trade of a third party or affect it injuriously were void at common law, without exception, and there were no reasonable contracts or combinations in restraint of trade of that kind. When one party to such a contract sought to enforce it against another the Court left both where it found them and gave no aid to either.

Our anti-trust statute, however, now makes such restraints, which were thus only void and unenforceable at common law, positively and affirmatively illegal, actionable, and indictable.

It has been frequently said that at common law a combination among laborers to raise their wages was illegal. I think this untrue. There were statutes punishing laborers for combining in this way, but it was not illegal at common law. Lord Bramwell, in *Mogul Steamship Company vs. McGregor,* said, "I have always said that a combination of workmen, an agreement among them to cease work except for higher wages, and a strike in consequence, was lawful at common law."

And, while cases can be found in this country in which the illegality of combinations of laborers for this purpose has been asserted, they cannot be sustained.

But it is one thing to say that a combination of laborers to cease work in order to secure a raising of wages or more favorable terms of employment is not actionable, and it is quite another thing to say that such combination for other purposes and to accomplish other results may not have been actionable at common law. The great weight of authority is that in certain cases they were.

It may reduce the employer's profits if he is obliged to pay his workmen on a higher scale of wages when they combine to leave his employment. The loss which he sustains, if it can be called such, arises merely from the exercise of their lawful right to work for such wages as they choose and to get as high rate as they can. The loss is caused by the workmen, but it gives no right of action against them.

Again, if workmen are called upon to work with the material of a certain dealer and the material is of such character as to make their labor greater or more dangerous than that sold by another, they may lawfully agree that they will refuse to work with such material. The loss caused by such joint action of the workmen to the employer or the material man is not a legal injury, and not the subject of action. The issue the workmen make and the purpose they have relate normally and directly to the terms of their employment and the work they have to do.

But on this common ground of common rights, where participants in business and manufacture and trade, employers and employees, are lawfully struggling against each other in peaceful methods for their respective interests and where losses suffered in the struggle must be borne, there are losses which are actionable, when willfully caused by combinations in the exercise of what otherwise would be a lawful right, because of the indirect and unjustifiable means taken to accomplish the end sought. They may not use a lockout or a strike or a threat of either, or a withholding of patronage, or a threat of it, to compel third persons to join them in the fight which they are lawfully making with their competitors, their employees, or their employers.

This is a secondary boycott, so called. The essence of its illegality is in the coercion of third persons to lend assistance in a legitimate competition in business, or a perfectly lawful contest between employers and employees, in which each may use against his rival or opponent his right of patronage, his right of labor, or his right of employment as he will. He may not by the same means coerce others to join him in the fight against their will. This view of the law has been taken in many cases in this country, and, while there have been some dissenting opinions, it has now been embodied in many statutes. A person injured by such a secondary boycott may invoke the action of the common-law courts in a suit for damages, or the courts of equity by way of injunction against the wrong-doers.

A secondary boycott has such possibilities in the way of injuring the whole community, of bringing into contests that are none of their own making so many indifferent and innocent persons, that ethics and law and public policy all require the recognition of the distinction which makes lawful the combination of workingmen against employers in their natural controversies over wages and terms of employment, but condemns the use of combination by either party to compel third persons against their will to come into the fight.

The suggestion is made that the workingmen ought to be allowed to use the secondary boycott, because if they do not, then they will resort to force. This seems to be a very poor argument. It assumes that militancy and the use of criminal means to further a cause should be recognized as an effective method of changing law.

The proper reason for the legality of a combination of laborers to raise prices is to be found in the necessity for enabling them to deal on an equality with their employers. If they did not have this power they would be at the mercy of employers who have capital and resources and who are not compelled to live from day to day on their daily earnings. The power to cease employment together—that is, to strike—is a most useful and legitimate weapon to bring their employers to terms. But why should they be permitted to use the strike to threaten third persons, and to compel such third persons to cease association with the employers on pain of being brought into the controversy and of themselves being subjected to similar treatment?

But it is said the right of labor is free. It is like any other right: it is free to use for a lawful purpose. But it is not free when it is used in a combination that effects such injustice as that I have described. To use the language of Mr. Justice Holmes speaking for the Supreme Court in *Aikens vs. Wisconsin*, 194 U.S. 205:

> No conduct has such an absolute privilege as to justify all possible schemes of which it may be a part. The most innocent and constitutionally protected of acts or omissions may be made a step in a criminal plot, and if it is a step in a plot, neither its innocence nor the Constitution is sufficient to prevent the punishment of the plot by law.

And so why should the right of labor be used to coerce third persons and thus bring about a result which will terrorize a community, as it did in the *Debs* case when the combination of the American Railway Union took the public by the throat and said, "We will starve your babies, we will prevent your food coming to you by stopping these railroads unless you intervene between Pullman and his employees and compel Pullman to pay higher wages than he is now willing to pay them"?

2

General Function of Constitution and Courts in
Protection and Limitation of Individual Rights
of Property, Contract, and Labor

In the first chapter I considered the state of the common law with reference to its limitations upon contracts and combinations in the exercise of the right of property and right of labor in the field of business, commerce, and industrial employment. It seems to me wise now to take up, in the course of discussion and as germane to it, a very general subject—to wit, the function of the courts in our system of government in the enforcement and limitation of such rights.

The United States Supreme Court's decisions under the Sherman law have been made the basis for a general attack upon our courts and for arguments in favor of grotesque and revolutionary changes in our judicial system which bear the name of "the recall of judges and the recall of judicial decisions." We have heard much denunciation of what is called "judicial legislation" and "judge-made law." It will aid, at this point, before we attempt to state the result of judicial construction of the great anti-trust statute, to examine into the utility and indispensable character of the office that courts have performed in the history of the common law, in the construction of statutes, and in the application of written constitutions.

For purposes of discussion we can say that our municipal law is divided into three branches. The first is the customary or common law, inherited from England, and varied to meet our differing conditions here; the second is the statutory law, which, whenever the legislative branch of the government desires to change the customary or common law, is substituted for that law; and the third, the fundamental or constitutional law, which lays down the permissible limits of legislative discretion in enacting statutes.

In respect to the common law, we must have some official authority to say what it is. It was the judges in England who were learned in the customs of the realm that in litigated cases between individuals adjudged what their rights and duties were by that custom; and their decisions, covering century after century, preserved in reports, made up the body of the common law.

As times changed in England, as new conditions arose for the application of the law of rights and duties and the lawmaking power of Parliament was silent, the judges exercised a wise discretion on principles of justice and morality to determine new forms for the application of old principles, by way of analogy, following so far as they could interpret it the prevailing morality and the predominant public opinion. From time to time it was found that the progressive quality of the law did not keep pace with enlightened public opinion and obvious public necessity, and then changes occurred both by statutory provision and by direct action of the king.

The customary law has been handed down to us, and its history one can trace in much detail for six hundred years. Indeed, if one will consult the great books on this subject like Holmes on the Common Law, Pollock and Maitland's *History of English Law,* and other works of similar character, he can note the interesting development and progress that has been made in the English law from time to time under the necessities that the changing conditions in society imposed.

Sometimes the law has lagged behind public reforms and popular judgment. It generally lags behind the moral rules, but not so much now as in the past. The growth of equity in the English law presents one of the most inspiring histories that I know of, and the rules of equity, with some exceptions, represent as high a moral tone as we can hope to reach in municipal law.

If one would realize the growth of the common law in this respect he should read an article by that jurist and professor of law, James Barr Ames, on "Law and Morals," in the twenty-second volume of *The Harvard Law Review,* page 97. Dean Ames points out that the English law has squared itself more and more with the moral law and with the progress of society through two great instrumentalities.

The one was the statute of Westminster, Thirteenth Edward I, which, after all, was only a statute of procedure, by which the clerks in chancery were authorized to form new writs for new cases, by analogy to old writs. This elasticity gave power to the lawyers as the initiators of new writs and declarations, on the one hand, and to judges in the consideration and approval of such writs and declarations on the other, to give progress to the principles of law under the common-law system and to adapt its rules and its remedies to the public and social needs.

The other instrumentality grew out of the king's executive interference with the common-law courts to abate their rigid technicalities and injustice through his Chancellor. This exercise of the royal prerogative was regarded by common-law lawyers as a great abuse. It settled down, after many years, into a judicial system grafted on to that of the common-law courts. In the greater variety of remedy in the Courts of Equity, in the opportunity to compel the defendant to act by way of restitution and specific performance, there was offered a means, which was fully improved by the great Chancellors stimulated by high ideals, to give the law a much more practical moral result than it ever had before. That is why equity seems more all-embracing than law.

Professor Pound, of Harvard, has given the legal profession a great deal of aid in his discussion of the comparative jurisprudence of the various countries and of progress which the law has made. He thinks that in the adaptation of the common law to our new country and its development between the first years of the nineteenth century and the close of the Civil War a wonderful work was done by our courts, but that since the war they have not advanced the law as rapidly as they ought to have done, and he attributes it to the introduction of the elective judiciary and the failure to maintain experts of the law in independent judicial position since that time.

He points out that recent criticisms of courts based on their alleged failure to follow the changes in public opinion and to shape and adapt that law to the progressive needs of the people find their chief ground in the decisions of courts in which the judges are elective. His view is that great judges are those who understand so fully the fundamental principles of the law which must be retained, and have so clearly the sense of proportion which expert legal knowledge gives, that they are able to keep the law abreast of the times by rejecting from it what is casual and retaining those fundamental principles in its administration the departure from which would involve disaster to society.

Judges are men. Courts are composed of judges, and one would be foolish who would deny that courts and judges are affected by the times in which they live, as well by the defects of those times as by the higher ideals prevailing.

The first half of the nineteenth century, ending in the Civil War, resulted in a great moral elevation of the people in the struggle over slavery and its final excision. Afterward we settled down to a tremendous material expansion, in which all the people had their attention focused on the extended applications of invested capital to further development. It was a period in which the political duties of the people were negligently exercised and in which the influence of wealth over politics became greater and greater, until plutocracy threatened; and if the attitude of the courts reflected the attitude of the people, and the law did not make as much moral progress in that time, it is only because the courts were doing what it is denied they do now—i. e., keeping pace with society.

Now the people have waked up. Now the courts have waked up. Now Congress has waked up and the legislatures have waked up to the danger that was before us, and a great reform in public spirit has come. It infuses not only the people, but legislatures and the courts.

Remedies for the ills that have developed in society, for the injustices that exist, are being suggested and pressed into operation with all the enthusiasm and all the lack of discretion that such a popular uprising as we have had at first inspires. The leviathan, the People, cannot thus be given a momentum that will not carry them in their earnestness and just indignation beyond the median and wise line. The excesses, which we may hope are only temporary, are part of the cost that we have to pay in curing the original disease. Therefore I think we may take heart in reference to the administration of our laws, and have confidence that in the end and after some possibly serious mistakes we shall bring it into wise conformity with public needs and continue the courts as an effective instrument for the highest good.

I would not by anything I may say seem to uphold the diatribes and unjust and ignorant attacks that for demagogic and other purposes have been made upon our courts. All I mean to say is that they in their administration of the law have not been unaffected by the condition of the public mind, both for better and for worse, in the latter half of the nineteenth century.

Coming now to the field of statutory law, we find that while Congress has many lawyers, they are not always great jurists, they are not always exact in their knowledge of existing law, or statesmanlike in their appreciation of the operation of new law, and it is impossible for them to anticipate the myriad phases of transactions and points of contest between members of society that have to be decided in litigated cases. The necessity for filling the lapses that may occur in a statute, the inconsistencies that the statute has in itself and that it often has in concurrent operation with other statutes, require, in order to secure any reasonable working of the law, a tribunal which shall supply these lapses by reasonable inference as to the intention of the legislature, and shall reconcile the inconsistencies.

Of course, it is impossible that such a function as this could be performed by judges, who are only men, without at times exceeding their just discretion, without at times stepping over the line which is very hard to draw between judicial construction and judicial legislation. But it must always be remembered that the legislature has complete power in this regard, and that if the courts in their construction of law miss the intention of the legislature there is immediate relief at hand in a new law which may be made more clearly to set forth the legislative will.

Finally, we are brought to the function of courts in reconciling statutes to constitutional limitations and in declaring when the permissible discretion of the legislature conferred by the Constitution has been exceeded in seeming laws which must be declared to be invalid. This requires a short consideration of our form of government and what the object of government is. We believe in popular government in this country. But we insist that its duration and usefulness can only be secured in the long run by a recognition on the part of all the people that they must impose restraints upon themselves in order that the rule of a majority of the electorate, which is the only possible form of rule under a popular government, shall certainly be just and fair to the minority and the individual.

We believe that government is, of course, for the benefit of society as a whole, but that society is composed of individuals and that the benefit of society as a whole is only consistent with the full opportunity of its members to pursue happiness and their individual liberty. This, in its broadest and proper sense, includes freedom from personal restraint, right of free labor, right of property, right of religious worship, right of contract.

The people have imposed upon the electorate that represents them—and that is only a comparatively small percentage of all the people—certain restraints intended to preserve individual liberty and embodied in a written constitution. Were these restraints to be removed, and were a majority of the electorate, acting through temporary passion or before the formation of a settled public opinion based on real knowledge and deliberate consideration, to do injustice to the minority or to the individual in the supposed interest of the majority or society, then the knell of popular government would be sounded. The injured minority would ultimately drift into forcible resistance to the authority of laws the outgrowth of the selfish exercise of power and of not doing justice; and, after chaos, we would have the "man on horseback."

Therefore those of us who insist upon the preservation of constitutional limitations upon the action of a majority of the electorate are convinced that we are the best friends of popular government. Popular government is only an instrument to be used in promoting the opportunity for the pursuit of happiness by society and its members. It is not an end; it should not be a fetish.

When men have capacity to govern themselves popular government offers greater benefit to them than the government by one or a few. When they do not have that capacity as a whole, then, as in the past and as in many parts of the world today, government by one or the few is better.

Indeed, it is only a matter of degree. As I have already said, we are governed by the majority of an electorate. The minority of that electorate takes part, and therefore it cannot be said that it has not a voice in the government, because the minority changes into a majority and the majority into a minority in the practical operation of popular elections from time to time. But perhaps 80 percent of all the people never have any actual vote at all, and they are governed by the action of the 20 percent of the electorate. The electorate in a sense represents them, and, because their interests are similar or the same, in the long run the electorate carries out the public opinion of the whole body of the people—men, women, and children.

What we must keep clearly in mind, however, is that the end is the pursuit of community and individual happiness, that the means is popular government. There is not, therefore, the slightest reason *a priori* why we should not maintain in such a government the constitutional limitations upon the temporary action of the majority of that comparatively small percentage of the whole people which constitutes its electorate.

The electorate, of course, must ultimately control the fundamental law containing these restraints. They may amend it in parts or revise it as a whole. But it is essential to a wise revision or amendment that the changes proposed be carefully weighed by constitutional conventions or legislatures in the light of their general application, and that they be considered abstractly and from a statesmanlike standpoint, with a wide vision of their probable operation, not only in the immediate present, but in the far future. Such a discussion of constitutional limitations excludes the possibility of a narrow partisan or one-sided view, stimulated by particular cases of a sensational and exaggerative color which lead to hasty and ill-advised generalizations.

Having fixed our constitutional limitations, we need somebody to keep us within them. We need somebody to whom the individual or the minority, unjustly treated by the majority, may appeal, and who will enforce the limitations that it was intended by the Constitution to impose.

This calls for an independent judiciary, for a judiciary whose tenure and salary and learning and ability and character are such that they can face temporary unpopularity with the majority in defending the rights of the individual or the minority. That is the federal system, and while it has been criticized and attacked with ill-disguised vituperation from Mr. Jefferson to Mr. Roosevelt, a calm review of history made by independent observers, not of our country, shows that there has been nothing in our form of government so admirable and useful in its workings as the Supreme Court of the United States and the authority which it has exercised, in its steadying opinions, in the security it has given to life, liberty, and property, in its keeping open, as far as the Constitution can secure it, the equal opportunity of all men.

Its peculiar functions undoubtedly make it the most powerful tribunal in the world. The fact that it has been able to maintain its authority against such attacks as those we had at the birth of the nation and that are being renewed today is a sufficient proof of the sound sense, the underlying conservatism, and the clear governing capacity of the American people. The governing capacity of a people is measured by its self-restraint, by its recognition of the rights of the minority, and by its willingness to admit its liability to err and to lessen its liability to such error through fundamental restrictions upon its own action.

No one can read the judgments of the Supreme Court of the United States without realizing that no small or narrow prejudices contract their judicial views, or without recognizing that its members are, as they ought to be, not only great jurists, but great statesmen, and discharge their duties with the broadest appreciation of their responsibility and their duty not to substitute their opinion for the discretion which under our system it was intended that Congress and the State legislatures should exercise. The whole trend of their judicial decisions is as progressive as possible, and those who do not see it and assert the contrary are not familiar with them and speak in ignorance.

The Supreme Court of the United States is the final tribunal in all the critical issues of the present day arising out of the Fifth and Fourteenth Amendments. Under those amendments Congress and the States are forbidden to pass any laws depriving a person of life, liberty, or property without due process of law.

The rights included in these amendments are all the individual rights that we have come to regard as valuable in the pursuit of happiness. They embrace the right of personal freedom, the right to labor, the right to property, and the right to contract. Now it has always been recognized that these rights are not absolute rights, that they have to be exercised with reference to the exercise of similar rights by other individuals in the same community, and with due regard to community welfare, and that the permissible limitations upon their enjoyment must be affected by the changing conditions prevailing in society.

Three generations ago this was a sparsely settled country with a small population to the square mile, with small cities and towns and villages, with the great bulk of the population living in the country and most of them entirely independent in supplying themselves with the means of living. They raised their own food and prepared it, raised their own clothing and made it, they cut their fuel from the forest, and the mutual dependence of one upon the other was far less than it is today. The urban population has greatly increased in proportion to the rural population, while the feeding of the people, and their clothing, their education, their health, and their domestic comfort have necessarily cut down somewhat the free exercise of individual rights, which was wider half a century ago; and the courts have recognized the change.

Consider the restraints upon personal freedom of action contained in the modern health laws. Take, for instance, the compulsory vaccination laws sustained by the Supreme Court. I have had an opportunity to witness the effect of such laws in the Philippines upon a people that had not had popular government and had been steeled to arbitrary rule, and yet they resented the health laws as savoring of intolerable tyranny.

What is true of personal restraint is true also of the right of property, of the right of labor, and of the right of contract. Tenement-house acts frequently require a destruction of income-producing property, and this without any compensation to the owner. We now have statutes which affect the rights of contract, like that preventing the truck system, and like those which affect the character of insurance contracts that can be made.

Then there are statutes that change the law of agency and create liability against employers and limit their power to exempt themselves from it by contract.

Then we have the limitation upon the right of labor in the statutory inhibition against work for more than a certain number of hours and in child-labor laws.

In *Lochner vs. New York,* 198 U.S. 45, a statute of New York, which attempted to limit the hours of bakers' labor on the ground that baking was an unhealthful employment, was held by the Supreme Court, by a vote of five to four, to be unconstitutional. With the changed personnel of the Court and the present trend of their decisions, I am inclined to think that a similar case before that court would meet a different fate.

The truth is that the Court as at present constituted has shown itself as appreciative of the change of conditions and the necessity for a liberal construction of the restrictions of the Constitution, with a view to such changes of conditions, as any court could be.

Mr. Justice Brown, in *Holden vs. Hardy,* 197 U.S., in considering the question whether the legislature of Utah had the right to prescribe hours of labor for miners, referred to the changes in the statutory law affecting individual rights which had been recognized as valid and as not transgressing constitutional protection of those rights. Speaking of those instances, he says:

> They are mentioned only for the purpose of calling attention to the probability that other changes of no less importance may be made in the future, and that, while the cardinal principles of justice are immutable, the methods by which justice is administered are subject to constant fluctuation, and that the Constitution of the United States, which is necessarily and to a large extent inflexible and exceedingly difficult of amendment, should not be so construed as to deprive the States of the power to so amend their laws as to make them conform to the wishes of the citizens as they may deem best for the public welfare without bringing them into conflict with the supreme law of the land.

Of course, it is impossible to forecast the character or extent of these changes, but, in view of the fact that from the day Magna Charta was signed to the present moment amendments to the structure of the law have been made with increasing frequency, it is impossible to suppose that they will not continue, and the law be forced to adapt itself to new conditions of society, and particularly to the new relations between employers and employees, as they arise.

This shows the state of mind and the view of its duty in which the Supreme Court has approached the construction of the anti-trust law and the recognition that it has given to the fact that under the changes of business and social conditions limitations of the Constitution affecting the right of property, the right of free contract, and the right of free labor may be qualified in a limited way without a breach of individual liberty and without removing or disregarding the fundamental ancient landmarks set by the Constitution of the United States. It is not that the Court varies or amends the Constitution or a statute, but that, there being possible several interpretations of its language, the Court adopts that which conforms to prevailing morality and predominant public opinion.

It is before such a court that a great number of instances of monopoly and attempted monopoly, prosecuted by indictment and conviction or by bill in equity and decree in the inferior federal courts, have been brought, and it will be my effort in the chapters following to show how thoroughly the Court has responded to settled public opinion in the construction and application of the anti-trust law and that the criticisms of those who attack that great court on this account are born of ignorance or demagoguery.

3

The Sugar Trust Case, Its Narrowing Effect on the Usefulness of the Statute—Justice Harlan's Dissent Now the Law

The text of the first and second sections of the Sherman Anti-trust Act, in so far as they are important for consideration, are as follows:

> Section 1. Every contract, combination in the form of trust or otherwise, or conspiracy, in restraint of trade or commerce, among the several States or with foreign nations, is hereby declared to be illegal. Every person who shall make any such contract or engage in any such combination or conspiracy shall be deemed guilty of a misdemeanor, etc.
>
> Section 2. Every person who shall monopolize or attempt to monopolize or combine or conspire with any other person or persons to monopolize any part of the trade or commerce among the several states, or with foreign nations, shall be deemed, etc.

The act was passed in Mr. Harrison's Administration in 1890. The first important case under it was known as "In *re* Greene" (52 Fed. Rep. 104). It arose in August, 1892, on a petition for a writ of *habeas corpus* presented to Circuit Judge Jackson, afterward Mr. Justice Jackson, to test the legality of a warrant of removal under an indictment found in Massachusetts

197

against Greene as one of the officers of the Whisky Trust, for violating the first and second sections of the act.

The indictment charged that the distilling company had acquired seventy distilleries in the whole country, had united them for the purpose of controlling the business of distilling whisky, and one count contained the specification that for the purpose of controlling the business and prices and establishing a monopoly it had sold its whisky with a contract for a rebate on the price to those who would maintain retail prices, and that by this restraint of trade it sought to compel purchasers in the market to maintain the price of its whisky. In this case Mr. Justice Jackson narrowed the application of the statute in such a way that it is interesting to read his language in the light of the present condition of the law, as follows:

> It is very certain that Congress could not, and did not, by this enactment attempt to prescribe limits to the acquisition, either by the private citizen or state corporation, of property which might become the subject of interstate commerce, or declare that, when the accumulation or control of property by legitimate means and lawful methods reached the magnitude or proportions that enabled the owner or owners to control the traffic therein, or any part thereof, among the States, a criminal offense was committed by such owner or owners.

He further says:

> All persons, individually or in corporate organizations, carrying on business avocations and enterprises involving the purchase, sale, or exchange of articles, or the production and manufacture of commodities which form the subjects of commerce, will in a popular sense monopolize both state and interstate traffic in such articles or commodities just in proportion as the owner's business is increased, enlarged, and developed. But the magnitude of a party's business, production, or manufacture, with the incidental and indirect powers thereby acquired, and with the purpose of regulating prices and controlling interstate traffic in the articles or commodities forming the subject of such business, production, or manufacture, is not the monopoly or attempt to monopolize which the statute condemns.

He follows then with a discussion of what monopoly means. After defining engrossing, he says:

It will be noticed that in all the foregoing definitions of "monopoly" there are embraced two leading elements—*viz.,* an exclusive right or privilege on the one side, and a restriction or restraint on the other, which will to operate to prevent the exercise of a right or liberty open to the public before the monopoly was secured.

Then, referring to the facts as averred in the indictment, he says:

In this acquisition and operation of the seventy distilleries which enabled the accused, or said Distilling and Cattle Feeding Company, to manufacture and control the sale of seventy-five per cent. of the distillery products of the country, it does not appear, nor is it alleged, that the persons from whom said distilleries were acquired were placed under any restraint, by contract or otherwise, which prevented them from continuing or re-engaging in such business. All other persons who chose to engage therein were at liberty to do so. The effort to control the production and manufacture of distillery products by the enlargement and extension of business was not an attempt to monopolize trade and commerce in such products within the meaning of the statute, and may therefore be left out of further consideration.

It would be very difficult to reconcile this case with *Miles Medical Co. vs. Park Sons & Co.,* 220 U.S. 373, in which just such a contract for maintaining retail prices was held a restraint of trade under this statute. Mr. Justice Jackson's view of the monopolies and restraints affected by the law was a much too narrow one. He evidently felt that the Constitution did not extend to Congress the power so to qualify the right of acquiring and of disposing of the property as to make the acquisition of property for the purpose of controlling interstate commerce in it or in the products of it a criminal monopoly. He further took the ground, which we shall see elaborated and insisted upon in *United States vs. E. C. Knight Company,* 156 U.S. 1, that the mere acquisition of plants in different States for the ultimate purpose of using this ownership to control and restrain interstate commerce was a subject only within the jurisdiction of the States and not within the control of Congress.

In the *Knight* case the statute was fully considered in the Supreme Court for the first time. It was argued in October, 1894, and decided in January, 1895. The opinion of the Court was delivered by Mr. Chief Justice

Fuller, the Attorney-General was Mr. Richard Olney, and he with the Solicitor-General, Mr. Maxwell, and a former Solicitor-General, Mr. Phillips, represented the Government.

The bill in the *Knight* case alleged that the defendant, the American Sugar Refining Company, was engaged in the refining and sale of sugar; that the other four defendants were corporations separately engaged in refining and dealing in sugar at Philadelphia; that the product of their refineries amounted to 33 percent of the sugar refined in the United States; that they were competitors of the American Sugar Refining Company; that the products of their several refineries were distributed among several States of the United States, and that all the companies were engaged in trade or commerce with several States and with foreign nations; that prior to March 4, 1892, the American Sugar Refining Company had obtained the control of all the sugar refineries of the United States with the exception of the Revere of Boston and the refineries of the other four defendants above mentioned; that the Revere produced annually about 2 percent of the total amount of sugar refined; that the American Sugar Refining Company in order to obtain complete control of the price of sugar in the United States entered into an unlawful scheme to purchase the stock, machinery, and real estate of the other four members defendant, in pursuance of which on March 4, 1892, the defendant Searles, an agent of the American Sugar Refining Company, made a contract with each of the other companies by which for shares in the stock of the American Sugar Refining Company the American Sugar Refining Company received the shares of stock of these four companies.

It was averred that the American Sugar Refining Company, thus becoming the owner of refineries refining 98 percent of the sugar refined in the United States, monopolized its sale in the United States and controlled its price; and by these contracts of sale of the stock Searles and the American Sugar Refining Company combined and conspired with the other defendants for the purpose of restraining, and in fact restrained, commerce in refined sugar among the several States and foreign nations in violation of the statute.

The prayer of the bill was as follows:

1. That all and each of the said unlawful agreements made and entered into by and between the said defendants on or about the 4th day of March, 1892, shall be delivered up, canceled, and declared to be void,

and that the said defendants, the American Sugar Refining Company and John E. Searles, Jr., be ordered to deliver to the other said defendants respectively the shares of stock received by them in performance of the said contracts, and that the other said defendants be ordered to deliver to the said defendants, the American Sugar Refining Company and John E. Searles, Jr., the shares of stock received by them respectively in performance of the said contracts.

2. That an injunction issue preliminary until the final determination of this cause, and perpetual thereafter, preventing and restraining the said defendants from the further performance of the terms and conditions of the said unlawful agreements.

3. That an injunction may issue preventing and restraining the said defendants from further and continued violations of the said act of Congress, approved July 2, 1890.

4. Such other and further relief as equity and justice may require in the premises.

The view which the Court took, in holding that the bill did not state a case affecting interstate commerce so directly as to constitute a violation of the statute was evidently much influenced by the emphasis laid in the bill and in the main prayer for relief on the acquisition of shares of stock by the American Sugar Refining Company in sugar-refining plants in Pennsylvania. The court could not apparently look beyond the acquisition of property in one State to its ultimate purpose, which certainly was the control of the sale of refined sugar in countrywide trade.

The court said:

> The contracts and acts of the defendants related exclusively to the acquisition of the Philadelphia refineries and the business of sugar refining in Philadelphia, and bore no direct relation to commerce between the States or with foreign nations. The object was manifestly private gain in the manufacture of the commodity, but not through the control of interstate or foreign commerce.

It is true that bill alleged that the products of these refineries were sold and distributed among the several States, and that all the companies were engaged in trade or commerce with the several States and with foreign nations; but this was no more than to say that trade and commerce served manufacture to fulfil its function. Sugar was refined for sale, and sales were probably made at Philadelphia for consumption, and undoubtedly for re-sale by the first purchasers throughout Pennsylvania and other States, and refined sugar was also forwarded by the companies to other States for sale. Nevertheless, it does not follow that an attempt to monopolize, or the actual monopoly of, the manufacture was an attempt, whether executory or consummated, to monopolize commerce, even though in order to dispose of the product the instrumentality of commerce was necessarily invoked.

There was nothing in the proofs to indicate any intention to put a restraint upon trade or commerce, and the fact, as we have seen, that trade or commerce might be indirectly affected was not enough to entitle complainants to a decree. (WHT's italics.) The subject-matter of the sale was shares of manufacturing stock, and the relief sought was the surrender of property which had already passed and the suppression of the alleged monopoly in manufacture by the restoration of the status quo before the transfers; yet the act of Congress only authorized the Circuit Court to proceed in the way of preventing and restraining violations of the act in respect of contracts, combinations, or conspiracies in restraint of interstate or international trade or commerce.

The dissenting opinion of Mr. Justice Harlan was a very strong statement, and I don't think it is too much to say that it represents much more fully the present view of the Court as to what may constitute a direct restraint upon interstate commerce than does the opinion of Chief Justice Fuller. Mr. Justice Harlan, in his dissenting opinion, comments on the fact that the prayer of the bill was not wisely framed, for he says in the close of his opinion:

> While a decree annulling the contracts under which the combination in question was formed may not, in view of the facts disclosed, be effectual to accomplish the object of the act of 1890, I perceive no difficulty in the way of the court passing a decree declaring that that combination imposes an unlawful restraint upon trade and commerce among the States, and perpetually enjoining it from further prosecuting any business pursuant to the unlawful agreement under which it was formed or by which it was created. Such a decree would be within the scope of the bill, and is appropriate to the end which Congress intended to accomplish—namely, to protect the freedom of commercial intercourse among the States against combination and conspiracies which impose unlawful restraints upon such intercourse.

But the truth is, as is shown by the above quotation from the opinion of Chief Justice Fuller, the case for the Government was not well prepared at the circuit. No direct evidence that the sales of sugar across State lines, and the control of the business of such sales and of prices, were the chief object of the combination was submitted to the court. Nor was this chief feature of the Government's real case sufficiently set forth in the bill of complaint. And yet these facts must have been easily capable of proof. Especially noteworthy was the failure of the bill to pray for specific action by the Court to enjoin the continuance of the combination.

The effect of the decision in the *Knight* case upon the popular mind, and indeed upon Congress as well, was to discourage hope that the statute could be used to accomplish its manifest purpose and curb the great industrial trusts which, by the acquisition of all or a large percentage of the plants engaged in the manufacture of a commodity, by the dismantling of some and regulating the output of others, were making every effort to restrict production, control prices, and monopolize the business. So strong was the impression made by the *Knight* case that both Mr. Olney and Mr. Cleveland concluded that the evil must be controlled through State legislation, and not through a national statute, and they said so in their communications to Congress.

4

Error of Mr. Justice Peckham in his Opinions for
the Majority in the Trans-Missouri Freight and
Joint Traffic Cases in Refusing Aid of Common
Law in Interpretation of the Statute—Confusion
in Terms but Not in Ultimate Result

I wish now to point out an error which the majority of the Supreme Court
at first made in rejecting as an aid in construing the statute the common-
law rule for determining reasonable, valid, and enforceable restraints of
trade.

In 1891 a suit was begun to enjoin continued performance of a contract
between eighteen different railroads by which the contracting parties
agreed through common action to fix the rates of traffic in all the vast
territory west of the Missouri River and to abide by the rates thus fixed.

In the Circuit Court of Appeals there was a divided court, two of the
judges holding that the anti-trust law was intended to strike down only
those combinations in restraint of trade which would be unreasonable and
so invalid at common law, and that it did not appear that the provision for
fixing the rates, or that the rates themselves, were unreasonable or would
have been so regarded at common law, and therefore that the agreement
was not a restraint of interstate commerce within the statute. Judge Shiras,
of Iowa, dissented, holding that the contract was a restraint of trade denounced by the statute, and differing from the majority in their view as to
its validity at common law.

When the case came to be decided by the Supreme Court, *United States vs. Trans-Missouri Freight Assoc.,* 166 U.S. 290, the Court divided, five judges holding that the bill ought to have been sustained below, reversing the decree of the Circuit Court of Appeals. The two great points considered were, first, whether the terms of the anti-trust law in regard to combinations applied to interstate-commerce carriers whose regulation was especially provided for by the interstate-commerce law, and, second, whether, assuming the contract to have been valid at common law, the statute was to be construed as striking at only those restraints of interstate-commerce trade which would be held to be unreasonable at common law. A majority of the Court held that the anti-trust law did apply to interstate railroads and supplemented the regulation of them by the interstate-commerce law; and, second, Mr. Justice Peckham, speaking for the majority, used language declaring that the inquiry whether the restraints were reasonable or unreasonable at common law was unimportant because the statute denounced all restraints.

What I wish to emphasize in respect to this case, as well as in respect to the opinion in the case of the *United States Joint Traffic Association,* 171 U.S. 93, which presented almost identically the same issues, and was decided soon after, is that, while the majority of the Court did say that Congress intended to include in the condemnation of the statute restraints of interstate trade, whether reasonable or unreasonable at common law, they in fact, by express language in their opinion excluded from the operation of the statute all restraints which would be reasonable at common law.

The truth is, the lower court in the *Trans-Missouri* case erred in holding the contract reasonable at common law, and the Supreme Court gave little attention to this point, assuming its correctness. This error Mr. Justice Brewer subsequently pointed out, as we shall see. The judges misconceived the effect of the decision of the highest English courts in the *Mogul Steamship Company* case and failed to note the difference I have already pointed out between the affirmative illegality and indictability of the combination in restraint of trade in that case which the House of Lords denied, and its void and unenforceable character at common law, because it was unreasonable, which the House of Lords admitted. Now the anti-trust law destroys this distinction by making restraints of trade unenforceable at common law, both criminal and actionable, when affecting interstate commerce. It must have been this *Mogul Steamship Company* case and a failure to note the distinction I have pointed out that temporarily drove the majority of the Court away from the rule of reasonableness at common law in construing the terms of the statute. Mr. Justice Jackson in "In *re* Greene," 52 Fed. Rep. 104, already cited, made the same error. Mr. Justice Peckham, in speaking for the majority, used this language:

> Proceeding, however, upon the theory that the statute did not mean what its plain language imported, and that it intended in its prohibition to denounce as illegal only those contracts which were in unreasonable restraint of trade, the courts below have made an exhaustive investigation as to the general rules which guide courts in declaring contracts to be void as being in restraint of trade, and therefore against the public policy of the country. In the course of their discussion of that subject they have shown that there has been a general though great alteration in the extent of the liberty granted to the vendor of property in agreeing, as part consideration for his sale, not to enter into the same kind of business for a certain time or within a certain territory.

So long as the sale was the bona-fide consideration for the promise and was not made a mere excuse for an evasion of the rule itself, the later authorities, both in England and in this country, exhibit a strong tendency toward enabling the parties to make such a contract in relation to the sale of property, including an agreement not to enter into the same kind of business, as they may think proper, and this with the view to granting to a vendor the freest opportunity to obtain the largest consideration for the sale of that which is his own.

A contract which is the mere accompaniment of the sale of property, and thus entered into for the purpose of enhancing the price at which the vendor sells it, which in effect is collateral to such sale, and where the main purpose of the whole contract is accomplished by such sale, might not be included within the letter or spirit of the statute in question. (WHT's italics.)

In this language it will be seen that Mr. Justice Peckham concedes that a contract which is the mere accompaniment of the sale of property, entered into for the purpose of enhancing prices at which the vendor sells it, and where the main purpose of the whole contract is accomplished by such sale, was not included within the letter or spirit of the statute. As I attempted to demonstrate in my first article, such a contract and analogous contracts involving the same principle were the only kind of contracts in restraint of trade which were regarded as reasonable at common law, and all other contracts in restraint of trade were unenforceable. It follows, therefore, that the position of the Supreme Court as shown by Mr. Justice Peckham's opinion in these two cases in fact admitted that the statute might properly be construed not to include in its denunciation contracts in restraint of trade that were held reasonable and valid at common law.

This is shown even more clearly by the language he uses in the *Joint Traffic* case, 171 U.S. 93, in which in the lists of restraints excepted by him from the operation of the statute are the five classes of contracts that were the only restraints regarded as reasonable at common law, and they are all described by him as restraints "incidental or indirect."

The same view was enforced by the opinion of the Court given by Mr. Justice Holmes in the *Cincinnati, etc., Packet Co. vs. Bay,* 200 U.S. 879. In that case the owner of a line of steamboats on the Ohio River, engaged in interstate trade, sold his steamboats, and, as part of the contract of sale, agreed that he would not go into that trade for a period of years. One of the parties sought to avoid obligation under the contract on the ground that it was illegal, being a contract in restraint of interstate trade, and a violation of the anti-trust law.

The Court held that the effect was incidental to the contract of sale and not within the statute.

As already said, the combinations in the *Trans-Missouri* and *Joint Traffic Association* cases were both void at common law because they restrained the members of the combination from charging different prices from those fixed by the Joint Committee, they prevented the operation of free competition, and thus they restrained trade, and this was the main purpose of the contract. The fact, if it was a fact, that the rates which were fixed were reasonable did not make the contract reasonable or change its void character at common law.

I am strongly sustained in this view by the opinion of Mr. Justice Brewer in the case of the *Northern Securities Company vs. the United States,* 193 U.S. 197, where he concurred with the majority in a separate opinion in which, after stating that he was one of the majority in the *Joint Traffic Association* and *Trans-Missouri* cases, he said that, while a further examination had not disturbed his conviction that those cases were rightly decided, he thought in some respects the reasons given for the judgments could not be sustained, and that instead of holding that the anti-trust act included all contracts, reasonable or unreasonable, in restraint of interstate trade, the ruling should have been that the contracts there presented were unreasonable restraints of interstate trade, and as such within the scope of the act; that that act, as appears from its title, was leveled at only "unlawful restraints and monopolies"; that Congress did not intend to reach and destroy those minor contracts in partial restraint of trade which the long course of decisions at common law had affirmed were reasonable and ought to be upheld; that the purpose rather was to place a statutory prohibition which prescribed penalties for those contracts which were in direct restraint of trade, unreasonable, and against public policy; that whenever a departure from common-law rules and definitions was claimed, the purpose to make the departure should be clearly shown; that such a purpose did not appear and such a departure was not intended.

5

Cases after the Sugar Trust Case and before the
Standard Oil Case in Which the Effect of the Sugar
Trust Decision Was Practically Eliminated

We now begin a building up of authority which finally has destroyed the obstructing effect of the *Sugar Trust* case in the effort of the Executive Department to reach these industrial trusts which by combining manufacturing plants have monopolized countrywide trade in the products made. The first of these was the *Addyston Pipe Company* case, 175 U.S. 211, 85 Fed. Rep. 271 (Feb., 1898, Dec., 1899).

The bill of complaint in this case struck at a contract between various manufacturing companies in iron pipe which, except for the contract, were independent companies and retained their separate corporate lives. This was a much easier case to bring within the purview of the statute and the direct field of interstate commerce, because the subject-matter of the contract embraced what the Supreme Court in a long series of decisions had held to be interstate commerce.

The purposes and action of the combination, through the treachery of a stenographer, were laid before the court, so that minute dissection was possible. It was, in short, an agreement by which all the iron-pipe companies in the Ohio Valley and the Mississippi Valley, from which manufacturers in other parts of the country were naturally excluded by freight rates, agreed that they would maintain prices and share profits, and that in pursuance of these purposes no one of them would offer iron pipe to any intending purchaser, who was usually a municipal corporation, inviting public competitive bids, without the permission of the combination, and only after there had been a secret bidding among the members of the combination to see which member would make such a bid as would from the profits of the contract allow the best bonus to be divided among the other members of the combination.

It would be difficult to state a case of contract for sales among vendors more certainly restrictive and more selfish and monopolizing in character than this was. The Circuit Court of Appeals, of which Mr. Justice Harlan was the presiding justice, and Judge Lurton and I were the associate judges, held that as a large part of the sales to be made necessarily involved, in the geographical location of the plants and indeed in the division of territory that also appeared as a feature of the combination, interstate commerce, the combination was certainly a restraint within the jurisdiction of Congress.

We referred to the language of the opinions in the *Joint Traffic Association* and *Trans-Missouri* cases, declaring that every restraint was aimed at in the statute, whether reasonable or unreasonable at common law; but in spite of that we thought it wise to show by an extended examination of the authorities that this combination would have been regarded as unreasonable at common law and pointed out the distinction that I have emphasized in what I have said, that the only contracts in restraint of trade that were regarded as reasonable at common law were those incidental contracts strictly commensurate with the needs of a principal lawful contract of sale of good will or concerning the making or dissolution of partnerships.

The case went to the Supreme Court, and the Supreme Court unanimously affirmed the judgment of the court below. Neither in the Court of Appeals nor in the Supreme Court was any difficulty found with the opinion of the Superior Court in the *Sugar Trust* case, for in the *Addyston* case the subject-matter of the contract was not acquisition of title to property; it was actual and intended sales in interstate commerce. The relief sought was injunction against continuance of the combination, and the right to such a remedy was plain.

The next important case in the history of the proper construction and application of the law was the *Northern Securities* case, entitled *"Northern Securities Company vs. the United States,"* 195 U.S. 197. That, stated shortly, was an agreement between the owners of the majority of stock in the Great Northern Road and in the Northern Pacific Road, which were two railway lines extending from the Lakes to the Pacific coast through the northern tier of States, to unite their interests in a holding company organized in New Jersey which should take over into its possession not only a majority of stock in each of these roads, but also stock of the Chicago, Burlington & Quincy Railway Company, which owned a network of lines between Chicago and Minneapolis and Omaha, and made a convenient terminal union of the two longer lines.

The individuals who had to do with making the arrangement and the combination by which it was to be carried out, together with the three corporations, were made party defendants, and the relief sought was an injunction against the further execution of this arrangement and the rending of it asunder so far as it had been carried out, and this on the ground that it was a combination to restrain commerce among the northern tier of States.

Relying on the Sugar Trust decision, the defendants resisted the suit on the ground that it sought to nullify the acquisition of property and bring about the *status quo* before the consummated transfer of title, as in that case. It was insisted that the transaction in railway stock here had no more direct effect upon interstate commerce than had the acquisition of stock in the various sugar-refining plants there. It was pointed out that the Northern Securities Company was a State corporation authorized by a State to hold stock in other railways and that it was not within the power of Congress to interfere with acquisition of such property, that this transfer of property was preliminary to interstate commerce and did not directly affect it, and there was nothing to show in actual running of the railroads and fixing of rates that any restraint had been put upon either, growing out of the project.

The majority of the court, however, held that what this whole arrangement amounted to was an arrangement between the actual controllers of the property of the three great railroad systems to run them as one system, and thus acquire power to avoid competition and to monopolize interstate railroad transportation in a large section of the United States.

This decision, delivered by Mr. Justice Harlan, was a most important step forward in the useful application of the anti-trust act, because it brushed away many of the difficulties that were presented in the opinion of the *Sugar Trust* case in enforcing the act. With the *Addyston Pipe* case making clear the application of the law to any restraint by combination upon sales from one State to another, and with this *Northern Securities* case laying down the rule that courts might imply the intention and purpose of such a combination from its necessary effect to monopolize and control, and might enjoin its consummation before actual execution, the wide application of the statute became manifest.

There was nothing in this *Northern Securities* case that varied from the common-law rule as to reasonable and unreasonable contracts. This was made clear by the language of Mr. Justice Brewer, which I have already quoted.

The court, as courts of equity do, looked through the form of the transaction to its real essence and treated all the transfers of stock and the various corporate organizations as mere steps in the carrying out of a combination intended or calculated to secure a monopoly of interstate-commerce business. Such a contract as between its makers would certainly have been unenforceable at common law, and so the decision in this case was not inconsistent with the view that the statute was to be interpreted in the light of the common law.

The existence of the intent to gain power of control over interstate commerce is given more importance as cases proceed, as indeed it ought to be, and the circumstances that the particular transactions or steps alleged are immediately concerned with things or property or sales within a State does not prevent their being treated as part of a scheme to control interstate commerce if the intent to do so is averred and clearly made manifest by the evidence. We see this clearly in the next case to which I wish to refer, decided in 1905, just after the *Northern Securities* case. This was the *Meat Packers' Trust* case, 196 U.S. 375, in which the bill charged a dominant proportion of the dealers in fresh meat throughout the United States with maintaining a combination not to bid against one another in the livestock markets of the different States at Chicago, Omaha, St. Joseph, Kansas City, East St. Louis, and St. Paul; to bid up prices for a few days in order to induce cattlemen to send their stock to the stockyards; to fix prices at which they would sell, and to that end to restrict shipments of meat when necessary; to establish a uniform credit to dealers and to keep a blacklist; to make uniform and improper charges for cartage; and, finally, to get less than lawful rates from the railroads, to the exclusion of their competitors, with intent to monopolize the commerce among the States and prevent competition therein.

The opinion is by Mr. Justice Holmes, and is very illuminating as to the attitude of the Court in adapting the principles of pleading and procedure to the new conditions presented by litigation under the act. It was objected that the bill did not set forth sufficient or definite or specific facts. He said:

> This objection is serious, but it seems to us inherent in the nature of the case. The scheme alleged is so vast that it presents a new problem in pleading. If, as we assume, the scheme is entertained, it is, of course, contrary to the very words of the statute.
>
> Its size makes the violation of the law more conspicuous, and yet the same thing makes it impossible to fasten the fact to time or place. The elements, too, are so numerous and shifting, even the constituent parts alleged are and from their nature must be so extensive in time and space, that something of the same impossibility applies to them.
>
> The law has been upheld, and we are bound to enforce it notwithstanding these difficulties. On the other hand, we equally are bound by the first principles of justice not to sanction a decree so vague as to put the whole conduct of the defendants' business at the peril of a summons for contempt.
>
> We cannot issue an injunction against all possible breaches of the law. We must steer between these opposite difficulties as best we can.

The sales described in the bill were actual sales and deliveries of cattle at the various stockyards, followed by slaughter and preparation of meats in slaughterhouses, none of which by itself was an act of interstate commerce. It was urged that as these constituted the real acts under attack, it was effect upon state commerce and not interstate commerce that was complained of, and so it was not within the statute.

Mr. Justice Holmes's opinion in this case develops the importance of intent under the statutes and answers the objection as to the interstate effect of the acts charged as follows:

The scheme as a whole seems to us to be within reach of the law. The constituent elements, as we have stated them, are enough to give the scheme a body, and, for all that we can say, to accomplish it. Moreover, whatever we may think of them separately, when we take them up as distinct charges they are alleged sufficiently as elements of the scheme.

It is suggested that the several acts charged are lawful and that intent can make no difference. But they are bound together as the parts of a single plan. The plan may make the parts unlawful (*Aiken vs. Wisconsin,* 195 U.S. 194, 206). The statute gives this proceeding against combinations in restraint of commerce among the States and against attempts to monopolize the same. Intent is almost essential to such a combination and is essential to such an attempt.

Where acts are not sufficient in themselves to produce a result which the law seeks to prevent—for instance, the monopoly—but require further acts in addition to the mere forces of nature to bring that result to pass, an intent to bring it to pass is necessary in order to produce a dangerous probability that it will happen (*Commonwealth vs. Peaslee,* 177 Massachusetts 262, 272). But when that intent and the consequent dangerous probability exists, this statute, like many others, and like the common law in some cases, directs itself against that dangerous probability as well as against the completed result.

What we have said disposes incidentally of the objection to the bill as multifarious. The unity of the plan embraces all the parts.

And, again, he says:

It is said that this charge does not set forth a case of commerce among the States. Commerce among the States is not a technical legal conception, but a practical one, drawn from the course of business. When cattle are sent for sale from a place in one State, with the expectation that they will end their transit, after purchase, in another, and when in effect (399) they do so, with only the interruption necessary to find a purchaser at the stock-yards, and when this is a typical, constantly recurring course, the current thus existing is a current of commerce among the States, and the purchase of the cattle is a part and incident of such commerce.

The whittling down of the scope of the *Knight–Sugar Trust* case goes on under the deft hand of Mr. Justice Holmes by bearing down on the general intent of the acts and plan. He says:

One further observation should be made. Although the (397) combination alleged embraces restraint and monopoly of trade within a single State, its effect upon commerce among the States is not accidental, secondary, remote, or merely probable. It is a direct object, it is that for the sake of which the several specific acts and courses of conduct are done and adopted. Therefore the case is not like *United States vs. E. C. Knight Co.,* 156 U.S. 1, where the subject-matter of the combination was manufacture and the direct monopoly of manufacture within a State.

However likely monopoly of commerce among the States in the article manufactured was to follow from the agreement, it was not a necessary consequence nor a primary end. Here the subject-matter is sales, and the very point of the combination is to restrain and monopolize commerce among the States in respect of such sales. The two cases are near to each other, as sooner or later always must happen where lines are to be drawn, but the line between them is distinct.

It thus becomes clearer and clearer that the Sugar Trust judgment, in the opinion of the Supreme Court, turns on the defect in the pleadings and evidence in that case, in the failure of the Government to aver and prove that the purpose of the purchase of the stock in the Philadelphia refineries was only a step in a great scheme to monopolize the business of selling refined sugar among the States of the United States, a fact that, it would seem, might have been easy to establish. No one can deny that a plan merely to monopolize manufacture of sugar would be a State affair and not involve commerce among the States. Suppose that the profit in refining sugar was in tolls charged for the refining, as in grist-mills for grinding flour; this would be clearly only a State matter. The criticism of the court's decision in the *Sugar Trust* case, therefore, should really be directed, not against the principle of constitutional law it lays down, but against the narrow inferences of fact the majority of the Court drew as to the necessary and controlling effect of the union of the sugar refineries of the country upon the business of selling and delivery of sugar among the States. The man in the street knew that the acts set forth in the bill were part of a plan to monopolize interstate trade in sugar. Why should the Court have refused to see it?

Thus by further consideration, in the *Addyston Pipe* case, in the *Northern Securities* case, and in the *Meat Trust* case, the Court now reached a conclusion in regard to the practical application of the statute that justifies one in saying that if the *Sugar Trust* case were again brought before the court, different inferences of fact would be drawn from the evidence and a more liberal construction of the pleadings and the prayer for relief would be given and a different result would be reached.

The breadth and efficacy of the common-law rule as to restraint of trade finds a clear exposition in the opinion of Mr. Justice Hughes in *Miles Medical Company vs. Park & Sons Company,* 220 U.S. 373. Contracts between manufacturers and wholesale and retail dealers under which the manufacturers attempted to control the prices of their products in future sales by their purchasers and subpurchasers, were held to be unenforceable at common law, and, if they affected interstate commerce, to be a violation of the anti-trust act. This is a most important case in demonstrating that the effort to control prices in interstate trade by contracts with retail men with penalties or threats of nondealing is in the teeth of the Sherman Act.

6

The Standard Oil and Tobacco Trust
Cases—Effect of Antitrust Law on Combinations
of Labor Obstructing Interstate Commerce

We next come to the great and crucial *Standard Oil* case, 221 U.S. 1, which applied the interstate-commerce law to the greatest monopoly and combination in restraint of trade in the world. Its making and building up covered a period from 1870 down to the date of the opinion in the spring of 1912. (The Standard Oil Trust was probably one of the chief reasons for passing the statute in 1890.) The record in the case covered twelve thousand printed pages. It took 184 printed pages just to tell the summary story of the birth and growth of the monopoly. It had resulted in nine different Standard Oil companies and sixty-two other corporations and partnerships operating oil-wells, refineries, pipe-line and tank-line companies. The ruling body was the Standard Oil Company of New Jersey, that held stock in the other companies and did 85 percent of all the business of the United States selling refined oils and other products of petroleum. It was indeed an octopus that held the trade in its tentacles, and the few actual independent concerns that kept alive were allowed to exist by sufferance merely to maintain an appearance of competition.

In this case Chief Justice White adopts for the Court the view of Mr.

Justice Brewer, expressed in his separate opinion in the *Northern Securities* case, that the terms of the statute, being words having common-law significance, are to be interpreted in the light of their meaning at common law and that the statute is thus to be construed by the rule of reason. The Chief Justice states the history of restraints of trade and of monopolies and engrossing and regrating at common law, and shows the ultimate significance given to those terms and then applies it to the statute. He shows how the great congeries of corporations and business interests that were concentrated in the Standard Oil Company under one management were plainly an attempt to monopolize the refining and sale of petroleum oil and its products throughout the country, among the States, and in the foreign trade, and concludes that they were therefore obviously within the statute.

Mr. Justice Harlan, in a concurring opinion, criticizes the language of the Court in its construction of the statute and calls the application of common-law meaning to the terms of the statute, judicial legislation.

In the next great case, reported in the same volume of the Reports, that against the American Tobacco Company for the monopoly of the tobacco business, the Court reached a similar decision. The evidence of intent to restrain country-wide commerce and to monopolize it was not quite so overwhelming as it was in the *Standard Oil Company* case, only because care had been taken through the advice of keen counsel to make the transactions appear more innocent.

These two great judgments gave the widest scope to the anti-trust law, as may be seen from two passages that I must quote, one from the *Standard Oil* case and the other from the *Tobacco* case. In the *Standard Oil* case the Chief Justice said:

> In view of the many new forms of contracts and combinations which were being evolved from existing economic conditions, it was deemed essential by an all-embracing enumeration to make sure that no form of contract or combination by which an undue restraint of interstate or foreign commerce was brought about could save such restraint from condemnation.

The statute under this view evidenced the intent not to restrain the right to make and enforce contracts, whether resulting from combination or otherwise, which did not unduly restrain interstate or foreign commerce, but to protect that commerce from being restrained by methods, whether old or new, which would constitute an interference that is an undue restraint.

In the *Tobacco* case the same great judge said:

> Coming then to apply to the case before us the act as interpreted in the Standard Oil and previous cases, all the difficulties suggested by the mere form in which the assailed transactions are clothed become of no moment. This follows because, although it was held in the *Standard Oil* case that, giving to the statute a reasonable construction, the words "restraint of trade" did not embrace all those normal and usual contracts essential to individual freedom, and the right to make which was necessary in order that the course of trade might be free, yet, as a result of the reasonable construction which was affixed to the statute, it was pointed out that the generic designation of the first and second sections of the law, when taken together, embraced every conceivable act which could possibly come within the spirit or purpose of the prohibitions of the law, without regard to the garb in which such acts were clothed. That is to say, it was held that in view of the general language of the statute and the public policy which it manifested there was no possibility of frustrating that policy by resorting to any disguise or subterfuge of form, *since resort to reason rendered* it impossible to escape by any indirection the prohibitions of the statute.

Notwithstanding the decrees for the United States in these cases and the all-embracing character of these decisions and the opportunity they afford through the statute to reach every conceivable trust or combination at which the statute could have been aimed, they were made the object of attack by many politicians.

A calm and considered examination of the opinions of Chief Justice White in the *Standard Oil* and *Tobacco* cases, and the use of the rule of decision which he laid down in applying the act to subsequent cases, will show that those who charged that the Court had narrowed the act, or had not comprehended the settled public opinion that found expression in it, spoke without knowledge. The verbal difference between the Court and Mr. Justice Harlan, however, was soon reflected in controversies carried on in Congress, in the press, and in political contests, and its echoes are still sounding. This issue was engendered merely by language and not by real differences in result, or, indeed, in principle. The too-sweeping sentences of Mr. Justice Peckham in the *Trans-Missouri* and *Joint Traffic Association* cases, as to the irrelevancy of common-law meanings, with express exceptions really based on the common law such as I have pointed out, was really a statement of exactly the same principle of reasonable construction as that upon which Chief Justice White proceeded in his opinion in the *Standard Oil* case. Indeed, the much-criticized "rule of reason" of the Chief Justice was only a change of phrase from the expression which Mr. Justice Peckham had himself used as the guide to a proper construction of the statute. For in the *Joint Traffic Association* case that Justice says:

> An agreement entered into for the purpose of promoting the legitimate business of an individual or corporation, with no purpose to thereby affect or restrain interstate commerce, and which does not directly restrain such commerce, is not, as we think, covered by the act, although the agreement may indirectly and remotely affect that commerce.
>
> We also repeat what is said in the case above cited [i.e., in his own opinion in the Trans-Missouri case], that "the act of Congress must have a reasonable construction, or else there would scarcely be an agreement or contract among business men that could not be said to have, directly or remotely, some bearing upon interstate commerce, and possible to restrain it." (WHT's italics.) To suppose, as is assumed by counsel, that the effect of the decision in the Trans-Missouri case is to render illegal most business contracts or combinations, however indispensable and necessary they may be, because, as they assert, they all restrain trade in some remote and indirect degree, is to make a most violent assumption, and one not called for or justified by the decision mentioned, or by any other decision of this court.

Again, the error which Mr. Justice Harlan made in his concurring opinion in the *Standard Oil* case, in saying that the use of the common law to interpret the meaning of the anti-trust statute was "judicial legislation," may be inferred by reference to his own course of reasoning in his very able and convincing dissenting opinion in the *Sugar Trust* case, which, as I have already said, has really become the position of the court. But when the Court came over to him and that opinion, he could not bring himself to see the real victory he had won.

In his dissenting opinion in the *Sugar Trust* case he used this language:

> The fundamental inquiry in this case is, What in a legal sense is an unlawful restraint of trade?
>
> Sir William Erle, formerly Chief Justice of the Common Pleas, in his essay on "The Law Relating to Trades-Unions," well said that "restraint of trade, according to a general principle of the common law, is unlawful"; that "at common law every person has individually and the public also has collectively a right to require that the course of trade should be kept free from unreasonable obstruction," and that the right to a free course for trade is of great importance to commerce and productive industry, and has been carefully maintained by those who have administered the common law. (Pages 6, 7, 8.)
>
> There is a partial restraint of trade which in certain circumstances is tolerated by the law. The rule upon that subject is stated in *Oregon Steam Navigation Company vs. Minor,* 20 Wall 64, 66, where it was said that "an agreement in general restraint of trade is illegal and void; but an agreement which operates merely in partial restraint of trade is good, provided it be not unreasonable and there be consideration to support it. In order that it may not be unreasonable, the restraint imposed must not be larger than is required for the necessary protection of the party with whom the contract is made (*Homer vs. Graces,* 7 Bingh. 735, 743). A contract, even on good consideration, not to use a trade anywhere in England, is held void in that country as being too general a restraint of trade."
>
> But a general restraint of trade has often resulted from combinations formed for the purpose of controlling prices by destroying the opportunity of buyers and sellers to deal with each other upon the basis of fair, open, free competition. Combinations of this character have frequently been the subject of judicial scrutiny, and have always been condemned as illegal because of their necessary tendency to restrain trade. Such combinations are against common right and are crimes against the public. To some of the cases of that character it will be well to refer.

The learned Justice then considers a great many cases at common law in this country to show that a case like the *Sugar Trust* would be an unlawful restraint in trade within a State, and so also in interstate trade, and so must be within the statute. In other words, he proceeded exactly as the Chief Justice did in the *Standard Oil* case, to find out what the common law was, and in the light of the common-law definition of undue or unreasonable restraints of trade to bring the case before him within the statute. Yet this course, which he himself took in the *Knight* case, he pronounces to be improper judicial legislation on the part of the eight Justices who voted for the majority opinion in the *Standard Oil* case.

In spite, however, of the breadth of the Court's decision in the *Standard Oil* case, and its useful reconciling of the inconsistencies of previous decisions, the phrase "the rule of reason" brought out the condemnation of everybody of demagogic tendencies prominent in politics, and evoked from statesmen of little general information and less law, proposals to amend the statute, "to put teeth" into it, and to eliminate from the power of the Court the right to use the rule of reason in the construction and application of the anti-trust law. Were it not for the then hysterical condition of the public mind, the futility and manifest absurdity of such a proposition, which its very words necessarily implied, would have aroused the sense of humor of the American people.

After the opinion was announced, I invited the gentlemen who were most stentorian in condemnation of the interpretation given to the statute by the Supreme Court to mention and describe a case in which they would have the statute apply to which it would not apply under the reasoning of the court, and up to this time I have never heard such a case stated, and I think I may infer that the reason is that there is no such case.

But those politicians and demagogues who, as they have said, wish to draw blood, and whom nothing would satisfy but the absolute annihilation of the capital used in the trusts, are not the only persons who have made mistakes in dealing with the subject. There are those who are utterly opposed to the spirit of the law and who take the view that Lord Justice Bowen of the English Court of Appeal evidently took, judging by his language in the *Mogul Steamship Company* case, that the only proper way to remedy the evil of trusts and combinations of this character is to let them run riot and cure themselves. The contention of these opponents of the law has been that it is impossible for business men to live under the anti-trust law because nobody can tell what it means. They have continued this cry until they have put it in the mouths of their extreme opponents, who, accepting their view, now come forward to say that the law ought to be changed so as to denounce specific acts as in themselves criminal, whether they are used to promote the real evil aimed at by the statute or not.

The truth is that the course of the construction of the statute in the last twenty years has been a valuable asset for the public. No man who reads this series of decisions need be doubtful whether, when he is making a business arrangement, he is violating the law or not. He can search his own heart and he can tell what his purpose is and what the effect of his act is going to be. If what he is dealing with is interstate commerce, if what he is going to do is to reduce competition and gain control of the business in any particular branch, if that is his main purpose and reduction of competition is not a mere incidental result, if except for that purpose he would not go into the arrangement, then he must know he is violating the law, and no sophistry, no pretense of other purpose need mislead him. It is a question of self-knowledge; it is a question of intention and necessary effect.

The operation of the act upon conspiracies of members of labor-unions to injure the interstate trade of employers by restraints that are direct and illegal—to wit, by a secondary boycott—should be considered. It is quite clear that the mere striking to secure better wages or other terms of employment, and thus embarrassing the operation of a railroad engaged in interstate commerce, would not be within the statute, because such a combined action was not unlawful at common law, and it has come in modern days to be recognized as a legitimate means by which workingmen through united action may put themselves on a level of resource and power with their employer. But when they go further and seek by striking and united withholding of patronage to coerce others who have no normal relation to the fight to assist them in it and injure their employer, they step over the line of lawfulness, and if by such means they obstruct the interstate trade of their employer they violate the act.

In the case of *Loewe vs. Lawler*, 208 U.S. 274, a hat-manufacturing company in Danbury, Connecticut, declined to accede to the demand of the hatters' union, consisting of nine thousand men, in respect to their terms of employment. Thereupon the hatters declared a boycott against the company, and the Federation of Labor, a federation embracing a number of trades-unions having a membership of one hundred and fifty thousand, declared a boycott against the Danbury company all over the country, and notified the hat dealers that they would not purchase hats made by the Danbury Hat Company, and threatened the dealers themselves with a boycott if they sold such hats. The Danbury company sued the leaders of the boycott and the hatters' union for damages under the anti-trust act. Their liability was declared by the Supreme Court of the United States. This boycott, it will be noted, was a secondary boycott, because, while it was directed against the original manufacturing company, it sought to compel the hat dealers of the country to range themselves on the side of the labor-unions and injure the manufacturing company.

This was held to be a combination in restraint of interstate trade, and a substantial verdict for the company has since been recovered under the statute. The recovery would have been sustained at common law, and I do not know any reason why it does not necessarily come within the statute.

Attempts are being made in Congress to exclude from the operation of the anti-trust act trades-unions and farmers. I hope this will never be done. It will be legislation establishing a privilege for a class that is supposed to be powerful in votes, without any real reason for the distinction. A law with a similar exemption was passed by the legislature of Illinois. It was held by the United States Supreme Court to be invalid because it denied to all the people of Illinois the equal protection of laws. While that case was under the Fourteenth Amendment, which prevents a State from denying equal protection of the laws to any persons within its jurisdiction, it would be a question whether the Supreme Court might not find in the first eight amendments of the Constitution a prohibition upon Congressional legislation having similar unjust operation.

7

Ten Cases under Trust Law, Following Standard
Oil and Tobacco Decisions, Showing Broad
Scope of Those Decisions

In order to justify my statement as to the comprehensive character of the
decisions in the *Standard Oil* and *Tobacco* cases I wish now briefly to state
the effect of the ten cases which have been decided since, and the further
application of the rule of construction as finally given in those two leading
cases all by a unanimous court.

The first of these involved the legality of a terminal association of railroads in unifying the terminal facilities of St. Louis, which, owing to the
geographical conditions, all railroads entering St. Louis were under compulsion to use. It appeared that the combination was made by less than all
the companies entering the city, and that an existing member could arbitrarily exclude new applicants for membership. It was held that such a
combination effecting exclusive ownership and control came within the
first and second sections of the act and was an attempt to monopolize commerce among the States which must pass through the gateway of St. Louis;
that a combination of all the companies for the purpose of giving every
company entering St. Louis the same treatment would not have been a

violation of the act. This case illustrates how the Court by use of the remedial process of equity can effect exactly the right result. The "insiders" were
required, on pain of being enjoined from doing any terminal business
under the agreement, to let every other railroad entering St. Louis into the
agreement on exactly equal terms as a member.

In the *Bath-tub* case, 226 U.S. 20, the defendants, sixteen manufacturers controlling 85 percent of the trade in enameled iron ware, were shown
to have united to destroy competition, fix prices and terms of sale, and
establish penalties for violation of the agreement. This was quite within
the inhibition of the *Addyston Pipe* case. An attempt was made to escape
the statute on the ground that some of the parties had patents covering the
goods whose sale was the subject of the agreement. But the Court held
that, while rights made by patents are extensive, they do not give any more
than other rights a universal license against positive prohibitions of the
statute. In answer to the proposition that the defendants had a good motive
in their combination, Mr. Justice McKenna said that the cases in the Court
had demonstrated the sufficiency of the statute to prevent evasions of its
policy by resort to any disguise or subterfuge of form or the escape of its
prohibitions by any indirection, nor could the defendants escape by proof
of good motives, adding that the law is its own measure of right and wrong,
of what it permits or forbids, and the judgment of the courts cannot be set
up against it in a supposed accommodation of its policy with the good
intention of the parties. It should be said that the good motives here
averred and sought to be proved were the desire through a monopoly and
control of the market and prices to prevent the sale to the public of inferior
enamel for bath-tubs.

In the *United States vs. Union Pacific Railroad Company,* 226 U.S. 61,
the bill in equity was directed against the consummated acquisition of 46
percent of the Southern Pacific stock by the Union Pacific Company when
the two railroads were competing systems. Mr. Justice Day delivered the
opinion of the Court and held that the purchase was within the anti-trust
act, and that the mere purchase of stock by one corporation in another if
the intent and effect are to restrain commerce and obtain power to control
competition is within the statute.

In *United States vs. Reading Company,* 226 U.S. 324, decided December
16, 1912, the defendants, a number of coal-carrying railroads and mining

companies producing and transporting 75 percent of the annual supply of anthracite coal, combined to prevent the construction of an independent and competing line of railway into the anthracite region. The plan devised was to acquire for the Temple Iron Company, a corporation all of whose stock was owned by the defendants, the coal properties and collieries controlled by the largest independent producer whose support had been promised to the proposed new independent competing line of transportation. The plan succeeded, for, the independent properties having been acquired by the Temple Iron Company, the projected competing railroad was abandoned. It was contended that because the new line had been abandoned it would be idle to enjoin the doing of an act already accomplished. In answering this contention, Mr. Justice Lurton for the Court said:

> The combination by means of the Temple Company still exists. It has been and still is an efficient agency for the collective activities of the defendant carriers for the purpose of preventing competition in the transportation and sale of coal in other states. . . .
>
> So long as the defendants are able to exercise the power thus illegally acquired it may be most efficiently exerted for the continued and further suppression of competition. Through it the defendants in combination may absorb the remaining output of independent collieries.
>
> The evil is in the combination. Without it the several groups of coal-carrying and coal-producing companies have the power and motive to compete.
>
> It is, of course, obvious that the law may not compel competition between these independent coal operators and defendants, but it may at least remove illegal barriers resulting from illegal agreements which will make such competition impracticable. Whether a particular act, contract, or agreement was a reasonable and normal method in furtherance of trade and commerce may in doubtful cases turn upon the intent to be inferred from the extent of the control thereby secured over the commerce affected as well as by the method which was used.
>
> Of course, if the necessary result is materially to restrain trade between the States, the intent with which the thing was done is of no consequence. But when there is only a probability the intent to produce the consequence may become important.

Here we see the important principle announced that when a combination necessarily effects a monopoly it is no defense that the combiners did not intend a monopoly; but when the result is not complete or controlling as a monopoly, the intent is the important factor.

In *United States vs. Patten,* 226 U.S. 525, decided in January, 1913, the defendants were indicted for a conspiracy to run a corner in the available supply of the staple commodity of cotton, normally a subject of trade and commerce among the States, and thereby to enhance artificially its price throughout the country and compel all who had occasion to obtain it to pay the enhanced price or else leave their needs unsatisfied. The court held that the indictment was good in the terms of Section I of the act, that to run a corner is to acquire control of all or the dominant portion of a commodity with the purpose of artificially enhancing the price, and that one of the important features of the corner is the purchase for future delivery, coupled with a withholding from sale for a limited time. Mr. Justice Van Devanter pronounced the judgment of the court. He said:

> It may well be that running a corner tends for a time to stimulate competition; but this does not prevent it from being a forbidden restraint, for it also operates to thwart the usual operation of the laws of supply and demand, to withdraw the commodity from the normal current of trade, to enhance the price artificially, to hamper users and consumers in satisfying their needs, and to produce practically the same evils as does the suppression of competition.
>
> Upon the corner becoming effective, there could be no trading in the commodity save at the will of the conspirators and at such price as their interests might prompt them to exact. And so, the conspiracy was to reach and to bring within its dominating influence the entire cotton trade of the country.

The case of *United States vs. Winslow,* 227 U.S. 202, came to the Supreme Court on a judgment sustaining a demurrer to an indictment. The indictment charged that three companies engaged in different lines of business and not competing, but making respectively 60, 80, 70, and 80 percent of the lasting machines, welt-sewing machines, heeling machines, and metallic-fastening machines made in the United States, organized a new company to which they turned over their several businesses.

The Court affirmed the judgment of the court below in sustaining the demurrer. Mr. Justice Holmes in delivering the judgment said:

On the face of it the combination was simply an effort after greater efficiency. The business of the several groups that combined, as it existed before the combination, is assumed to have been legal. The machines are patented, making them a monopoly in any case, the exclusion of competitors from the use of them is of the very essence of the right conferred by the patents, and it may be assumed that the success of the several groups was due to their patents having been the best.

As by the interpretation of the indictment below and by the admission in argument before us, they did not compete with one another, it is hard to see why the collective business should be any worse than its component parts. We can see no greater objection to one corporation manufacturing 70 percent of three noncompeting groups of patented machines collectively used for making a single product than to three corporations making the same proportion of one group each. The disintegration aimed at by the statute does not extend to reducing all manufacture to isolated units of the lowest degree.

It is as lawful for one corporation to make every part of a steam-engine and to put the machine together as it would be for one to make the boilers and another to make the wheels. Until the one intent is nearer accomplishment than it is by such a juxtaposition alone no intent could raise the conduct to the dignity of an attempt.

This brings out clearly that mere bigness, not used to effect monopoly, but only to increase efficiency, is not a violation of the statute.

In the criminal case of the *United States vs. Pacific and Arctic Railway & Navigation Company and Others,* 228 U.S. 87, the defendants, a railroad company and two steamship companies, who were not competitors, but together formed a continuous line of transportation by water and rail from Seattle to the interior of Alaska, had combined in order to put out of business a steamship company that was competing with one of the defendants on part of the through route and to throw all trade into the hands of the defendant steamship companies. The steamship defendants agreed with the defendant railroad company to establish through routes and joint rates with them, and the latter agreed to refuse to do so with the competing steamship company. Defendants with like purpose so fixed the local rates that the combination of local rates was greater than the through rate agreed upon.

It was held that this was an infringement of the anti-trust law, and was something more than the exercise of the common-law right of selecting connections, and that the scheme was therefore illegal.

In *Nash vs. the United States,* 229 U.S. 373, a criminal case and conviction under the statute, the chief argument for the defense was that the anti-trust law was so indefinite and vague as to be inoperative on its criminal side. The Court held that there was no merit to this contention. Mr. Justice Holmes said:

> The objection to the criminal operation of the statute is thought to be warranted by the *Standard Oil Company vs. United States,* 221 U.S. 1, and the *United States vs. American Tobacco Company,* 221 U.S. 106. Those cases may be taken to have established that only such contracts and combinations are within the act as, by reason of intent or the inherent nature of the contemplated acts, prejudice the public interests by unduly restricting competition or unduly obstructing the course of trade. . . . We are of the opinion that there is no constitutional difficulty in the way of enforcing the criminal part of the act.

In that case the Court also held that a conspiracy indictment under the act need not aver the commission of an overt act, "as the Sherman act punishes the conspiracies at which it is aimed on the common law footing, and we can see no reason for reading into the Sherman act more than we find there."

The last exposition of the Supreme Court's broad view of the purpose of the statute and practical enforcement of it is in the case of *Straus vs. the Publishing Company,* 231 U.S. 222. There it appeared that a publishers' association, composed of probably 75 percent of the publishers of copyrighted books in the United States, and a booksellers' association, including a majority of the booksellers throughout the United States, entered into a combination and agreement by which their members bound themselves to sell copyrighted books only to those who would maintain the retail price on copyrighted books. It further appeared, as a result of this combination, that competition on copyrighted books at retail was almost completely destroyed and that the plaintiffs in the case, who conducted a department store in New York and because of their methods of business had been able to undersell other bookstores, were put on a "cut-off" list and were unable to secure a supply of such books in the ordinary course of business because dealers who had supplied them were wholly ruined by the combination. Applying the principle of the *Bath-tub* case, that the monopoly of a patent did not enable those who dealt in the patented device to enjoy immunity under the Sherman law, which was to be regarded as a limitation of rights which might be pushed to evil consequences, the Court said:

> So in the present case it cannot be successfully contended that the monopoly of a copyright is in this respect any more extensive than that secured under the patent law. No more than the patent statute was the copyright act intended to authorize agreements in unlawful restraint of trade and tending to monopoly, in violation of the specific terms of the Sherman law, which is broadly designed to reach all combinations in unlawful restraint of trade and tending, because of the agreements or combinations entered into, to build up and perpetuate monopolies.

From this review of the Supreme Court's decisions, it is perfectly clear that the Court has no disposition to narrow the effect of the statute or to exclude any case that is properly within the evil which Congress intended to strike down.

The effect of the cases is that a mere union of capital in the same branch of industry for the purpose of promoting economy and efficiency, though it uses interstate commerce, and though to the extent of the business of the two firms or companies it suppresses the competition of each against the other, is not within the statute unless what is done necessarily has the effect to control all the business or can be shown by the character of the acts to be intended to effect that purpose or to be a step in the plot to bring it about. Mere bigness is not an evidence of violating the act. It is the purpose and necessary effect of controlling prices and putting the industry under the domination of one management that is within the statute. This evil is to be punished or restrained under the statute, no matter how ingenious or varied the device for bringing it about may be. The Court will look through the form of the device adopted to evade the effect of the law to its essence, to the intent, and to the result.

8

Popular Misconception of Supreme Court's
Attitude in Constructing Anti-trust Law—No
Assumption of Power to Enforce Economic or
Political Views of Judges—Merely Following a
Common-Law Standard—Admirable Adaptability
of Decrees in Equity to Enforcement
of Statute—Efficacy of Standard Oil
and Tobacco Decrees

One might well infer from the unfair and false strictures upon the attitude of the Supreme Court in construing the statute that it had asserted its power to say, "It is true that this contract restraining trade and this monopoly it effects are within the literal terms of the statute, but, on the whole, we think, from our views of political economy, it would be unwise and unreasonable to include them, and so we limit the operation of the express words of the act those things we believe to be injurious to the public weal."

I have said little to my purpose if I have not made clear that the only reasonableness in the application of the statute which the Court assumes to consider and decide is that of the restraint of trade, ancillary to a main contract with a different purpose and which the common law has for years furnished practical and definite legal rules for determining. The idea of the Supreme Court's ignorant but enthusiastic critics is that the Court has said, "There are good trusts and bad trusts, and we have the power to say what are the good trusts and what are the bad trusts, according to our economic and political views." Now, of course, the Court has asserted no such power.

It would be unwise to intrust this power to the courts. It would be legislative power, not judicial power. What the Court has said in effect is this:

> It is evident what the Congress had in its mind from the language it uses. We know from current history the evil it sought to remedy. It has used terms that had a well understood meaning at common law—to wit, restraint of trade, monopoly, combination, and conspiracy. It is a settled rule of all American and English courts in construing statutes and constitutions that common-law terms are to receive common-law meaning unless there is good reason to the contrary. In the light of reason, and applying common-law meaning to such statutory terms, we hold that such incidental restraints as were reasonable at common law were not intended to be included within the term "restraints of trade" used in the statute.

That is not assuming legislative power at all. It is only exercising the function that courts have exercised in applying a well-measured and definite yardstick to contracts incidental and ancillary for now more than three centuries.

The legislators and political orators who rejoice in outradicaling everyone else object to the courts using the rule of reason in construing statutes and say that in this regard the courts of our country exercise more power than in any other country. They are wrong. I commend them to the statute which has been passed in Australia, the home of radicalism and fads and nostrums, on the subject of trade restraints.

The Australian act makes it a criminal offense to enter into any combination in relation to trade or commerce among the States of the Commonwealth (*a*) with intent to restrain trade or commerce to the detriment of the public, or (*b*) with intent to destroy or injure by means of unfair competition any Australian industry the preservation of which is advantageous to the Commonwealth, having due regard to the interest of producers, workers, and consumers. The act also makes it a criminal offense to monopolize, or attempt to monopolize or combine or conspire with any other person to monopolize, any part of the trade or commerce among the States with intent to control to the detriment of the public the supply or price of any service, merchandise, or commodity.

It seems to me that this is conferring on the judges and courts a power that ought never to be intrusted to them. It is submitting, not to their legal, but to their economic and business judgment questions for decision that are really legislative in character. I regret to say that this is the tendency of the pending bills in Congress, in which it is proposed to leave first to an executive board and then to the courts to declare and forbid what in their judgment is unfair competition. If this means more than what is included in unreasonable restraints of trade at common law now denounced by the anti-trust law, it would seem to be conferring legislative power.

By misrepresentation, ignorant or malicious, the public in this country have been given the impression that the power which the Australian courts are thus given, and which it is now proposed to give to the new trade commission and the courts, our Supreme Court has assumed to exercise. If I have made clear the unjust and unfounded character of this impression I shall count what I have written worth while.

Before concluding a discussion of the State, I wish to say something on the chief civil remedy provided by the anti-trust law for reaching the evil aimed at—to wit, the elastic and many-sided remedies afforded by procedure in equity.

The first advantage in dealing with a trust by decree of a court of equity is that the power of punishment by summary contempt proceedings for violation of the provisions of the decree insures their performance. No jury trial need intervene between a disobedience of its terms and deterrent punishment.

The second advantage is that the decree can be shaped to suit the situation so as to stamp out the evil of monopoly and restraint, and yet to leave the capital and plant ably organized, to reduce the cost of production, and to carry on legitimate business for the benefit of the public. The court of equity can take hold of a trust and use the varying form of its remedies by injunction and receivership to squeeze the unlawfulness out of a trust and retain for the benefit of society those features of it that great business energy and genius have created and that can be continued entirely within the law.

This leads me now to the consideration of the decrees in the *Standard Oil* case and in the *Tobacco* case. Both of them have been referred to as altogether ineffective and of no use in preventing the continuance of the evil which the Court found to exist and against which it entered its decree. I am firmly convinced from an investigation of the decrees in these cases that this charge is altogether unfounded and that the decrees were quite as effective to bring about the result desired as any decree in equity ever was.

In the *Standard Oil* case the decree required a dissolution of the company holding stock in the many other companies constituting the congeries of agencies for the monopoly of the trade and followed the language of the prayer of the bill asking the dissolution of the trust. The holding company was enjoined from continuing its control and its stock was distributed to the various stockholders, and they were enjoined from maintaining any further concert or combination. The argument against the effectiveness of this decree is based on the fact that after the decree was put into operation the stock of the individual companies increased greatly in value. In other words, because the decree did not destroy or injure the value of the property, it shows that it was not effective to destroy the combination.

Nothing has been cited to show that the parts into which the combination was divided have violated the decree. Such violation could be promptly met and summarily punished by contempt proceedings before the Circuit Court. The mere fact that the business of the separate corporations into which the combination was divided has been good since the decree is no evidence that the decree is not effective to relieve the business of refining and selling oil from the heavy hand of the old monopoly.

In the first place, the increase in the market value of the stock of the old constituent companies is easily explained by two circumstances which have nothing to do with the decree. The first one is that the judicial investigation into the affairs of these companies disclosed what was not known to the public—that each company had a large surplus which did not appear in the published statements and which made its stock much more valuable than its previous market quotation had shown it. And the second is that the very large increase in the consumption of gasoline, a product of petroleum, due to the substitution of automobiles for carriages and wagons, has so increased the demand, and thus the price, as naturally to make the gasoline business more profitable.

But there are two circumstances that show beyond question the influence of the decree to accomplish the purpose of the act, which is to rid trade from restraint and give way to free competition. One of the manifestations of the power of the Standard Oil Company, when it was a monopoly, was the power it exercised to keep down the price of crude oil. The Standard Oil Company owned only a small percentage—less than 15 percent—of the oil-wells of the United States. It purchased the crude oil, and there was no circumstance showing its complete power over the trade more clearly than its keeping down to a point almost below cost of pumping the price of the crude oil. Under the influence of the decree the price of crude oil has gone up 100 percent beyond what it was in the halcyon days of the trust.

Again, the percentage of the amount of oil refined and sold by the independent companies that never were in the Standard Oil combination, as compared with the percentage of those companies into which the Standard Oil was dissolved, has increased to 44 percent from 15 percent, as it was before the decree. Indeed, counting as an independent the Waters-Pierce Company, which was controlled by the Standard Oil Company and is now in litigation with and in the bitterest opposition to its former associates, the independents refine and sell considerably more than half the oil of the country. An inquiry made of any leading independent oil-refiner will lead to confirmation of the view that the decree has been in every way most effective to help them to a free and profitable business. But it is said prices have not been reduced. Gasoline has increased in price for reasons that have been explained. Other products of oil remain at about the same price. The increase in the price of crude oil, which the trust had kept down, easily explains this. Moreover, if competition is restored the statute has accomplished its purpose. The effect of this upon prices, to keep them lower, is an economic result dependent on so many causes that failure to reduce them can certainly not be charged to the form of the decree or the character of the remedy.

The *Tobacco* decree has been even more severely criticized than the *Standard Oil* decree. The fact is it was far more drastic. In it the Supreme Court for the first time recognized as a possible step in the equitable remedy against a monopoly the appointment of a receiver and the sale of the company's assets, if it be necessary to protect the public.

The details of the decree were left to the three judges of the Circuit Court to settle. They did so. It was not taken to the Supreme Court again.

The decree divided the trust into four large companies, and the result has been a genuine and strong competition between these four companies by advertising and lowering prices, so that the small so-called independent companies, in the face of the competition between the large companies, have been less comfortable than under the tolerance of the Tobacco Trust. But this furnishes no ground for criticizing the decree or its effect. These companies are not affected by illegal methods in the competition. They are only not able to keep the pace in modern business methods of selling and economical production. The object of the statute is to give opportunity for free and genuine competition.

There was found in the working of the Tobacco Trust the same feature as appeared in the case of the Standard Oil Trust. This was the concerted suppression of competition in the purchase of the raw product. The result in bearing down the price of white burley tobacco caused the night-riders and their lawless violence in Kentucky and Tennessee, intended by them to curtail the crop and compel higher prices. The price of that important raw product in the tobacco field of business under the effect of the *Tobacco* decree soared to 100 percent more than it had been. The four companies into which the trust was divided are trying to get business one from the other. They are not trying to drive independent companies out of business, but their purpose to win business in competition with one another leads them to great effort and expense. The mere fact that smaller companies are unable to keep the pace is an indication that they must have greater capital in order to keep down their cost of production so that they can sell with the other and larger companies. The objection to the decree, then, is that it did not divide up the companies into small enough pieces to prevent effective competition. In this view it is the aim of the anti-trust law not to free trade from obstruction or restraint, but rather to destroy the larger businesses whose capital and large plants enable them to produce goods cheaply, in order that small plants that cannot produce them as cheaply may live. This is not the purpose of the statute, and those who insist that it ought to be true misunderstand its useful intention.

The criticism of the *Standard Oil* and *Tobacco* decrees is that the dissolution into its parts of each trust left the old shareholders owning aliquot shares in each corporation of those into which the trust was divided. That is true, but it was thought that the monitory effect of the decree and contempt proceedings and the motive for independent action would necessarily compel a voluntary separation of the interests when they could not be united for direct control of the whole business. Restrictions in the decree as to interlocking directorates and other limitations preventing the resumption of a common management justified this belief. In spite of the unjust criticism and misrepresentation, these anticipations have been vindicated.

9

Summing up of the Effect of Anti-trust Law on
Big Business—Value of First Two Sections
as Construed—Danger in Amendments
Looking to Greater Severity

What, then, is the result as to the lawful business, and especially the big business, of our country under the statute and these decisions? It is this: It is possible for the owners of a business of manufacturing and selling useful articles of merchandise so to conduct their business as not to violate the inhibitions of the anti-trust law and yet to secure to themselves the benefit of the economies of management and of production due to the concentration under one control of large capital and many plants.

If they use no other inducement than the constant low price of their product and its good quality to attract custom, and their business is a profitable one, they violate no law.

But if they attempt, by a use of their preponderating capital and by a sale of their goods temporarily at unduly low prices, to drive out of business their competitors, or if they attempt, by price-controlling contracts with their patrons and threats of nondealing except upon such contracts, or by other methods of a similar character, to use the largeness of their resources and the extent of their output compared with the country's total output as a means of compelling custom and frightening off competition, then they disclose a purpose to restrain trade and to establish a monopoly and violate the act.

The object of the anti-trust law was to suppress the abuses of business of the kind described. It was not to interfere with a great volume of capital which, concentrated under one organization, reduced the cost of production and made its profits thereby and took no advantage of its size by methods akin to duress to stifle competition with it.

I wish to make this distinction as emphatic as possible, because I conceive that nothing could happen more destructive to the prosperity of this country than the loss of that great economy in production which has been and will be effected in all manufacturing lines by the employment of large capital under one management. There is usually a limit beyond which the economy of management by the enlargement of plant ceases; and where this happens and combination continues beyond this point, the very fact shows intent to monopolize, and not to economize.

The original purpose of many combinations of capital in this country was not confined to the legitimate and proper object of reducing the cost of production. On the contrary, the history of most trades will show at times a feverish desire to unite by purchase, combination, or otherwise, all plants in the country engaged in the manufacture of a particular line of goods. The idea was rife that thereby a monopoly could be effected and a control of prices brought about which would inure to the profit of those engaged in the combination.

The path of commerce is strewn with failures of such combinations. Their projectors found that the union of all the plants did not prevent competition, especially where proper economy had not been pursued in the purchase and in the conduct of the business after the aggregation was complete. The unemployed wealth of the country soon was devoted to the construction of new competing plants. In such cases they found they had, in order to keep out or destroy new competition, to resort to deep underselling, to exclusive dealing with retailers, to buying and dismantling competing plants, to making preferential contracts with railroads, and to doing many other things of an unfair character, which their capital and their control of a large part of the trade enabled them to make effective weapons for the purpose.

The statute has been on the statute-book now for two decades, and the Supreme Court in more than twenty opinions has construed it in application to various phases of business combinations and in reference to various subjects-matter.

The Sugar Trust escaped dissolution not because it was not held to be a trust, but because it was thought by the Court to be a case within State jurisdiction. Every other important trust that has been haled before the Supreme Court in the twenty years which have elapsed since that decision has been condemned, and the terms of the statute have been given a scope which leaves little doubt that every other one of these octopuses, as its organization and methods are disclosed and analyzed, will be subjected to the heavy hand of the law.

A statute which is rendered more and more certain in its meaning by a series of decisions of the Supreme Court is more and more valuable. This furnishes a strong reason for leaving the act as it is, to accomplish its useful purpose, even though if it were being newly enacted useful suggestions as to change of phrase might be made.

The effect of this series of decisions to prevent new organizations of this kind is already manifest. New combinations of large capital are few in number, and when projected they are made with the greatest circumspection to avoid breach of the law.

Existing organizations that feel themselves near the line of illegality have abandoned practices that would give color to the claim that they seek to restrain competition or aspire to monopoly. Many companies, rather than stand the test of litigation, are consenting to dissolution by agreement with government authorities.

How strongly this result makes manifest the thorough manner in which the Supreme Court has construed the statute to reach the evil aimed at! But for these decisions of which I have attempted to give a résumé the work of concentrating all business of the country in a few hands would have gone on and we would have had our being and our comfort largely under control of a small number of iron monopolies.

What now of the proposed amendments to the anti-trust act? I have already referred to one or two features of them. As I write, though they have passed one House, it is so certain that they will be much changed in the other House that it would not be worth while to discuss them. I can, however, properly refer to the disposition of some members of Congress to make the statute more severe. It has even been proposed to require sentences of imprisonment for conviction under the anti-trust law. I quite agree that a few prison sentences would have put a wholesome fear of violating the statute earlier into the hearts of promoters of trusts. Some such sentences have been already pronounced. But my impression is that an amendment leaving no discretion between fine and imprisonment to the Court would make convictions very much harder to secure. Even the fear of jail sentences when the Court has had such discretion has led to many acquittals where the proof was conclusive and where the jury convicted the corporation but acquitted the president and other officers who really did the work. The fear of the law now is much greater than it was. The Supreme Court decisions have made it so. In theory, members of the public wish to draw blood, but when they are in a jury-box they do not like to send their fellow-citizens to jail for doing what some years ago was only regarded as shrewd business, unless there are some elements of outrageous defiance of public sentiment in what they have done. And even then, as in the meat-packers' indictments in Chicago after the civil suits were won, a complete case before the jury against men whose attitude cannot be said to have been contrite resulted in an acquittal lest a prison sentence should follow. A change of the law in the direction of greater severity or more specific definition of criminal acts would demonstrate its lack of wisdom by experience without perhaps doing much harm, except as it would frighten capital and business men at a time when business conditions are by no means satisfactory. A change of the first two sections of the existing statute would be most harmful, however. The very value of the statute under the view the Supreme Court has taken of it is its general and widely inclusive language, which embraces every form of scheme to suppress competition and control prices and effect monopoly. What else does the legislator desire? If the law interpreted by the Supreme Court remains on the statute-book as it is, it will continue to free business from its real burdens.